Understanding Global Media

By the same author:

New Media: An Introduction (2005)

Understanding Global Media

Terry Flew

First published 2007 by
PALGRAVE MACMILLAN
Houndmills, Basingstoke, Hampshire RG21 6XS and
175 Fifth Avenue, New York, NY 10010
Companies and representatives throughout the world

PALGRAVE MACMILLAN is the global academic imprint of the Palgrave Macmillan
division of St. Martin's Press, LLC and of Palgrave Macmillan Ltd. Macmillan® is a
registered trademark in the United States, United Kingdom and other countries.
Palgrave is a registered trademark in the European Union and other countries.

ISBN-13: 978–1–4039–2048–5   hardback
ISBN-10: 1–4039–2048–6   hardback
ISBN-13: 978–1–4039–2049–2   paperback
ISBN-10: 1–4039–2049–4   paperback

This book is printed on paper suitable for recycling and made from fully
managed and sustained forest sources.

A catalogue record for this book is available from the British Library.

Library of Congress Cataloging-in-Publication Data
Flew Terry.
 Understanding global media / Terry Flew.
  p. cm.
 Includes bibliographical references and index.
 ISBN-13: 978–1–4039–2048–5 (cloth)
 ISBN-10: 1–4039–2048–6 (cloth)
 ISBN-13: 978–1–4039–2049–2 (pbk.)
 ISBN-10: 1–4039–2049–4 (pbk.)
  1. Communication, International. 2. Globalization. I. Title.

P96.I5F59 2007
302.2–dc22   2006052503

10 9 8 7 6 5 4 3 2 1
16 15 14 13 12 11 10 09 08 07

Printed in China

Contents

List of Figures, Tables and Case Studies

Figures

Tables

Case Studies

Preface

I have gained considerable insights into developing this book through my work with staff and students at the Creative Industries Faculty at the Queensland University of Technology in Brisbane, Australia. Stuart Cunningham, John Hartley, Christina Spurgeon, Brad Haseman, Jinna Tay, Jiannu Bao, Axel Bruns, Abdullah Khayrallah and Tania Lim have been among those whom I have worked with in developing the ideas that inform this book. I would particularly like to thank Michael Keane for his contribution as a reader of drafts and a source of ideas, and whose own work on Chinese media and creative industries has provided considerable insight in developing the key themes of this book.

I would like to thank Kirsty Leishman and Callum Gilmour in their research contributions to the book, and Stephi Donald for providing a base from which to work on the book at the University of Technology, Sydney. Elizabeth Jacka, Tom O'Regan, John Sinclair and Graeme Turner are among those working in Australia whose work has provided touchstones for the development of my own analysis.

I have benefited from the opportunity to present some of the ideas developed in this book at international conferences in Barcelona, Sheffield, Wellington and Seattle, as well as national conferences and staff symposia in Sydney, Brisbane and Perth. Some parts of this book have been published in earlier forms in the *International Journal of Cultural Policy* 10 (3), 2005, and *Television and New Media* 8 (3), 2006.

Thanks also to the team at Palgrave Macmillan for supporting me during the writing of the book, including Sheree Keep, Emily Salz and Lara Woodward.

Finally, my deepest gratitude to Angela Romano for bearing with me during the writing of the book. During the latter stages of book completion, our first child, Charlotte Sophia Flew, came into the world, meaning that while one project was nearing completion, a much larger and more challenging one was commencing.

Acknowledgements

I am grateful to the following authors and publishers for permission to use their work in this book:

Figures

Figure 1.1: Sage Publications, 2002, published in Robert G. Picard (ed.), *Media Economics*, p. 21.

Figure 4.1: AusFILM, 2000, published in *A Bigger Slice of the Pie*, Malcolm Long Associates, p. 13.

Figure 4.2: Sage Publications, 2004, published in Allen J. Scott, Cultural-Products Industries and Urban Economic Development: Prospects for Growth and Market Contestation in Global Context. *Urban Affairs Review* 39 (4), p. 476.

Tables

Table 3.1: UNCTAD, 2003, *World Investment Report*. New York and Geneva: United Nations, p. 2.

Table 3.2: Taylor and Francis, 2001, published in John Dunning, *Global Capitalism at Bay?*, p. 17.

Table 3.4: UNCTAD, 2003, *World Investment Report*. New York and Geneva: United Nations, p. 5.

Table 5.1: Rowman and Littlefield, 2004, published in Jan Nederveen Pieterse, *Globalization and Culture: Global Mélange*, p. 55.

Introduction to Global Media: Key Concepts

Introduction

Communications media have been central to the major developments of modern societies. Their role has been seen as critical to the emergence of nation-states and conceptions of national identity; ideas of citizenship, democracy and associated human freedoms; the development of political culture and the public sphere; and the growth of capitalist commercial enterprises. They constitute the principal means through which people worldwide are informed and entertained, and develop an understanding of their local, national and global social and cultural environments. Historically, communications media have been integral to the rise and fall of empires, to diplomacy, war, the spread of languages and cultural norms, and to the processes we refer to today under the general terms of globalization and modernity.

When we refer to media, the term is understood in a three-fold sense. First, it refers to the *technological means of communication*. The term 'media' is an extension of 'medium', or the technical means through which a message is sent and received. The process of human communication over time and across distances has always required a technical means through which a message can be transmitted to others. Technical media that have been prominent through modern human history have included print (paper and movable type), broadcasting (radio and television), telephony and the Internet. In relation to the media of *mass communication*, Thompson defines mass communication as 'the institutionalized production and generalized diffusion of symbolic goods via the fixation and transmission of information or symbolic content' (Thompson, 1995, p. 26). He argues that mass communication forms have five characteristics (Thompson, 1995, pp. 18–31):

1. the development of technical and institutional means of production and diffusion, which includes the development of communications infrastructure as well as media industries;
2. the commodification of symbolic forms, or the capacity of media to be bought and sold, and to acquire economic as well as symbolic value;
3. the existence of a structured break over space as well as time between the production and reception of symbolic forms;

4. extension of the availability and durability of symbolic forms across space and over time;
5. the public circulation of symbolic forms, and their role in ordering public space and public culture through being 'made visible and observable to a multiplicity of individuals who may be, and typically are, scattered across diverse and dispersed contexts' (p. 31).

The technological means of communication constitute the *infrastructure* that makes media communication possible. As Thompson's analysis indicates, however, it is the case that while the component elements of this infrastructure may be technical – printing presses, TV and radio antennas, copper wires, broadband cables, satellites orbiting the globe, and so on – their impacts are clearly social and cultural. While the questions arising from 'how to infrastructure' have frequently been approached from a technical or engineering perspective, rather than through its impacts upon social relations and human interactions (Star and Bowker, 2005), there are influential traditions in media and communications studies which take the technical properties of a medium to be a key starting-point for understanding its social impacts and implications. *Medium theories* are those which, according to Joshua Meyrowitz, 'focus upon the particular characteristics of each individual medium or each particular type of media', in order to examine variables such as 'whether the communication is bi-directional or uni-directional, how quickly messages can be disseminated, whether learning to encode and decode in the medium is difficult or simple, [and] how many people can attend to the same message at the same moment' (Meyrowitz, 1994, p. 50). The technical media of communications and their supporting infrastructure play a central role in processes of media globalization through the role played by globally networked communications infrastructures in enabling not only the international circulation of cultural commodities, texts, images and artefacts, but also their centrality to global commerce, global politics, global war and conflict, the globalization of organizational communication, and the general global circulation of ideas, information and ideologies.

The second sense in which we refer to media is in relation to *the institutional and organizational forms through which media content is produced and distributed*. At its simplest, this refers to the *media industries*, and it will be argued in this book that there was a generalization in the course of the 20th century of the corporate form as the dominant institutional arrangement for the management of media production and distribution. Yet the media institutions operate within circuits of production, distribution and reception. An important and complex role is played by those who generate original creative content, and the workplace and professional values of those involved in the production of media content: such professionals include actors, animators, producers, directors, journalists, photographers and camera people.[1] There is also the relationship of 'core' media industries to those who are providers of content (e.g. developers of digital content), aggregators of audiences (e.g. marketing agencies, audience research analysts), and the industries the media symbiotically depends upon for the provision of regular content (e.g. administrators of major sports) as well as revenue (e.g. companies that use media for advertising). In all of these relationships, the media industries operate in a range of *markets*. The term 'market' is used here to incorporate a variety of forms of transactions between agents – formal and informal, monetized and non-monetized – and the nature of media markets will be discussed in more detail below.[2]

The third sense in which the term 'media' needs to be understood is as *the informational and symbolic content that is received and consumed by readers, audiences and users*. This is of course the 'common sense' understanding of what the media are, as it refers to the content that comes to us through our newspapers, magazines, radios, televisions, personal computers, mobile phones and other reception devices. Importantly, none of this content exists independently of the technical infrastructures and institutional forms through which it is produced and distributed. Consideration of the nature and significance of media content as it is received by a wider public draws attention to how media are integrally connected to culture. 'Culture' is a notoriously slippery term, having been famously identified by British cultural theorist Raymond Williams as 'one of the two or three most difficult words to define in the English language' (Williams, 1976, p. 87), and its relationship to media will be discussed in more detail below. At this point, it is worth following Thompson (1991) in identifying the two principal conceptions of culture. One is the *descriptive* conception of culture as what people do in a particular place or at a particular time, or 'the varied array of values, beliefs, customs, conventions, habits and practices characteristic of a particular society or historical period' (Thompson, 1991, p. 123). The other is the *symbolic* conception of culture, or the underlying system of social, cultural, linguistic, and psychological relationships through which people, in different places or at particular times, are engaged in making sense of their wider social environment and acting within it.

These three interconnected elements of the media – technical infrastructures, institutional forms, and socio-cultural contexts of reception – draw attention to three further relationships in which media are engaged, although they are certainly not exclusively media-related.[3] First, there is the question of *media power*. If communications media can be understood as constituting one of the forms of social action that 'structures culture, politics and economics ... [and] determines how a life may be lived' (Jordan, 1999, p. 1), then theories of global media need to engage with how media power shapes, and is shaped by, the capacity to engage in purposive social action in order to further one's aims and interests, and what the distribution of resources is which enable or inhibit the occurrence of such action. Second, there is need to develop an understanding of *media markets*. On the one hand, it is frequently argued that the media are 'not just another business' (Schultz, 1994), on the basis of their centrality to contemporary public communication. At the same time, the predominant role played worldwide by privately owned commercial media, with their patterns of corporate ownership and reliance upon realizing profits through the sale of media commodities by various means, requires an understanding of both the general nature of economic markets in which the media industries and related agents operate, and the distinctive features of both media commodities and media markets as compared to other lines of capitalist commerce and industry. Third, we need to consider the relationship between *media and culture*. This requires an understanding of the extent to which culture is increasingly 'mediated', that is, the distribution of informational and symbolic content is increasingly distanced over both space and time, and reception increasingly occurs in private as well as public contexts, to the point where the public/private distinction is itself increasingly blurred. It also involves recognition of the extent to which culture, understood here as the deep structure of relations, understandings and symbolic systems of people within communities in particular times and places, can act as a mitigating factor upon the potential for global communication arising from the development of seemingly 'borderless' information and communications technologies (ICTs).

The remainder of this chapter will elaborate upon each of these themes. The themes to be considered are:

■ media and power;
■ media markets;
■ media institutions and policy;
■ media and culture;
■ new media technologies.

This will provide the context for an introduction to the issues arising from media globalization, including the consideration of whether this constitutes a new form of cultural imperialism. It will lead on to the evaluation in Chapter 2 of how these key concepts and issues are approached through different intellectual traditions in relation to global media.

Media and Power

One of the reasons why we consider the study of global media to be important, and a central factor in framing different theories of the media, is because we associate its international circulation with questions of *power*. Thompson has defined power as 'the ability to act in pursuit of one's aims and interests, the ability to intervene in the course of events and to affect their outcome' (Thompson, 1995, p. 13). He proposes that communication can be understood as a social activity, where communicating agents engage in purposive activity in structured social contexts. If communication is thus understood as purposive social action, and not simply as the transmission of information, then communication can also be understood as one of the forms through which power can be exercised. In her study of applications of power in international relations, Susan Strange has proposed that power is never simply *relational*, or 'the power of A to get B to do something they would not otherwise do', but is also *structural*, understood as 'the power to decide how things shall be done, the power to shape frameworks within which states relate to each other, relate to people, or relate to corporate enterprises. The relative power of each party in a relationship is more, or less, if one party is also determining the surrounding structure of the relationship' (Strange, 1988, p. 24, 25). The work of French philosopher Michel Foucault has also drawn attention to the need to study, not simply power in the abstract, but *power relations*, or 'the strategies, networks, the mechanisms, all those techniques by which a decision is accepted and by which that decision could not but be taken in the way it was' (Foucault, 1988, pp. 103–4).

Table 1.1 Forms of power

Forms of power	Resources	Paradigmatic institutions
Economic power	Material and financial resources	Economic institutions (e.g. commercial enterprises)
Political power	Authority	Political institutions (e.g. nation-states)
Coercive power	Physical and armed force	Coercive institutions (e.g. military, police, prisons)
Symbolic power	Means of information and communication	Cultural institutions (e.g. religious institutions, schools and universities, media industries)

Source: Thompson (1995), p. 17

Thompson (1995) has observed that media are associated with forms of *cultural power* or *symbolic power* that arise from the capacity to control, use and distribute resources associated with the means of information and communication. Symbolic power matters because it is the principal means by which the actions of others can be shaped through transformation of values, beliefs and ideas, or the practices and institutions of *culture*. Thompson contrasts symbolic power with economic power, political power, and coercive power in the manner shown in Table 1.1.

Media are particularly important in terms of Thompson's schema, since they are not only institutional sites through which cultural or symbolic power may be exercised, but also major corporations that invest in resources, employ people, and produce goods and services, and therefore exercise significant economic power. As Stuart Hall observed, the combination of economic, technical, social and cultural resources held by media organizations means that 'quantitatively and qualitatively ... the media have established a decisive and fundamental leadership in the cultural sphere' (Hall, 1977, p. 341). Consideration of the nature of *media power* draws attention to two sets of issues. One is the extent to which power is seen as relational, and primarily connected to the nature of influence, or whether it is seen as structural, and connected to the question of ideology. The second is the extent to which media power is largely reflective of other systems of social power (economic, political and coercive), or has its own internal dynamics. It has been the process of drawing the interconnections between these two dimensions of media power – the cultural-symbolic and the political-economic – that has historically defined *critical media theories*.

The emergence of *mass communications* as a field of academic knowledge in the 1950s and 1960s was strongly connected to the dominance of liberal pluralism in the social sciences during this period, and equated power with *influence*. According to liberal-pluralist models of society, power was primarily about the capacity of 'A to influence B to make decision X' and, as a result, its focus was upon the impact of media upon behavioural change.[4] In his critical overview of mass communications and the liberal pluralist tradition, Hall argued that it ultimately promoted a functionalist model of society where:

> The media were held to be largely reflective or expressive of an achieved consensus. The finding that, after all, the media were not very influential was predicated upon the belief that, in its wider cultural sense, the media largely reinforced those values and norms which had already received a wider consensual foundation. (Hall, 1982, p. 61)

The development of critical media theories was in part a reaction to this apparent sanguinity about media power found in the mass communications paradigm. While the critique of the mass communication paradigm was multi-faceted,[5] there were two particular critiques of the ways in which the relationship of media to power, and the nature of media power, had been approached. First, the idea that power was equated with influence, and associated primarily with the behavioural effects upon individuals arising from particular media messages, was demonstrated to be inadequate when the point was raised that power operated in a structural as well as a relational sense. As Hall (1982) observed, social and cultural power was about the 'power to define the rules of the game' and to determine what was 'deviant' behaviour, as well as the capacity to define social reality through processes of representation, which were never simply the reflection of events, but the active production of meaning. Hall argued that:

> If the media were not simply reflective or 'expressive' of an already achieved consensus, but instead tended to reproduce those very definitions of the situation which favoured and legitimated the existing structure of things, then what had seemed at first as merely a reinforcing role had now to be reconceptualized in terms of the media's role in consensus formation. (Hall, 1982, pp. 63–4)

In other words, while the mass communications tradition had approached the relationship of media to power in terms of influence, which was behavioural, individualized, and empirically measurable in relation to particular media messages, the critical media studies tradition understood the question of media power in terms of *ideology*, and the complex relationship of dominant ideologies to questions of representation, consent and the social construction of reality, or what Hall termed the 'reality effect' (Hall, 1982, pp. 74–5).

The second critique of the mass communications tradition concerned its failure to connect media power to other power relations. In particular, while the mass communications tradition tended to approach economic, political, coercive and symbolic-cultural power as relatively discrete in their nature and operations, the critical paradigm saw these as being interconnected. Examples included relations of structural inequality through which the dominant interests in capitalist societies – particularly dominant class interests – maintained their control or hegemony over subordinate social groupings or, on a global scale, how dominant Western interests maintained political and economic power over the 'less developed' or 'Third World' nations. In doing so, they drew upon the Marxist critique of structural inequality in capitalist societies to argue that 'property ownership, economic control and class power were inextricably tied together' (Murdock and Golding, 1977, p. 28). The distinctiveness of the media in such a critical paradigm required an understanding of how the media had increasingly become a central part of the capitalist economy, with two issues being central. First, it involved a mapping of patterns of concentration of media ownership and control, in order to establish both that 'the media are first and foremost industrial and commercial organizations which produce and distribute commodities' (Golding and Murdock, 1973, p. 207), and that their economic significance in capitalist economies is both large and increasing over time. Second, it required an analysis of the relationship between these structures of economic control and processes of cultural production and distribution, in order to assess the claim made by Murdock and Golding that 'it is only by situating cultural products within the nexus of material interests which circumscribe their creation and distribution that their range and content can be fully explained' (Murdock and Golding, 1977, p. 36).

The critical media studies tradition has drawn attention to two issues concerning the nature of media power, and the relationship of media power to other forms of power, that have been central to defining two approaches to understanding global media, that will be discussed in more detail in Chapter 2. The first is the relationship of the economic to the ideological in understanding the nature and significance of cultural or symbolic power as it arises through the media. The *political economy* approach has tended to attach explanatory primacy to economic factors, seeing these as shaping cultural developments, with varying degrees of direct determination or relative autonomy. By contrast, *cultural studies* approaches have tended to draw attention to the distinctiveness of language and systems of signification, arguing that their articulation to systems of economic or political power is by definition particular, contingent, and contested, since the nature of meaning as it is produced and understood is rarely the same between senders and receivers in complex communications systems.[6] The second issue is the extent to which media power is largely reflective of other forms of power, or possesses its own institutional relations, capacities and dynamics. In an important recent contribution to these debates, Couldry and Curran (2003) distinguish between the conception of media power as simply a component in a wider and more intense mass, where the power of media only matters insofar as it is connected to other forms of power (economic, political, social, cultural, coercive and so on), and an understanding of media power as an entity in its own right, with its own dynamics of production and distribution that is nonetheless connected to other power sources. The significance of this distinction is that it draws attention to how contestations about the media in itself – how it is produced, distributed, consumed, and regulated – can shape other institutional and power relationships, thereby questioning the implicit hierarchy found in many accounts of media power, where it is in some sense 'reflective' of other power relations, such as control over economic resources or governmental authority.

Media Markets: Audiences, Advertisers, Finance and Creative Content

Media organizations operate in three markets. First, there is the *market for creative content*, or the ability to produce and/or distribute material which is sufficiently compelling to audiences, readers or users for them to exchange money and/or time for access to such content. Second, there is the *market for financial resources*, or the ability to finance their ongoing operations as well as new investments in technology, distribution platforms, or territorial expansion of their operations. Some of these revenues can be generated internally, from profits reinvested in production and distribution activity, but funds are also generated from loans through financial institutions, equity investment (shares), and from government through subsidies, tax incentives and other means. The balance between these sources varies, on the basis of whether the media organization in question is a commercial operation that is privately owned, a publicly owned and funded organization, or a hybrid in terms of either its ownership structure or its sources of funding. Examples of the latter include public service broadcasting (PSB) organizations that nonetheless rely upon commercial advertising for at least part of their revenue, and privately owned media organizations that draw upon forms of government funding. Third, there is the *market for audiences/readers/users*, or the competition for both the expenditure of consumers and the time and attention devoted to accessing the content of the media organization. Garnham (1987) proposed that industries and companies in the media and cultural sectors compete in four ways: (1) for consumer expenditure; (2) for advertising expenditure; (3) for consumption time, in what has been termed the 'attention economy' (Pine and Gilmore, 1999); and (4) for talent and specialist labour.

The market for audiences has been discussed at length in the field of *media economics*. One of the distinctive features of the media industries is that they operate in *dual product markets* (Picard, 1989). Media organizations compete in the market for audiences' or users' time and money with the products and services which they circulate. They also compete in the *advertising market*, selling access to audiences for the producers of other goods and services, on the basis of the size and characteristics of the audiences or users that their products and services attract. The types of advertising which they attract can vary from classified advertising, local advertising, to specialist advertising services such as publication inserts, and national advertising. Media organizations compete in particular *geographical markets*, which may be local, national or international. In some instances, particularly in relation to the allocation of broadcasting spectrum, government regulatory authorities determine the geographical reach of the market area. In other instances, most notably in relation to the Internet, the global reach of the medium enables media organizations to compete in a market space that is at least potentially borderless and global. Media markets take the form shown in Figure 1.1.

An understanding of the structure, financing and control relations in media industries has been an ongoing issue for critical media theorists, particularly from the political economy perspective. There exist four broad means by which a media organization can finance both its ongoing activities and any new investments it wishes to make:

1. *retained earnings*, or revenue derived from sales (including advertising sales) that is reinvested into the organization;
2. *debt financing*, or borrowing from financial institutions to finance expansion and new investments;
3. *equity investment*, or the sale of shares in the company;
4. *government financing*, which can range from direct subsidy to special loans and tax incentives.

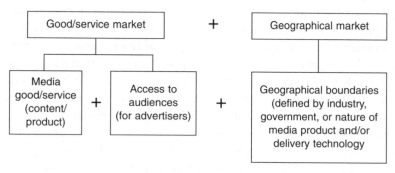

Source: Picard (1989), p. 21

Figure 1.1 The nature of media markets

While financing growth through retained earnings is the option which ensures that control over media organizations remains with those who currently have it, both the need to invest in new technologies to remain competitive and tendencies towards expansion as a means of capturing new markets and achieving greater control have necessitated the use of other financial instruments in the sector, most notably debt and equity. These external financial instruments present new forms of risk. In the case of debt, the risk is that the debt will not be able to be serviced, and control over the media organization will pass to banks and other financial institutions, while the risk associated with equity is that the company can be subject to a takeover bid.

Expansion in the media sector has involved not only competitive strategies to expand market share within particular markets, but producing and selling in multiple markets. Forms of expansion include:

1. *horizontal expansion*, through takeovers, mergers and acquisitions of competitors within the industry in which they are dominant, or the development of new products and services within that industry;

2. *vertical expansion*, or takeovers, mergers and acquisitions of related production and distribution interests within the industry supply chain, or the development of new enterprises in related areas. Doyle (2002a, 2002b) identifies three core elements to the media supply chain: *production*, or the creation of original media content; *packaging*, or the bundling of content into marketed media products or services (for example, newspapers, magazines, music CDs, videos and DVDs, television and radio networks with programming schedules, and Internet portals); and *distribution*, or final delivery of media products to consumers;
3. *diagonal expansion*, or *conglomeration*, which involves expansion into complementary activities, either through mergers and acquisitions or the development of new enterprises, that enable productive synergies to be developed;
4. *diversification*, or expansion into non-media activities or, correspondingly, non-media companies expanding into media industries.

The final significant media market is the *market for creative content*. In many ways, this is the market that is least understood not only by media economists, but by media theorists from across all academic disciplines. An understanding of the market for creative content requires that consideration be given to the distinctive features of both the media commodity and the creative industries. *Media commodities* possess three characteristics which mark them out as distinctive when compared to other commercial products. First, there is a high level of *risk* attached to investment in the production and distribution of media products. As media products are in many case *experience goods*, producers have a very unclear understanding of consumer preferences, and consumers often have a poor understanding of the nature of the creative product before consuming it, and their satisfaction results from an experience which cannot be predicted with any accuracy prior to the act of consumption.[7] Second, many media commodities are *immaterial* in their form. Collins *et al.* observed that 'it is the message not the medium that provides value to the user and the message is immaterial or intangible' (Collins *et al.*, 1988, p. 7). There are, however, different degrees of materiality to music, broadcast media and print. One can hear a song or view a TV programme in a relatively fleeting, and often quite contingent, moment of consumption; this may take a more tangible material form if one buys a CD that the song is on, or a DVD set of the TV series. Books are very tangible and material, but other print media forms, such as newspapers and magazines, may be casually consumed and discarded on the same day or in the same wait for the services of a dentist, a hairdresser or a lifestyle consultant. Third, there is an ongoing *demand for originality and novelty*, which relates to what Ryan (1992) has identified as the truncated product life cycle for many cultural commodities.

The combination of high levels of risk, relative immateriality, and inexorable demand for innovation and novelty, means that many media and cultural commodities have both high initial production costs and near-zero costs of reproduction. As a result, the development of new media and cultural commodities can be seen as a process of continuous research and development to generate new prototypes, so that 'rapid product innovation [is] a central condition of existence' of the media industries (Collins *et al.*, 1988, p. 9). There are risk management strategies that have been developed over time to deal with these contingencies, such as the development of content streams or *repertoires*; the use of genres, formats, established stars and long-running programmes or serials to provide background information to audiences about content; time-based forms of distribution (for example, broadcast television screens the programmes likely to attract the largest audiences at 'prime time' on certain days at key points in the year); and corporate expansion strategies such as vertical integration and conglomeration, which can provide greater regularity to content development and distribution (Garnham, 1987; Hesmondhalgh, 2002).

Features of the media commodity such as high risk associated with experience goods, relative immateriality of consumption, and the requirement for ongoing innovation and novelty are more general characteristics of the *creative industries*. Richard Caves defines the creative industries as those industries 'supplying goods and services that we broadly associate with cultural, artistic, or ... entertainment value' (Caves, 2000, p. 1). They include, for Caves, book and magazine publishing, the visual and performing arts, music, film, TV, fashion and games. Caves identifies seven distinctive economic properties of creative activities:

1. a high degree of *demand uncertainty*, as they are experience goods for which consumer preferences are unknown and, except in an *ex post* sense, largely unknowable to producers. This is what Caves terms 'symmetrical ignorance' or the 'nobody knows' principle (Caves, 2000, p. 3): producers don't know what consumers want, and consumers don't know until consuming the product what producers have given them;
2. creative product combines the care and commitment which creative people typically attach to their creative work, with the need for 'humdrum' commercial skills which enable creative product to be produced and go to market;
3. the need to bring together a large number of people with highly diverse skills on a contract basis in order to produce creative product, or what is termed the 'motley crew' element of team-based production;
4. the *infinite variety* principle, whereby there is not only 'horizontal' product differentiation (for example, action movies differ from romantic comedies,

animated films or Westerns), but no two creative products are the same, and there is 'vertical' product differentiation (no two action movies are the same, and whether action movie A is better than action movie B – Is a Vin Diesel film better than a Steven Seagal film? Is one Vin Diesel film better than another? – will be based upon the highly subjective preferences of individual consumers);

5. the existence of *vertically differentiated skills*, or the 'A-list'/'B-list' phenomenon, where small and often intangible differences in skill, originality, proficiency and talent can lead to vastly different levels of income for two creative people undertaking a similar activity, such as singers or actors, on the basis of differing 'marketability' of the creative talent;

6. the need to co-ordinate the activities of complex creative teams according to tight time schedules, raising issues of co-ordination, project management and time management;

7. the *durability* of creative products, and the capacity of the most successful creative products to continue to derive *economic rents* over a long period of time (for example, the back-catalogue of Beatles songs continue to be purchased, played on the radio, used in films, re-recorded by other artists and so on, long after their original composition and commercial release).

For Caves, risk and uncertainty in the creative industries are principally managed by two means: contracts and institutions. *Contracts* are essential to the creative industries, and take a multiplicity of forms, but nonetheless present two major issues. One issue is that of *asymmetrical information*, where one signatory may have less information than another, and can therefore be exploited or disadvantaged through the contract. The other major issue is the *allocation of decision rights*, or the question of who has final decision-making control over the different aspects of producing, distributing and selling a creative product. *Institutions* therefore become central to the ongoing management of projects, contracts, risks and rewards, particularly since the production of complex creative products (for example, feature films or TV series) typically has high fixed costs that are best distributed across a range of projects. Media corporations are the most obvious institutional form through which risks and contracts in the creative industries are managed, but others, such as unions representing artists and other creative personnel, also play an important role. At the same time, the market for creative content is, as Caves noted, far more volatile and unpredictable than traditional capital and consumer markets, since the competition for creative content is ultimately a competition for the skills and talents of creative people, and it has always proved difficult to institutionalize creativity, since it is notoriously hard to either quantify or routinise.[8] The complexities associated with managing and commercializing creativity will be returned to below, but Richard Florida outlines the issues in his analysis of the rise of a *creative class* when he observes that 'Creativity comes from people. And while people can be hired and fired, their creative capacity cannot be bought and sold, or turned on or off at will' (Florida, 2002, p. 5).

Media Organizations and Policy

Analysis of both media power and media markets draws attention to the nature of *media institutions*, or what occurs within the institutions that solicit, produce, manage and distribute media content. It also points to the importance of *media policy* as a system of institutionalized governance mechanisms over the structure, conduct and performance of media organizations by, for the most part, national governments.

Large-scale corporate organizations came to dominate the media and related industries in the 20th century, as they did in most sectors of the economy, as there was both greater concentration of media ownership and the absorption of small-scale commercial media producers and distributors by larger corporate conglomerates. The historical process of media concentration and conglomeration within national media markets has been well documented (for example, Golding and Murdock, 1973; Curran, 1977; Sánchez-Tabernero *et al.*, 1993; Meier and Trappel, 1998; McChesney, 1999; Bagdikian, 2000; Doyle, 2002a), and will not be dwelt upon here. We can observe five factors that have been both cause and consequence of the increasing enmeshment of media production and distribution within the corporate institutional form.

The first is the nature of the corporation as a *distinctive legal form of property*. Company law has given a permanent legal status to the incorporated company that is separate from that of its shareholders, and the principle of limited liability has meant that shareholders in a company cannot be legally accountable for more than the amount of money represented by the value of their shares. This legal safeguard has dramatically promoted investment in corporations over many years, and has in particular promoted the growth in institutional investment by banks, insurance companies and other financial institutions in corporations of all sectoral types, meaning that the amount of capital able to be invested in corporations through either loans or shares has grown dramatically, thus enabling corporations to operate on a much larger scale than unincorporated businesses.[9]

Second, the corporate form of enterprise has engendered a tripartite division of power within the corporations between shareholders, company directors and corporate managers, and has raised the question of *who controls the corporation*. While *legal ownership* has entailed the right to receive revenues from the corporation in the form of dividends, *economic ownership* has involved the capacity to exercise powers of control over the corporation's assets and, under modern company law, these powers reside with the corporation itself as a legal entity (Herman, 1981; Scott, 1985; Clegg *et al.*, 1986). The capacity to exercise *strategic control* within a corporation, which involves the capacity to undertake longer-term planning rather than administer day-to-day administration, may rest with dominant shareholders, power blocs of investors and directors (for example, through indirect control by financial institutions), or with corporate managers within the organization. In any case, the capacity to exercise such power is never absolute: it is always contingent upon overall corporate performance, the trading of shares in the corporation, the corporation's overall financial position, and the ability to retain majority support among the board of directors.

Third, the growth in the size and scale of modern corporations has been accompanied by the increasing *complexity* of managing production, distribution and consumption, and the problem of *how to control* such processes in order to minimize risk, maximize profits, and manage uncertainty. Beniger (1986) and Mulgan (1989) have argued that a *control revolution* took place in industrial societies in the late 19th and early 20th centuries, that was premised upon the increasing centrality of corporate planning to the management of economic relations, and the interaction between innovations in technologies of information, communication and transportation on the one hand, and organizational reform on the other. The bureaucratization of organization promoted the development of the multidivisional corporation, which marked the triumph of what the business historian Alfred Chandler termed the 'visible hand' in corporate management, whereby 'control in the sense of co-ordination and the stabilization of markets passed from the external, dispersed control of the market to the internal bureaucracies of the corporation' (Mulgan, 1989, pp. 79–80). A critical question in the 21st century, to be considered in Chapter 4, is whether there has been a further mutation in the locus of control from the organization and the internalization of control, to networks as a more fluid and provisional site for concentrated decision-making, itself promoted by new developments in the technologies and infrastructures of communications media.

Fourth, the rise of the corporate form gave new significance to the role of legal *contracts* as a means of managing risk and co-ordinating diverse activities. While the corporate form has provided the primary institutional framework for managing projects, contracts, risks and rewards, particularly in those instances where production processes have high fixed costs distributed across a range of projects, *contracts* have constituted the other significant set of mechanisms through which such social relations are managed. Williamson

(1975, 1985) has understood the corporation as a *nexus of contracts*, or an institutional means of managing transaction costs and pooling capabilities in order to maximize benefits, and minimize risks, associated with organizing interdependent relations in a context of market failure, imperfect information and endemic uncertainty. The relationship between institutions and contracts is particularly pressing in the media industries as a means of managing endemic risk, economic uncertainty, and organizational complexity, due to the complex and contingent division of labour and the time-constrained nature of projects, and the unique difficulties involved in combining the personally driven and non-conforming elements of creative work with bureaucratic and commercially oriented forms of corporate organization.

Fifth, the *bureaucratic organizational form* has presented itself as both a central, and yet deeply problematic, means of managing creativity in the media industries. The classical model of bureaucracy, derived from the German sociologist Max Weber, defines it as an organizational form characterized by: (1) a highly complex hierarchy or authority; (2) a highly developed division of labour and role specialization; (3) a formalized set of rules and procedures; (4) employment and promotion based on performance and technical qualifications (for example, professional managers make most of the decisions); (5) rationalized and codified decision-making procedures; and (6) formal, rule-bound relations between workers and managers (Demers, 2002). Davis and Scase (2000, p. 55) have drawn attention to the rise of bureaucracy in both the commercial and publicly supported media industries. In the bureaucratic model, the mechanisms of control and co-ordination are explicit and hierarchical, and creative people are motivated by both conventional measures of income and status within the organization, and by some degree of 'internalized commitment' to the organization and its values. Nonetheless, the bureaucratic corporate model does not sit easily with creative workers since, as Caves observes, 'the inner and individualistic aspect of creative production mixes badly with the orderly, rule-driven routines of the large, bureaucratic firm' (Caves, 2000, p. 16). Davis and Scase have observed that the characteristic modes of organizing creative work, which assume high degrees of personal autonomy, non-conformity and a degree of indeterminacy in how such practices can be generalized within organizations, profoundly challenge bureaucratic, norm-driven models of work organization (Davis and Scase, 2000, pp. 17–21).

Policy institutions have a central role in regulating the ownership, production and distribution of media in all forms, and as James Michael has observed, the regulation of the media of communication is 'as old as blood feuds over insults, and ... as classic an issue as deciding whose turn it is to use the talking drum or the ram's horn' (Michael, 1990, p. 40). At its simplest, media policy can be understood as a set of laws and regulations, whose precise forms differ from one country to another, but typically address such issues as:

1. control over market entry in order to ensure planned development of media services;
2. limits on the concentration of media ownership, in order to set limits to media power and influence;
3. limits on foreign ownership of national media, that may be connected to concerns about national security or territorial sovereignty;
4. promotion of local or national content, that is in some sense more reflective of the local or national culture, particularly in mass media such as broadcasting;
5. promotion of programming which caters to the needs of particular audiences, such as children, older people, minority populations (for example, indigenous communities) or people living in remote areas;
6. promotion of programming that is reflective of the cultural, linguistic and other forms of diversity found in the wider society;
7. programme standards that ensure fair, accurate and responsible coverage of matter of public interest, that do not vilify or offend particular groups in the community or unreasonably undermine community harmony;
8. programme standards that prevent the distribution of material that is deemed harmful to the community as a whole, as well as placing restrictions upon distribution and access to content that may be particularly harmful to sections of the community.

In this respect, media policy could be approached as a specific sub-branch of public policy, with its own set of relations between policy objectives, policy instruments and policy outcomes, and its own forms of policy actors, institutions, communities and cultures (cf. Considine, 1994; Hill, 1997). Two specific factors give policy considerably more salience in relation to media, and a central role in understanding global media. First, the corporate form of organization in the media sector has attached to it a series of *legal and governance requirements*, that include both generalized forms of law and regulation (for example, company law, workplace relations law, competition policy), and specific forms of policy and modes of regulation applied to media corporations as socially and culturally influential institutions. Price (1995), Streeter (1995) and Donald (1998) have observed how, in relation to broadcast media in particular, both the nature of property (the licence to broadcast) and broadcasting markets are artefacts of government policy and the ways in which industry structure and conduct are shaped through law and regulation, so that the institutional forms media organizations take are very much shaped by media policy. Price has referred to the role of government in structuring broadcast television, since 'government structuring refers to the specific efforts by governments to determine the ownership, management, and content of systems for the distribution of television signals and the associated aspects concerning the production of programmes' (Price, 1995, p. 16). This structuring of the right to broadcast through government-sanctioned property regimes can be seen as an example of how 'the state shapes an economy's organizational structure – the different institutional arrangements that actors use to co-ordinate exchange and production' (Campbell and Lindberg, 1990, p. 634).

Second, the media have been considered to possess a unique role in the development of national citizenship, and the linking of populations to nation-states and forms of national identity through culture. Gellner observed that a defining feature of modern nationalism has been 'the striving to make culture and polity congruent, to endow a culture with its own political roof, and not more than one roof at that' (Gellner, 1983, p. 43). In a historical sense, Anderson linked media as cultural technologies to the emergence of modern nationalism, drawing attention to the rise of print capitalism in the emergence of the modern nation-state. Anderson understood the nation as 'an imagined political community' (Anderson, 1991, p. 6), and proposed that the symbolic dimension of nationalism as a series of 'myths' grounded in representations and everyday practices became crucial in extending the boundaries of community, promoting a symbolic unification through common allegiance to a 'deep, horizontal citizenship' that seeks to transcend divisions within the nation-state. In a similar vein, Schudson (1994) drew attention to the ways in which the modern nation-state self-consciously uses language policy, formal education, collective rituals such as national events, cultural policy and the public exhibition of 'high' culture in galleries and museums, and the mass media, to promote national cultural integration. In the context of media globalization, national media and communications policies constitute a form of what Schlesinger has termed 'communicative boundary maintenance', regulating and mediating the relationship between global media flows and local cultural impacts (Schlesinger, 1991a, p. 162; cf. Flew and McElhinney, 2005).

Media and Culture

Media are central to the provision of cultural or symbolic resources globally, and therefore integral to the exercise of cultural or symbolic power. Hall observed that the combination of economic, technical, social and cultural resources held by media organizations had meant that 'quantitatively and qualitatively ... the media have established a decisive and fundamental leadership in the cultural sphere' (Hall, 1977, p. 341). Debates about the cultural impact of global media are at the forefront of current considerations surrounding globalization, and yet the linking of these debates to culture is highly complex. Hartley (2002, p. 51) has observed that culture is *multidiscursive*, as 'it can be mobilised in a number of different discourses ... you cannot import a fixed definition into any and every context and expect it to make sense'. In a similar vein, Poster (2005, p. 134) has drawn attention to how, with particular reference to new media, 'culture has become a problem for everyone' and how, in the absence of an explicit theorization of culture, there are strong tendencies to adopt the default settings of the *status quo*. The relationship between media and culture as it has been understood in different theoretical approaches to global media will be explored in depth in Chapter 2, but it is important to establish three conceptual preliminaries that lie behind such discussions.

First, there is the relationship, and the associated tension, between the aesthetic and anthropological understandings of culture. The word 'culture' is derived from cultivation, and was extended in Europe from the 16th to the 18th centuries from an association with crops and animal husbandry to the cultivation of the mind. By the 19th century, culture had become linked to civilization, and the idea that the development of the human mind and the advancement of a civilization could be linked through promotion of the production and distribution of great works of scholarship and art among a wider population (Bocock, 1992). This led to the question of what constituted 'great works', and to the intellectual traditions associated with *aesthetics*, and the development of criteria for attaching and ascribing different forms of artistic and cultural value to the myriad cultural products that had been created and distributed among a wider population (Cooper, 1992). The anthropological sense of culture, by contrast, did not concern itself with what are or are not canonical works of art and literature, but rather with culture as the lived experience of people and communities, or what Edward Tylor described in 1903 as 'that complex whole which includes knowledge, belief, art, morals, law, custom, and any other capabilities acquired by man as a member of society' (quoted in Thompson, 1991, p. 128). In such a definition, culture is not about 'What is good?' or 'What is excellent?', but is rather about *culture as lived experience*, or what people do in a given social situation, with the resources available to them, to both produce and consume culture, understood here not as a show case for excellence, but as a diverse repository of symbolic forms.

The second key issue in considerations about culture, and its relationship to media, concerns what Hall (1986) described as the *two paradigms* of cultural studies, culturalism and structuralism. Hall drew attention to the formative texts of British cultural historians such as Richard Hoggart, Raymond Williams, and E. P. Thompson, and how they developed an understanding of culture as lived experience that moved beyond dichotomies between 'high' and 'low' culture, to instead 'conceptualize culture as interwoven with all social practices, and those practices, in turn, as a common form of human activity ... through which men and women make history' (Hall, 1986, p. 39). While this understanding of culture has been central to cultural studies as it has subsequently evolved, what Hall terms the *culturalist* tradition – with its focus upon the lived experience of ordinary people – was challenged by the various forms of structuralism that developed over the same period. *Structuralism* was concerned less with what people did than with the overarching social conditions under which they did it. It drew attention to the ways in which individuals were not 'free agents' in a society and culture, but were rather the 'products' of a system of social, cultural, linguistic and psychological relationships that existed independently of the actions of particular individuals, which possessed an underlying structural 'code' that was not in itself immediately accessible to those individuals who were expected to adopt it. Structuralism was strongly influenced by developments in cultural anthropology associated with Claude Lévi-Strauss, the field of semiotics and its understanding of language as a system or code whereby, as Umberto Eco argued, 'every act of communication ... presupposes a signification system as its necessary condition' (Eco, 1976, p. 9), and by Marxist adaptations of structuralism to the theory of *ideology*, particularly through the work of the French Marxist philosopher Louis Althusser. Althusser proposed a radical rethinking of the Marxist theory of ideology along structuralist lines, proposing that while ideology was a 'system of representations', it was not so much a false presentation of social reality in order to serve dominant class and other interests, but rather an 'imaginary relationship' developed by individuals in relation to their historical conditions of lived experience. This 'imaginary relationship' was, nonetheless, so deeply embedded structurally in the consciousness of individuals that – in the absence of a radical intellectual and/or political rupture – they would, unconsciously and on a daily basis, reproduce the conditions of social life that maintained structures of power and domination (cf. Barrett, 1991).

The relationship between culture as lived experience (culturalism), and culture as a complex signifying system (structuralism), generates some interesting tensions when applied to popular mass media forms, and in particular to the question of the relationship of critical media and cultural theories to popular media and culture. Cultural studies has sought to occupy this space, differentiating its understanding of the relationship of media to its audiences from both empirical studies of how people use the media, such as the *uses and gratifications* approach to audience studies in mass communications research

(Curran, 1990; McQuail, 2005, pp. 423–8), and the *dominant ideology* thesis, where it is argued that the dominant meanings of popular media reflect the class interests of those who own and control these institutions. It has done so through the deployment of three key concepts (cf. Hall, 1986; Fiske, 1987, 1992; Turner, 1990; Hall, 1993b):

1. *hegemony*: the complex, but nonetheless contested, processes through which 'a dominant class wins the willing consent of the subordinate classes to the system that ensures their subordination' (Fiske, 1992, p. 291). In particular, theories of hegemony have drawn attention to the ways in which symbols that are signifiers of unity – such as nationalism, the 'national interest' and 'common sense' – can be deployed in ways that disguise and elide other markers of social differentiation and conflict within a given population;
2. *negotiated readings*: the extent to which a media text may possess a 'preferred reading' that is consistent with the dominant ideology, but such interpretations, or readings, are contested by sections of the population. In particular, those in subordinate relations to the dominant structures of cultural and political-economic power, such as working-class people, young people, and racial and sexual minorities, may develop more 'negotiated' or even 'oppositional' readings of the dominant text, on the basis of their own social experience;
3. *textual polysemy*: semiotic theory argues that the meaning of a text is never simply given by the intentions of its author, but is rather subject to a wider social negotiation through structures and systems of interpretation. The texts of popular culture, and particularly popular media, are required by this interpretation to be polysemic, or open to a range of interpretations by a socially diverse and mixed population, in order to be popular and, in a capitalist context, to be commercially successful.

New Media Technologies

At their simplest, theories of new media propose that the information and communications technology (ICT) revolution that has gained momentum from the 1980s onward has so transformed the global media environment that we are witnessing the twilight of the 'old' media of print and broadcasting, and the rise of the 'new' media associated with digital technologies, convergence and networking. The global popularization of the Internet in the 1990s marks out the critical point in this debate, as it most clearly exemplified the qualitatively distinct properties associated with new media, but a considerable range of digital devices – most notably mobile phones – have displayed core characteristics of new media such as:

1. the convergence of ICTs, communications networks and media content, combined with the exponential growth in the processing capabilities of computer microchips (also known as Moore's Law – Verhulst, 2005, p. 333);
2. the digitization of all forms of text, speech, image and sound, into informational content that is manipulable and changeable at all stages of creation, storage, delivery and use, can be delivered at speed across physical distances, and is able to be stored in very small physical spaces;
3. networked distribution on a global scale, through communications infrastructures that are open, flexible, adaptable, and able to expand without limits as long as codes and protocols are shared across the network;
4. dramatically reduced access barriers to being a producer as well as a consumer of content, which has a potentially global reach in terms of audience;
5. interactivity between producers and users, with multiple feedback loops and media texts that remained continuously 'open' for re-use, repurposing and other forms of modification;
6. the scope for multiple modes of communication, ranging from one-to-one to many-to-many, in contrast to the one-to-many form characteristic of 20th-century mass communications media, and the potential this entailed for 'disintermediation', or more direct forms of communication not subject to the 'gatekeeping' functions of powerful interests or trained media professionals such as journalist and editors.

While all of these trends have been real and substantive in their impacts at all levels of society and social interaction, it is nonetheless the case that some of the more significant secondary claims made for new media – particularly in the 'boom years' of the 1990s – have failed to eventuate. For example, the claim that these new media would mark the death of television and other forms of broadcast media (for example, Gilder, 1994) was always dubious, and it has long been apparent that rapid adoption of the Internet worldwide in no way meant the mass migration of either audiences or advertisers away from mass media. Similarly, the idea that there would be a decline in the power of the traditional media giants, and the rise of a new generation of leaders in the digital content industries, not only overestimated the quality of the business models developed by some of the 'dot.com' darlings of the period (as brutally exposed in the collapse of the NASDAQ new-technology share index in April 2001). It also underestimated the capacity of the traditional 'big media' to respond to media convergence, the scope for strategic partnerships between 'old' and 'new' media corporations, and the extent to which digital media content is as often recombinant of existing media forms as it is qualitatively new (Bolter and Grusin, 2000). In all of these cases, there was a lack of awareness of lessons of media history, and the extent to which it reveals an adaptive capacity on the part of those involved in established media in dealing with the challenges of new media; the case of both radio and cinema in relation to the rise of television is one of many cases that reveal the limits of technological determinist readings of media futures (Flew, 2005a).

Lievrouw and Livingstone (2005) have argued that thinking about new media broadens the traditional concerns of media and communication studies by shifting the dominant concerns of the latter with media production, texts and audiences to a focus upon 'the *artefacts or devices* used to communicate or convey information; the *activities and practices* in which people engage in communication or share information; and the *social arrangements or organizational forms* that develop around those devices and practices' (Lievrouw and Livingstone, 2005, p. 2, authors' emphasis). Lievrouw and Livingstone identify a key limitation of many analyses of new media as being their failure to get beyond the level of artefacts and devices, or technologies in the narrow sense. To understand why a new media device, or indeed a new content form, is new, one always needs to ask not why this is a new device or form, but what is new *for society* about it (cf. Livingstone, 1999). Using this criterion, we could argue that the mobile phone that enabled SMS messaging was more new than the Digital Video Disc (DVD) player, as the mobile phone significantly changed the spatial, temporal and social dimensions of interaction through communications media, whereas the DVD player allowed for an enhanced version of an already established mode of personal interaction with prepackaged media content. In other words, mobile telephony has a significantly greater degree of impact upon communication activities and practices, with further impacts across the wider society, ranging from family relations to the construction of urban space. In a similar vein, it could be argued that the impact of the Internet on journalism and news production emerged with a time lag. For much of the 1990s, the impact of the Internet on journalism was understood through the frame of Computer-Assisted Reporting, or how journalists could use the new media to better perform their traditional roles. It was not until the rise of phenomena such as blogging, 'open news' sites and collaborative online news production in the 2000s that it became apparent that the Internet was not simply a useful tool for doing traditional journalism better, but was potentially corrosive of a long-established series of activities and practices associated with the 'gatekeeping' functions of traditional journalism (Bruns, 2005). In other words, the critical question in relation to new media is the impact of these new media artefacts and devices and new communications activities and practices upon both social arrangements and organizational forms, or 'the ways that new media technologies and practices are organized and governed' (Lievrouw and Livingstone, 2005, p. 2).

Media in Space: Understanding Global Media

It is worth concluding this chapter by considering the relationship that media have in relation to space, as a prelude to considering how various theories of media and communications address issues related to global media. Debates about new media are an example of the ways in which media and communications theories have certainly addressed the significance of changes in media forms, relations and practices over time. As a first pass, one can draw from the available summary literature on new media (see for example, Di Maggio *et al.*, 2001; Harries, 2002; Gauntlett, 2004; Marshall, 2004; Wellman, 2004; Flew, 2005a; Lievrouw and Livingstone, 2005) a series of propositions on how various social, economic and cultural relations have changed in the context of developments in new media have been developed and debated, including the following possible shifts from 'old' to 'new' media environments, as shown in Figure 1.2.

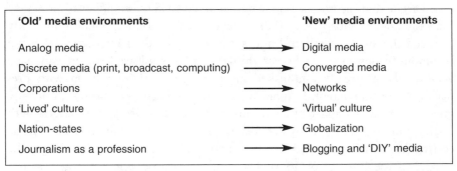

'Old' media environments		'New' media environments
Analog media	⟶	Digital media
Discrete media (print, broadcast, computing)	⟶	Converged media
Corporations	⟶	Networks
'Lived' culture	⟶	'Virtual' culture
Nation-states	⟶	Globalization
Journalism as a profession	⟶	Blogging and 'DIY' media

Figure 1.2 Scenarios for transition from 'old' to 'new' media environments

All of the authors listed above recognize that these trends are the subject of debate, and none uncritically endorses a transition from 'old' 20th-century media to 'new' 21st-century media. My point is rather that there is a deeply rooted tradition in media and communications studies across its various intellectual paradigms of thinking about developments over time in media technologies and forms and their impacts upon the wider political-economic and socio-cultural environment.

What is less clear, and which becomes an important issue in thinking about global media, is that there has been an equally strong commitment to thinking through the *spatial* dimensions of media in relation to these environments. One of the recurring themes – indeed, traps – in the literature on globalization generally, and media globalization in particular, is the tendency to assume that we have moved in a relatively seamless fashion over a relatively short time from a system based upon locally or nationally based media to one of global media. The argument is typically grounded primarily in an understanding of the global reach of new media technologies, and secondarily in either the transnational expansion of media corporations or the increased availability of a common repertoire of media images and experiences to more and more people worldwide. It is a particularly seductive line of argument when it is combined with understandings of new media that place these technological developments at the forefront of a wider set of trends and tendencies associated with knowledge-based economies, the rise of networking, uses of the Internet and satellite television among diasporic communities, the growth of global 'keywords' as factors underpinning political mobilization, and the internationalization of various forms of governance, including media governance. In the methodological framework that will be developed in this book, it will be such lines of argument concerning media globalization that will be scrutinized in some detail, from a mixture of economic, cultural, geographical, historical and political perspectives.

This is not to say that there are not approaches that explicitly foreground the spatial dimensions of media and communications. One of the most notable has been the Canadian tradition of communications studies, which has long linked the cross-border capabilities of communications technologies to questions of sovereignty, dependence, identity and global connectivity. Arguably the first theorists of global media were the Canadian communications theorists Harold Innis and Marshall McLuhan, who both stressed the importance of the technical properties of different media, particularly in relation to how their 'bias' was either towards the durability of information over time (time-bias) or towards the distribution of information over space (space-bias). Out of a complex and particular reading of the rise and fall of empires through history in relation to their primary systems of communication, Innis (1951) argued that the formation of empires in modernity was grounded in their capacity to rapidly distribute messages across space, thereby being able to maintain centralized rule over geographically dispersed spaces. From an Innisian perspective, the rise of media technologies that further deterritorialize global communications, such as satellite television and the Internet, could be seen as the furthering of such a 'project of Empire' (cf. Angus and Shoesmith, 1993; Acland and Buxton, 1999). A key counter-proposition in Canadian communications theory was that of Marshall McLuhan, who identified – naively in the view of his critics (for example, Stevenson, 1995) – the capacity of mass broadcast media distributed worldwide to contribute to a 'Global Village' (McLuhan and Powers, 1969), with the capacity to appeal to sensory experiences, and hence forms of literacy, that went beyond the place-bound and language-specific literacies associated with the written word (cf. Cohen, 2000; Marshall, 2000). McLuhan-inspired arguments have been developed in relation to new media by de Kerckhove (2001) and Levinson (2001).

Innis and McLuhan are useful representatives of what we may term the 'pessimistic' and the 'optimistic' strands of thought concerning the spatial dimensions of thinking about the impact of media, even if their arguments are quite specifically linked to particular media as they were disseminated in particular contexts, and neither of them was particularly empirically focused in their findings. There are other variants of speculative modes of theorizing about global media, mot notably in those approaches which draw out the implications of a historical link between development of the technologies of media and communication, information management, warfare and surveillance, such as the French political theorist Paul Virilio (for a useful summary of Virilio's ideas, see Redhead, 2004b; cf. Headrick, 1981). One media theorist who has drawn upon Virilio has been McKenzie Wark, with his notion of the *media vector* as a technological form that has fixed transmission properties, but tendencies towards 'ever greater velocity and flexibility, ever greater interconnection and abstraction' (Wark, 1994, pp. 222–3). In Wark's analysis, global media vectors draw people around the globe into a greater sense of interconnectedness driven by the technical means of communication, which in turn generates an increasingly significant set of disjunctures from culture as it is experienced locally through non-mediated forms of interaction, to the point where, as Wark puts it, 'we no longer have roots, we have aerials' (Wark, 1994, p. 64).

The approach being taken in this book to understanding global media is more of an empirical rather than a speculative one. The question of whether media are now best understood as operating on a global scale, constituting a qualitative break with the recent past where media were primarily local or national in their scope and operations, is a question that requires close scrutiny from a variety of perspectives. There is no doubt that the technologies of media and communication have created a situation where there is unprecedented capacity for global communication and exposure to global media flows. In order to establish whether this capacity has translated into an epoch of global media, and all that this implies in terms of other social, political, economic and cultural relations, we need to investigate more closely some of the key questions that have emerged in this chapter about what it would mean to say that we are experiencing a transformation towards global media:

1. Has there been a fundamental shift in cultural and symbolic power away from those forms which have national frames of reference, towards those which circulate through global mediascapes?
2. Are changes in the nature and scale of impact of media power reflected in other forms of power, such as economic, political and coercive power? Put differently, has there been a shift in the spatiality of power relations from national institutions and forces (for example, nation-states, national institutions, national military security systems) towards those of an international nature (for example, global governance laws and institutions, transnational corporations, global military and security systems)?
3. Do media markets increasingly operate on a global rather than a local or national scale?
4. Are media organizations increasingly operating according to a global logic of expansion, and is there a trend towards the colonization of national media spaces by global media corporations?
5. Have national forms of law, regulation and governance become increasingly ineffectual in the face of these globalizing forces?
6. Do we see the rise of an increasingly global form of culture, associated with the increasing role of media in the formation of identities and subjectivities?
7. Will the forces of new media, associated with digitization, convergence, networking and globalization, usurp the role and significance of the traditional forms of print and broadcast media, as well as cinema?

In the remainder of this book, there will be considerable critical scrutiny of these propositions. Chapter 2 undertakes an overview of two major intellectual traditions that have informed the study of global media – critical political economy and cultural studies. It is argued that both of these paradigms can draw significant and original insights from the perspectives derived from institutionalism, cultural policy studies, and cultural and economic geography. The chapter concludes with a consideration of the work of key theorists of 'strong globalization' such as Manuel Castells, and Michael Hardt and Antonio Negri, and how critiques of such work can be understood from such an interdisciplinary and multiperspectival approach.

In Chapter 3, an empirical analysis is undertaken of the extent to which the globalization of media corporations is consistent with the arguments of critical political economists that we have moved or are moving into an era of global media monopolies, where a small number of transnational media conglomerates dominate the media industry worldwide. The chapter draws upon empirical work on the 'transnationality' of global corporations (TNCs), and perspectives derived from institutionalism, international economics, and economic geography to question strong globalization claims such as those made by the critical political economists. It is also observed that while there has been a globalization of media production, we need to be careful about assuming that this involves a 'race to the bottom' driven by cost factors, as globalization driven by the clustering of locally specific skills and resources in particular locations is an equally significant factor.

Chapter 4 extends these arguments by considering some of the factors that drive new forms of clustering and location-specific resources as a counter-weight to globalization driven by cost-based dispersal and deterritorialization. The five factors identified as being of general relevance are: the rise of a knowledge economy; new competition theories that stress innovation as a driver of international competitiveness; the growing significance of network-based form of organization; the relevance of locational advantages to the emergence of industry clusters; and the rising importance of global production networks in the management of production and distribution by global corporations. Attention is drawn to the social embeddedness of market relations, and to theories of 'asymmetrical interdependence' and 'cultural reconversion', as providing bases from which to rethink theories of the local and the global from perspectives other than those of top-down cultural imperialism. Television-format trade and feature film production are used as case studies of the complexities of such global geo-economic flows.

Chapter 5 addresses the question of global media cultures. It discusses the difference between culture as lived experience and culture as mediated symbolic communication, observing that in the first case the concept of a global culture makes no sense, whereas if we consider the media dimension it becomes more plausible, particularly in the context of the globalization of modernity. It works through the relationship between these two dimensions of culture and two further ways of thinking about culture – as a resource and as a policy discourse – and uses these to discuss such issues as the rise of creative industries and creative cities discourses, the mediated nature of national and sub-cultural identity, and the rise of emergent transnational media cultures in Asia. It also discusses the relationship between culture and citizenship, both in relation to theories of nationalism and the rise of the modern nation-state, and questions of identity and cultural hybridity in a more globally fluid media-scape.

Finally, in Chapter 6, we consider some policy implications of these developments. While the claim that the nation-state has been rendered increasingly irrelevant by media globalization is strongly questioned, it is at the same time noted that media globalization presents significant challenges for media and cultural policy as it has been traditionally understood, which point in the direction of creative industries development strategies and a role for the state that is increasingly 'enabling' of industry development rather than 'protective' of national identities. It considers the rise of cultural policy at the sub-national level of cities and regions, as well as the supra-national level of international trade agreements and global civil society, concluding with a discussion of the UN-sponsored World Summits on the Information Society (WSIS) in Geneva in 2003 and Tunis in 2005.

Theories of Global Media 2

Introduction

We have identified in Chapter 1 a set of criteria through which developments in global media can be critically evaluated. These focused upon six issues of: the relationship of media to political, economic, coercive and cultural power; the nature and operation of media markets; developments in media organizations and public policy; the complex relationship between media and culture; the implications of new media technologies; and the spatial dimensions of global media. In Chapter 2, there will be an analysis of where different theories of the global media sit in terms of these criteria. The first part of the chapter will focus upon two influential academic paradigms for understanding global media: critical political economy and cultural studies. In considering the strengths and weaknesses of these approaches to developing an understanding of contemporary global media, there will also be consideration of some emergent perspectives that shed new light on issues raised from within these paradigms. The four alternative approaches which we will give consideration to are: institutionalism; cultural policy studies; cultural and economic geography; and globalization theories. All of these present questions about whether developments in global media need to be understood, not as an extension of well-established tendencies and hence understandable within existing paradigms of thought, but rather as qualitatively new phenomena which require the elaboration of new concepts and theoretical tools.

Critical Political Economy

Critical political economy has for at least three decades provided the most influential framework through which developments in global media are understood and interpreted. Its origins lay in a critique of mass communications theory as it had developed in the 1950s and 1960s, arguing that these approaches failed to give suitable weight to the significance of questions of power and ideology, particularly how economic, political and symbolic power interacted in the sphere of culture. It was argued that there exist economic structures of dominance in the media and communications industries that set limits to the diversity of ideas and opinions in circulation through the media, and that this in turn promotes the circulation of a hegemonic set of ideas, or a 'dominant ideology', among the wider population. This critique of mass communications theory was connected to a rediscovery of the Marxist critique of capitalism, which linked this critique of media in liberal-democratic societies to a wider conceptual understanding of the bases of social order in class-divided societies. Marxism also provided a means by which the fragmentation of knowledge arising from unconnected, discipline-based approaches to academic research could instead be reformulated as more integrated, interdisciplinary forms of research and scholarship (see for example, Blackburn, 1972). Political economists place a particular primacy upon the structure of economic relations under capitalism, because structures of domination based upon class relations have seen as the core element of what both defines a capitalist economy and generates its dynamics, including those of class conflict. Garnham (1995, p. 70) argues that 'political economy sees class – namely, the structure of access to the means of production and the structure of the distribution of the economic surplus – as the key to the structure of domination'.

The critical political economy approach to media and communications has developed four principal practices, or 'pillars', that inform research and academic practice in the field (Mosco, 1996; Golding and Murdock, 2000). First, there is the insistence that media research refer to the *social totality*, or the interconnection between systems of economic, political, coercive and symbolic power as they are related to the media sphere. This points to the need for interdisciplinary research and scholarship, and developing connections between media and communications research and a wider set of forces, determinants and social relations. Second, there is the need for a *historical perspective*, or what Golding and Murdock (2000, p. 74) refer to as the '"slow but perceptible rhythms" that characterize the gradually unfolding history of economic formations and systems of rule'. Golding and Murdock (2000, pp. 74–7) identify four historical processes as being central to a political economy of media: the growth of the media as both an economic sector and a site of cultural influence; the extension of corporate control over the media; the growing commodification of media forms; and the changing nature of government intervention in media industries. Third, critical political economists are concerned with the changing balance between the commercial media industries and the government sector – including public service broadcasters – over time. The question raised here, which will be explored in more detail in later chapters, is whether there has been a symbiotic relationship between media globalization and the moves since the 1980s, classified under the general tag-line of neo-liberalism, to reduce government regulation and to privatize state-owned enterprises in strategic sectors such as telecommunications and broadcasting. Finally, critical political economists have placed a strong emphasis upon the notion of *praxis*, or a relationship between academic research and practice and the wider contexts in which it seeks influence, that is founded in ethical norms. Golding and Murdock identify 'a communications system as a public space that is open, diverse and accessible … [as] a basic yardstick against which critical political economy measures the performance of existing systems and formulates alternatives' (Golding and Murdock, 2000, p. 77). The need to develop and present research findings in ways that reflect a wider dialogue with activists and community interests is also indicative of 'a broad conception of professional activity that envisions a wider public than scholars tend to accept' (Mosco, 1996, p. 9).

A fifth element can be added, which is that critical political economy must be *global*, as the insistence upon a global perspective has been central to the development of critical political economy. The exemplar of such an analysis of global media from the perspective of critical political economy was US scholar Herbert Schiller. Schiller argued in his first book, *Mass Communications and American Empire* (Schiller, 1969), that the international movement towards the commercialization of broadcasting was driven by the rise of the US *entertainment, communications and information (ECI) industries*, and that the ascendancy of the ECI industries in the US economy had reached a point where 'nothing less than the viability of the American industrial economy is involved in the movement toward international commercialization of broadcasting' (Schiller, 1969, p. 96). In an argument that remained remarkably constant over a 30–year period, Schiller emphasized three propositions. First, the growth, concentration of ownership and geographical spread of US media and cultural industries, or the ECI sector – as it clearly also included the telecommunications and information technology industries – needed to be viewed alongside broader strategies of United States political, military, economic and foreign policy. Second, the influence of the ECIs is never simply political or economic; these sectors differ from other branches of commercial enterprise through their 'direct, though immeasurable impact on human consciousness', as well as their capacity 'to define and present their own role to the public' (Schiller, 1996, pp. 115, 125). The result is that what Schiller terms 'American pop culture product' has been constructed as the cultural ideal to which people in other parts of the world aspire, resulting in 'the phenomenally successful extension of marketing and consumerism to the world community' (Schiller, 1996, p. 115). Third, Schiller argued that the economic power of the ECI sector, combined with the global reach of cultural commodities and media messages, led to *cultural imperialism*. In *Communication and Cultural Domination*, Schiller defined cultural imperialism in the following terms:

> The concept of cultural imperialism ... describes the sum of processes by which a
> society is brought into the modern world system and how its dominating stratum is
> attracted, pressured, forced, and sometimes bribed into shaping social institutions to
> correspond to, or even promote, the values and structures of the dominant centre of
> the system. (Schiller, 1976, p. 9)

In terms of the relationship between media, power and culture, the critical
political economy perspective has engaged in two critical dialogues. The first
is with liberal-pluralist media theories. In manifestations that vary from the
'modernization' theories popularised in the 1960s (Lerner, 1958; Schramm,
1964) to current thinking about the impact of American 'soft power' as a
force for consensus in the global political economy (for example, Nye, 2004),
critical political economists have argued that such models have been fundamentally flawed by their exclusion of media and communications research
from a broader consideration of structures of economic, political and cultural
power (see Mattelart, 1994, pp. 147–64; Thussu, 2006, pp. 42–50 for a
summary of these debates).

The second dialogue, and in many respect the more complex one, has been
with Marxism. Marxism has at a general level put forward the proposition
that the realm of culture and ideas cannot be understood independently of the
political and economic forces that shape it and ultimately constrain it. This is
why the concept of *ideology* is so central to a Marxist theory of culture. Two
key variants of this argument can be found from the work of Karl Marx and
Friedrich Engels. The first, and perhaps the most influential, was developed by
Marx in *The German Ideology*:

> The ideas of the ruling class are in every epoch the ruling ideas i.e. the class which
> is the ruling material force of society, is at the same time its ruling intellectual force.
> The class which has the means of material production at its disposal, has control at
> the same time over the means of mental production ... The ruling ideas are nothing
> more than the ideal expression of the dominant material relationships. (quoted in
> Barrett, 1991, p. 9)

Perhaps the boldest and most prominent restatement of the 'ruling class = ruling
ideology' equation has been in the *propaganda model* of media developed by
Noam Chomsky and Edward Herman (Chomsky and Herman, 1988).
Chomsky and Herman proposed that the United States media largely functioned
through a class-based monopoly of ideas, whereby 'money and power are able
to filter out the news fit to print, marginalize dissent, and allow the government
and dominant interests to get their messages across to the public' (Chomsky and
Herman, 1988, p. 2). For Chomsky and Herman, this has been the result of five
'filters' that impact upon the flow of ideas through the mass media:

(1) the size, concentrated ownership, owner wealth and profit orientation of the dominant media firms; (2) advertising as the primary income source of the mass media; (3) the reliance of the media on information provided by government, business, and 'experts' funded and approved by these primary sources and agents of power; (4) 'flak' as a means of disciplining the media; and (5) 'anti-communism' as a national religion and control mechanism. (Chomsky and Herman, 1988, p. 2)

In a post-Cold War and post-9/11 world, the model would still be seen as valid, with the 'War on Terror' replacing 'anti-communism' as the driver of US government-corporate priorities (see Chomsky, 2001).

The 'ruling class = ruling ideology' or propaganda model sits alongside a second approach, developed in Marx's Introduction to *A Contribution to the Critique of Political Economy*, where culture and ideology exist as a level in a social formation where economic relations are in a dominant, but not necessarily determinant, relationship to the political and ideological 'levels' through which social relations are largely understood and contested:

In the social production of their lives, men enter into definite relations that are indispensable and independent of their will, relations of production which correspond to a definite stage of development of their material productive forces. The sum total of these relations of production constitutes the economic structure of society, the real foundation, on which rises a legal and political superstructure and to which correspond definite form of social consciousness. *The mode of production of material life conditions the social, political and intellectual life process in general.* (quoted in Larrain, 1983, p. 42; emphasis added)

This approach to the relationship between media and power, that sees economic power relations under capitalism as dominant but not determinant, has been the most influential one in critical political economy. Two of its key proponents have been the British political economists Peter Golding and Graham Murdock. Golding and Murdock have stressed how analyses of the relationship between media texts and their audiences need to be framed by both 'an analysis of the way the cultural industries work ... as industries', and an examination of 'the ways in which people's consumption choices are structured by their position in a wider economic formation' (Golding and Murdock, 2000, p. 72). In their overview of the political economy of media, communication and culture, Golding and Murdock propose that there are three factors that set structural limits to the diversity of media forms and representations. In doing so, however, they stress that these are sites of contradiction and contestation, in a world where, in explicit contrast to Chomsky and Herman, 'Owners, advertisers and key political personnel cannot always do as they wish ... [but] operate within structures that constrain as well as facilitate' (Golding and Murdock, 2000, p. 74). The first is the power relationship between nation-states and corporations, as understood through public and private ownership and the issue of privatization of state-owned assets, as well as changes in the nature and forms of 'pubic interest' regulation of commercial media (cf. Curran and Park, 2000). Second, they argue that dominant economic interests strongly influence, if not necessarily determine, the range and diversity of textual forms available to audiences for interpretation, and that there are structural as well as rhetorical limits to the polysemy of media texts (cf. Condit, 1989; Budd *et al.*, 1990). Third, they draw attention to the extent to which income-based barriers to access to cultural and communications goods and services constitute a reiteration of class divides (cf. Murdock, 2000). This is not only a matter of who can access what – as seen in literature of the 'digital divide' in relation to new media – but is also a question about the range and relevance of 'value-added' media and communication resources to those who are not a part of higher-income demographics (Gandy, 2002). In relation to new media, Dan Schiller (1999) has argued that the rapid expansion of ICT networks worldwide in the 1990s was both cause and consequence of 'a powerful pan-corporate attempt to subject worldwide telecommunications policy to United States-originated, neo-liberal regulatory norms' (Schiller, 1999, p. 40). Readings of the rise of new media in terms of its emancipatory capacity lose sight of the extent to which the development of this 'digital capitalism' in fact reinforces pro-capitalist norms, values and policies on a global scale and – from the perspective of critical political economy – the resultant reinforcement of socio-economic and political inequalities, tendencies towards commercialization, and governance of a wider range of social spheres – ranging from telecommunications to education – under a pro-market, neo-liberal ideology (cf. McChesney and Schiller, 2003).

It is also important to note that some critical political economists argue that the current phase of capitalist development is one where the economic and media/cultural spheres increasingly overlap. A key theorist in this respect has been Nicholas Garnham, although elements of this approach can be identified in the later work of Raymond Williams (1977, 1980), who argued that:

> The major modern communications systems are now so evidently key institutions in advanced capitalist societies that they require the same kind of attention ... that is given to the institutions of industrial production and distribution ... these analyses force theoretical revision of the formula of base and superstructure and of the definition of productive forces, in a social area in which large scale capitalist activity and cultural production are now inseparable. (Williams, 1977, p. 136)

Garnham (1990) argued at a theoretical level that the base/superstructure model and its variants misunderstood Marxism, in conflating the 'material' with industrial production and the 'ideological' with cultural production. Garnham instead proposed that the key question for a materialist theory of culture was to understand the processes through which cultural forms became 'industrialized', or subject to the general forms and practices of capitalist commodity production. Analogous approaches to understanding the dynamics of commercial cultural industries can be found in the work of Miège (1989) on the relationship between cultural products and cultural work, Ryan's (1992) analysis of the contradictions between creative practice and corporate organization in the cultural sectors, and Hesmondhalgh's (2002) synthesis of this diverse literature into a practical understanding of the economics and sociology of the cultural industries.

The nexus between these themes and approaches is seen in recent work on the political economy of global media. Edward Herman and Robert McChesney's *The Global Media: The New Missionaries of Global Capitalism* (Herman and McChesney, 1997) restated many of the key themes of the cultural imperialism thesis as developed by Herbert Schiller and others in the 1970s, alongside a detailed overview of trends towards media concentration on a global scale that gained particular momentum in the 1980s and 1990s. Herman and McChesney's analysis will be discussed in more detail in Chapter 3, but they propose that the period from the early 1980s to the present has involved 'a dramatic restructuring of national media industries, along with the emergence of a genuinely global commercial media market' (Herman and McChesney, 1997, p. 1), with the consequences of concentration of media power on a global scale in the hands of a relatively small number of multinational corporations (MNCs), and a thoroughgoing commercialization of media worldwide. They argue that the global media system has become 'an indispensable component of the globalizing market economy as a whole', both because of the significance in the wider economic sense of global investments in the media, communications and information industries (or what Schiller referred to as the 'ECI complex'), but also because 'the global media provide a vital forum for advertisers and the promotion of demand and consumerist values that grease[s] the wheels of the global market' (Herman and McChesney, 1997, p. 189).

Global Hollywood (Miller *et al.*, 2001) is an important contribution to the critical political economy of global media literature, as it seeks to shift debates about global media from the 'cultural imperialism' thesis – and its attendant questions of ideology and influence – towards global production systems, or what Miller *et al.* term the *New International Division of Cultural Labour* (NICL). For Miller *et al.*, what is distinctive about the current phase of globalization of predominantly US-based audiovisual media industries is that they have been structurally separating the 'activities of the hand' – the production of films and television programmes as material artefacts – from the 'activities of the mind', or the development of ideas, concepts, genres and programme forms. In a mode of thought that is derived from Adam Smith as well as Karl Marx, Miller *et al.* argue that the production process ('activities of the hand') is being progressively globalized in search of lower labour costs and other costs of production, while the generation and ownership of intellectual property ('activities of the mind') that are associated with these new product concepts remain highly centralized. Miller *et al.* propose that the NICL as a concept explains and critically interrogates 'the differentiation of cultural labour, the globalization of labour processes [and] the means by which Hollywood coordinates and defends its authority over cultural labour markets' (Miller *et al.*, 2001, p. 52). The *Global Hollywood* argument developed by Miller *et al.* is distinctive in the critical political economy tradition, in that is not dependent upon the dominant ideology thesis, cultural nationalism, or an effects-based understanding of the media text–audience relationship. In that respect, their work cuts across the grain of many traditional arguments between critical political economy and other perspectives such as cultural studies, and will provide an ongoing touchstone for arguments developed in this book.

Cultural Studies

It is in some respects odd to juxtapose cultural studies to critical political economy as different ways of understanding global media. Both approaches share an understanding of social reality derived from critical theory and the work of cultural theorists such as Raymond Williams, both seek to identify and critique dominant interests in the media and cultural spheres, and both draw upon a range of intellectual resources that arise from the critical dialogue with Marxism that emerged from the rise of the 'New Left' and anti-colonial movements in the 1960s and 1970s. At the same time, however, the two approaches have clearly seen each other as exhibiting a serious lack, as seen in the protracted and sometimes venomous debate between academics representing the two approaches (see for example, Garnham, 1995; Grossberg, 1995; Mosco, 1996; Ferguson and Golding, 1997; Hartley, 2003).

Cultural studies has been particularly concerned with questions of *cultural power*, or the ways in which a multitude of cultural forms are produced, distributed, interpreted and contested through technical means of communication in an era where access to the technologies through which media are distributed is widely spread among populations. Nelson *et al.* (1992, p. 4) have defined cultural studies as 'an interdisciplinary field ... committed to the study of the entire range of a society's arts, beliefs, institutions and communicative practices'. It has been particularly concerned with the relationship between media, power and culture in modern, mass-mediated societies and cultures. As Stuart Hall observed, 'in twentieth-century advanced capitalism, the media have established a decisive and fundamental leadership in the cultural sphere ... They have progressively *colonized* the cultural and ideological sphere' (Hall, 1977, p. 340).

The differences between cultural studies and critical political economy have frequently revolved around the question of ideology, and the ways in which developments in the economic and cultural spheres are articulated and have mass-popular impact in contemporary societies. Hall argued that cultural studies addressed these question through the concept of *hegemony*, or 'the operation of one class upon another in *shaping and producing consent* (through the selective forms of social knowledge made available) ... [that is] one of the principal kinds of work that the dominant ideologies perform' (Hall, 1977, p. 339). The notion of ideology as hegemony is derived from the Italian Marxist Antonio Gramsci and, in contrast to the notion of ideology as reflecting the dominance of one class over another, it implies continually shifting power balances between social classes, so that 'the concept allows for the dimension of struggle and opposition, of confrontation between different cultures, where hegemony has to be negotiated and won' (Newbold, 1995b, p. 329). It also acknowledges that culture is never a given totality at any particular place and time as there is the significance of: ideas that do not have a necessary 'class belonging' (for example, nationalism or religious belief); intermediate social classes and groupings with their own values and professional ideologies (for example, intellectuals, state administrators, media professionals); as well as what Raymond Williams (1965) termed 'residual' and 'emergent' forms of cultural practice, that have a complex relationship to the dominant culture of any given historical period.

In an influential series of essays, Hall (1977, 1982, 1986, 1996) developed the concept of hegemony as one that was central to cultural studies as an interdisciplinary and politically engaged field of intellectual practice. For Hall, the concept of hegemony establishes that ideology and culture cannot be thought of as a 'superstructure' that is largely shaped through developments at the level of the economic 'base'. Since ideology is suffused through all aspects of society and social relations through its relationship to language, culture, lived experience and the unconscious, there can be no simple relationship of determination between the economic and the cultural. In other words, ideology is never simply a tool for class dominance through the promotion of erroneous ideas, since:

> Hegemony cannot be sustained by a single, unified 'ruling class' but only by a particular conjunctual alliance of class fractions ... hegemony is not a 'given' and perma-

nent state of affairs, but has to be actively won and *secured* ... there is no *permanent* hegemony: it can only be established, and analysed, in concrete historical conjunctures. (Hall, 1977, p. 333, author's emphasis)

Hall also saw hegemony as providing a way forward between the two major conceptions of 'culture' that had been informing cultural studies in the 1970s. These were the British historical tradition that sought to understand culture in terms of lived experience and 'the study of relationship between elements in a whole way of life' (Williams, 1965, quoted in Hall, 1986, p. 36), with its implied agenda of democratizing culture by revaluing the culture of subordinate classes or 'ordinary people'; and the European structuralist tradition, which stressed the influence of the determinant elements of culture upon lived experience, through its structuring into class relations, language and signifying systems. Hall proposed that it was in the relationship between these two elements, which draw attention to the complex terrain that is 'marked out by those strongly coupled but not mutually exclusive concepts culture/ideology', that the concept of hegemony could advance a materialist theory of culture by confronting in different, and sometimes opposed ways, 'the dialectic between conditions and consciousness' (Hall, 1986, p. 48). A central means of developing this understanding of hegemony in Hall's work is through the concept of *articulation*, which refers both to the complex unity formed between different elements in a particular historical conjuncture, and to the role played by discourse in establishing 'common sense' through the ordering and regulation of statements and meanings, as well as the extent to which social conflicts are expressed through language and the 'struggle over meaning' of particular terms and concepts (Hall, 1996). An example of the former notion of articulation could be the relationship between religion and the state in different societies, where it is strongly aligned to class power in some countries, and a source of political opposition in others. An example of the latter is the way in which terms such as 'democracy', 'the people', 'common sense' or 'national identity' have different and contested meanings at different times and in different places (Hall, 1982).

Contemporary mass media have provided rich terrain for analysis and testing of these propositions. At the same time, Hall has been criticized for having 'comparatively little to say about the institutions of mass communication' and lacking 'a detailed appreciation of how the economy and the state shape cultural production' (Stevenson, 1995, pp. 41, 43). There is a political economy of media developed within Hall's model of cultural studies through the *encoding/decoding model* of media messages. The process of *encoding* of media texts incorporates the institutional structures of media, organizational cultures and production practices, relations of production, and technical infrastructure, through which a media form, such as a newspaper or a television programme, is produced. Through this production process, a media text will have been produced which has encoded within it certain dominant meanings and, in order that the media text is able to reach an audience, it must be meaningful to them, or align itself to audience expectations about what constitutes a media text that they would wish to consume. In the process of receiving the media text, however, the audience engages in a *decoding* of that media text, or a 'reading' of its content that makes it meaningful or pleasurable in the act of consumption or use.

Key studies of media from a cultural studies perspective undertaken in the 1980s and 1990s (for example, Fiske, 1987, 1992; Morley, 1980, 1992; Ang, 1991) focused upon the latter aspect of this framework, differentiating between the 'preferred reading' of a media text, and practices of audience decoding that (i) operate within the 'dominant code' of the text; (ii) 'negotiate' the dominant code; and (iii) make oppositional readings or 'aberrant decodings' which interpret the text within an alternative frame of reference. These audience reading practices are then refracted back into questions of social structure, political orientation, and the capacity for resistance to dominant ideologies, as readings are 'founded on cultural differences embedded within the structure of society – cultural clusters which guide and limit the individual's interpretation of messages' (Morley, 1992, p. 118). For Fiske (1987), what resulted were 'two economies' in mass media – Fiske's particular interest was in broadcast television – as the nature of the cultural commodity means that it circulates within a 'financial economy', whose operations are largely explained by political economy, and a *cultural economy*, where the popularity of media texts is determined through 'the exchange and circulation of ... meanings, pleasures and social identities' (Fiske, 1987, p. 311). This work has been largely discussed in terms of the validity of its political conclusions, particularly the claim that mass popular media constitute a site of resistance to dominant ideologies rather than a site for their reinforcement (see esp. Fiske, 1987, pp. 316–26). What is equally notable, although less commented upon, is the way in which such an approach takes the analysis of the encoding process – the production and circulation of media texts in the financial economy – as largely given by the work of critical political economy. I will return to this point below, in considering the contributions of institutionalism and cultural policy studies to an understanding of media organizations and policy.

A different set of issues for cultural studies arise around whether its frame of reference is essentially national, and how well equipped it is for critical analysis of global media. This point has been raised by Stratton and Ang (1996) who observe how cultural studies emerged historically in response to particular issues emerging in Britain and how they were understood by a generation of cultural theorists,[1] as well as its methodological focus upon the specific and the conjunctural as the key points from which to understand the relationship between culture and power. Nelson *et al.* (1992, p. 8) define conjunctural analysis as being 'embedded, descriptive, and historically and contextually specific'. Stratton and Ang observe that, in this commitment to grounded, 'bottom-up' research methodologies, there nonetheless remain a given set of disciplinary concepts that have been derived from the British (or, more recently, British and North American) experience that are then applied in other national contexts. The problem is akin to that of the concept of 'society' in sociology, where the governing set of principles are taken as universal, and are then extended outwards to comparative studies of national societies ('American society', 'French society', 'Chinese society' and so on), where 'all these national particulars can be specified and described in terms of the presumably universal concepts and theories of a ... sociological master narrative' (Stratton and Ang, 1996, p. 364). They argue that the approach which emphasizes national cultural studies formations, while partially decentring 'master narratives' derived from the North Atlantic corridor, has the problem of over-emphasising nationalist preoccupations, and generating 'a lack of reflexivity concerning the presumed fit between cultural studies and the nation-state', so that 'the nation-state then becomes ... the taken-for-granted determining context within which particular versions of cultural studies develop' (Stratton and Ang, 1996, p. 380).

A capacity to move beyond the confines of the nation-state is particularly important for cultural studies in relation to media globalization, as media in their most advanced forms are now clearly operating outside of national formations in terms of their financing, production, distribution and reception. At the same time, however, it can be argued that there remain strong localizing and indigenizing tendencies to practices of cultural consumption, which act as a brake on the idea of a globalized and hegemonic mass popular culture. One influential approach to these questions, developed from cultural anthropology more than cultural studies, has been found in the work of Arjun Appadurai. Appadurai has provided conceptual underpinnings for theories of globalization and global culture that point to *cultural hybridization*, rather than cultural domination, as being its *raison d'être*. Appadurai (1990) argued that the global cultural economy was based upon a tension between forces promoting a common global culture (cultural homogenization) and those promoting cultural difference (cultural heterogenization). He proposed that global cultural flows operated across five planes:

1. *ethnoscapes* – movements of people across the world, as tourists, immigrants, refugees, exiles, guest workers, students and so on;
2. *technoscapes* – the movement of complex technologies around the world, and associated capital and skilled labour linked to investment projects;

3. *finanscapes* – the dramatic and unprecedented global movements of financial capital through currency markets, financial institutions, stock exchanges, and commodity markets;
4. *mediascapes* – the global flows of images, narratives, media content and so on through print, broadcast, film and video and, increasingly, the Internet and digital media;
5. *ideoscapes* – the global circulation of ideas, concepts, values and 'keywords', such as democracy, human rights, environmental consciousness and so on.

For Appadurai, what is distinctive about the current phase of global culture is the growing disjuncture between these flows, meaning that 'this new set of global disjunctures is not a simple one-way street in which the terms of global cultural politics are set wholly by … the vicissitudes of international flows of technology, labor and finance, demanding only a modest modification of existing neo-Marxist models of uneven development and state formation' (Appadurai, 1990, p. 306). In his later work *Modernity at Large: Cultural Dimensions of Globalization* (Appadurai, 1996), Appadurai developed a more focused account of the cultural elements of global communication and culture, proposing that the central elements which make the current era of globalization a culturally distinctive one are the globalization of electronic media and mass migration.

The emphasis upon mass migration and the lived experience of diasporic communities in multicultural societies allows Appadurai to construct a definition of culture that is based around (i) *situated difference*, or difference in relation to something local, embodied and significant, that (ii) can constitute the basis for a group identity, that (iii) can be mobilized as an articulation of that group identity in other arenas. What follows from such a definition is that cultures constituted as group identities based upon situated difference can engage in cultural politics, or 'the conscious mobilization of cultural differences in the service of a larger national or transnational politics' (Appadurai, 1996, p. 15). Global media flows insert themselves opportunistically into 'this fertile ground of deterritorialization, in which money, commodities and persons are involved in ceaselessly chasing each other around the world' (Appadurai, 1990, p. 303). Appadurai's work has sought to open up spaces from which 'globalization from below' can be understood and, with this, opportunities for the 'subaltern' to 'speak' about the multiplicities of globalization and its cultural impacts, thereby giving greater recognition to the work being undertaken 'from below' by activists around the world on how to renegotiate the terms of entry of these globalizing flows in order to achieve more empowering and democratic outcomes. By contrast, Appadurai argues that speculative theorizing which occurs independently of an understanding of these local struggles ignores the fact that 'the idea of an international civil society will have no future outside of these efforts to globalize from below ... in the study of these forms lies an obligation to academic research that, if honoured, might make its deliberations more consequential for the poorer 80 per cent of the world ... who are socially and fiscally at risk' (Appadurai, 2003, p. 3).

Institutionalism, Media Corporations and Public Policy

One criticism which can be made of both the critical political economy and cultural studies perspectives is that they have often worked with a fairly rudimentary analysis of the internal dynamics of media organizations. Hesmondhalgh (2002) has made the point that, in the case of critical political economy, this has arguably been more the case in the North American academic literature than in those – principally European – traditions that have been influenced by theories of the cultural industries. Hesmondhalgh argues that a critical political economy of media and cultural industries needs to focus not only upon questions of ownership and market structure, but also upon 'how such issues of market structure affect the *organization* of cultural production and the making of texts at an ordinary, everyday level' (Hesmondhalgh, 2002, p. 34). A capacity to move from the macro-dynamics of global media to questions of industrial organization and organizational culture is thus an important benchmark for the usefulness of theories of global media. In the case of cultural studies, there has sometimes been a tendency to view the production process as largely explained through political economy, in order to focus attention upon the politics of media consumption and use. Fiske's (1987) theory of the progressive possibilities of the cultural economy, for instance, rests very much upon its existence alongside a financial economy of media texts whose operations are largely explained through neo-Marxist political economy.

Institutions have been the dominant organizational form of modern societies. Whether it be the concentration of economic resources into large corporations, the growth of the nation-state as the principal regulator of economic, social and cultural life, or the ways in which we work in organizations, or join unions, guilds or professional associations to declare a common affinity with those in like occupations, institutions have been the central organizational form of capitalist modernity in the 20th and early 21st centuries. March and Olsen (1989, pp. 1–2) have observed that 'Social, political and economic institutions have become larger, considerably more complex and resourceful, and *prima facie* more important to collective life. Many of the major actors in modern economic and political systems are formal organizations, and the institutions of law and bureaucracy occupy a dominant role in contemporary life'. Institutions exist both as formal legal entities (such as corporations) and more informal mechanisms for combining individuals and organizing their relationships with others. W. Richard Scott (1995, p. 33) has defined institutions as 'cognitive, normative and regulative structures and activities that provide stability and meaning to social behaviour. Institutions are transported by various carriers – cultures, structures, and routines – and they operate at multiple levels of jurisdiction'. They have a *regulative* element, as mechanisms for setting rules, establishing routines, and offering rewards for compliance (or sanctions for non-compliance). They have a *normative* element, as their durability over time is dependent upon the willingness of those within an institution to accept a set of broadly shared values. As a result, they possess a degree of *path dependency* in their responses to the external environment, shaped by ideas, values and commitments held by key individuals and disseminated through the institution (Hall and Taylor, 1996; Peters, 1999). Finally, institutions have a *cognitive* element, as they confer identities, and provide the conditions through which individuals construct a shared discourse. The anthropologist Mary Douglas (1987) argued that institutions generate the cognitive and discursive conditions for the 'making up' of an individual *persona*, or a sense of social 'self', by framing situations, defining identities, and generating meaning out of a repertoire of available discourses.

A focus upon the importance of institutions as forms that both regulate individual conduct and enable collective action has been characteristic of *institutionalism*, which has a long and often dissident history as a methodology in the social sciences. Institutionalism has presented itself, from quite eclectic perspectives, as providing an alternative way of thinking to methodologies shaped by assumptions about the rational individual, such as neo-classical economics, or overly functionalist interpretations of how the behaviour of individual agents is largely shaped by their positioning in a social structure, as found in some versions of Marxism (Hindess, 1989). Institutionalism gives a central role to the interplay between technology and organizations, the exercise of power in markets, questions of ownership and control, and transformations in institutional behaviour and social organization over historical time (Hodgson, 1988; Stilwell, 2002). For example, Hodgson (1988, p. 208) has described the firm as 'an institution of power' that functions in part as 'a kind of protective enclave from the potentially volatile and sometimes destructive, even ravaging speculation of a competitive market'.

The institutionalist tradition is, by its very nature, a heterogeneous one. Its core elements have been a demand that relations of *power* be recognized in all forms of social theory, but particularly in economic theory (Galbraith, 1973), and that the *social embeddedness of markets* be given its rightful historical and contemporary significance. The latter concept of a mutually constitutive relationship between institutions and markets has been developed historically in the work of Karl Polanyi (Polanyi, 1944, 1957; cf. Jessop, 2002), who argued that an economy is by definition embedded in institutional and social processes:

> The human economy ... is embedded and enmeshed in institutions, economic and non-economic. The inclusion of the non-economic is vital. For religion or govern-ment may be as important to the structuring and functioning of the economy as monetary institutions or the availability of tools and machines themselves that lighten the toil of labour. (Polanyi, 1957, p. 34)

It is important to note that there are differences within institutionalist thought, or what has been referred to as 'weak' and 'strong' institutionalism (Hall and Taylor, 1996; Peters, 1999; Coriat and Dosi, 2002). At the 'weak' end of this spectrum is *rational choice institutionalism*, which understands the development of institutions as rule systems that rational individuals agree to in order to maximize personal benefits to be derived from collective action (Rutherford, 1996). This approach largely draws upon methodological indi-vidualism in the social sciences, and upon neo-classical economics in particu-lar, in developing a 'new economics of organization', that emphasizes the importance of property rights, rent-seeking behaviour, and transaction costs to the development of institutions (Williamson, 1985; Hall and Taylor, 1996).

At the 'strong' end, the French 'Regulationist School' of political economists (Aglietta, 1987, 1998; Boyer, 1987, 1988, 1990; Lipietz, 1987) have developed a model of capitalist economic dynamics that links Marxist, institutionalist and macro-historical methodologies. Coriat and Dosi (2002, p. 102) have observed that what the 'Regulationists' refer to as a *regime of accumulation*, a term derived from the Marxist theory of capitalist accumulation grounded in historical time, is based upon six sets of institutional arrangements:

1. the wage-labour nexus (types of employment, systems of governance of industrial conflict, union representation, wage formation and so on);
2. forms of competition in product and service markets;
3. institutions governing financial markets, including share and credit markets;
4. norms of consumption;
5. forms of state intervention in the economy (economic management poli-cies, regulation of conflict, industry development, taxation, welfare, health and education, public good provision and so on);
6. organization of the international system of exchange.

Coriat and Dosi identify regulation theories as a form of 'strong institutionalism' whereby institutions shape the cognitive processes and identities of individuals, where the identification of self-interest is linked to institutional maintenance, and where institutions are the 'carriers of history', whose decisions generate a path dependency in social development over time (Coriat and Dosi, 2002, p. 100).

It was observed in Chapter 1 that the relevance of institutional analysis to the study of global media arises from the centrality of the *corporate form* to media organizations in the 20th and 21st centuries. Five factors presented themselves as being of significance in promoting the increasing enmeshment of media production and distribution within the corporate institutional form:

1. the distinctive legal form of the corporation;
2. the question of who controls the corporation;
3. the growing complexity of corporate institutions and the move towards multidivisional organizational forms;
4. the role of contracts as a means of managing risk and co-ordinating diverse activities;
5. the role of bureaucracy as a means of managing creativity, and challenges to this within the context of creative work.

It was also observed that the corporate form of institutional organization generates particular questions related to policy and governance, and it cannot be assumed that the decisions made by the political institutions of the state simply reflect the structural alignment of forces that exist independently of it. *Historical institutionalists* such as Skocpol (1985) have critiqued the notion that policies are largely determined by the balance of forces and interests that lie outside of state institutions, arguing that 'the formation ... [and] political capacities of interest groups and classes depend in significant measure on the structures and activities of the very states the social actors, in turn, seek to influence' (Skocpol, 1985, p. 27). Such approaches address the problem of what Dunleavy and O'Leary (1987) have termed the *cipher image* of public policy, where policy development is largely seen as the reflection of outcomes already achieved through elite bargaining between powerful corporate and government interests. In such approaches, the institutional specificities of policy formation and implementation are largely erased, and policy outcomes are typically seen as the consequence of structural imperatives derived independently of the policy process. The result is that we are left with 'the uncomfortable inference that the study of state institutions is something of an irrelevance' (Johnston, 1986, p. 69). In a critique of neo-Marxist interpretations of Australian broadcasting policy, that engages with questions of how to best understand the relationship between structure and agency, Pearce (2000) observed that such accounts 'paid no attention ... to what the many interest groups involved in broadcasting policy *at the time* thought was in their interest', but rather 'assigned interests based on its own external, ideological understandings of the "public interest" and "business interest"' (Pearce, 2000, p. 371).

Pontusson (1995) has observed that institutionalism is commonly understood as a *middle-range theory*, problematizing relationships between agency and structure, or between methodological individualism and various forms of structuralism. The nature of being a 'middle-range' theory in the social sciences raises the question of what analyses outside of this framework it is anchored to. Pontusson argues that institutionalism should be aligned to the macro-social approach associated with critical political economy, in order to develop 'the comparative study of advanced capitalism' (Pontusson, 1995, p. 143). This is akin to Sayer's argument that regulation theory has emerged as 'a middle-range theory or analysis of capitalism which examines the different kinds of social embedding of macro-economic processes' (Sayer, 1995, p. 24), and is reflective of dialogues between institutionalism and Marxism that have taken place within the field of critical political economy (Dugger and Sherman, 1994; Stilwell, 2002).

Rethinking State Capacities: Cultural Policy Studies

State theory has been an important arena for debates between liberal-pluralist and critical theories of global media. There has been in recent years an important rethinking of how to understand state agencies in relation to global media, influenced by institutionalist theories and cultural policy studies. The political economy approach challenged claims arising from liberal-pluralist theory that the state was a neutral arbiter of competing interests, instead emphasizing the power and influence of corporate interests over government policy (Miliband, 1973). An important debate occurred within the study of political economy in the 1970s about the role and nature of the state in capitalist societies, where the 'instrumentalist' perspective – which saw the state as acting in the interests of the dominant classes because they possessed the most power and influence under capitalism – was challenged by *structuralist* approaches, which drew attention to the complex and contradictory nature of class interests, competition between competing fractions of capital, and the need for the state to be seen to be 'above' particular interests in order to maintain legitimacy (Poulantzas, 1972; cf. Jessop, 1990). From a political economy perspective, Mosco argues that 'the state has to promote the interests of capital even as it appears to be the independent arbiter of the wider social or public interest' (Mosco, 1996, p. 92). Kellner (1990) has drawn upon the Gramscian concept of hegemony to argue that this potential contradiction between state strategies to promote private capital accumulation and its need to retain some degree of popular legitimacy is managed in part by 'a logic of exclusion that condemns to silence those voices whose criticisms of the capitalist mode of production go beyond the boundaries allowed by the lords of the media' (Kellner, 1990, p. 9).

These approaches have been critiqued from the perspective of *cultural policy studies* for how they represent the relationship between media power, policy and culture. Tony Bennett, one of the leading theorists of cultural policy studies, has argued the need for a more institutionally grounded approach to understanding cultural forms and practices, which can identify opportunities for cultural politics that can impact upon the conduct of identifiable government agents and institutions (Bennett, 1992a). Bennett's call for a cultural studies that is *useful*, in the sense that it can connect to the discourses and institutional structures of cultural policy formation, has been echoed by cultural studies theorists such as McRobbie (1996), who identified cultural policy as the 'missing agenda' of cultural studies. It was also connected to a wider body of work, associated with Michel Foucault's notion of *governmentality* (Foucault, 1991), which shifted the locus of understanding of government from who controls formal state institutions and structures, towards the micro-politics of *technologies of government* that shape the understanding of political problems and the forms of action that can be directed towards them (cf. Miller and Rose, 1992). Hunter (1988) drew upon such work to argue that cultural studies needed to move towards more historically grounded and institutionally specific forms of engagement with cultural institutions, arguing that 'cultural interests and attributes ... can only be described and assessed relative to ... the actual array of historical institutions in which such attributes are specified and formed' (Hunter, 1988, p. 106).

Bennett (1992a, p. 26) proposed that culture was best thought of as 'a historically specific set of institutionally embedded relations of government in which the forms of thought and conduct of extended populations are targeted for transformation – in part via the extension through the social body of the forms, techniques, and *regimens* of aesthetic and intellectual culture'. For Bennett, this approach linked contemporary cultural policy advocacy to historical analyses of cultural formations in modern societies, by seeing the 'governmentalization' of culture as part of a broader trend towards the use of specific forms of knowledge as technologies for the management of populations. Bennett saw the implications of such a revised analytical framework for the study of cultural institutions as four-fold. First, it would shift the emphasis of cultural history away from the ways in which the development of these institutions was understood by cultural critics, towards a more fine-grained institutional analysis of the administrative goals, objectives and outcomes of the organizations themselves (cf. Hunter, 1988). Second, Bennett saw cultural policy, not as an optional add-on to cultural studies, but as rather being 'central to the definition and constitution of culture' (Bennett, 1992b, p. 397). Third, it pointed to cultural studies developing perspectives that would be 'conducted in a manner such that, both in its substance and style, it can be calculated to influence or service the conduct of identifiable agents within the region of culture concerned' (Bennett, 1992a, p. 23). Fourth, this clearly entailed establishing an ongoing dialogue between cultural theorists and what Bennett has termed 'cultural technicians', or cultural policy-makers and administrators (Bennett, 1992b, p. 397). The forms that this would take would vary according to the priorities of the institutions being engaged with and the issues in question, but it clearly meant talking to state agencies and institutions, rather than writing them off in advance as ideological state apparatuses, and then 'in a self-fulfilling prophecy' identifying their policy failures (Bennett, 1992a, p. 32).

Bennett's work, and that of related authors within the emerging field of Australian cultural policy studies (Cunningham, 1992; Hunter, 1994; Mercer, 1994; Bennett, 1995; Meredyth, 1997), has drawn a diverse range of responses. Lewis and Miller (2003) have argued that it is an approach to cultural policy studies that makes more sense in countries such as Britain and Australia, where there is a history of critical intellectuals and local authorities pursuing collaborative projects, than in the United States.[2] In the US, cultural policy studies has emerged out of fields such as cultural economics, which have had a relatively strong and direct connection to questions surrounding the public funding of the arts and cultural institutions (Di Maggio, 1983; Lewis and Miller, 2003). Some writers have endorsed the general aspirations of developing cultural studies in more institutionally oriented and pragmatic directions, while nonetheless questioning this particular approach to cultural policy studies. Miller (1994) observed that one outcome of cultural policy studies emerging out of a dialogue with cultural studies, rather than policy studies as it had developed in the social sciences, was that there was a lack of awareness of issues surrounding the ethics of consultancy, the problem of 'capture' of researchers by clients, and the relationship between policy rhetoric and implementation. McGuigan (1996) also noted that the capacity to advance cultural policy initiatives is also very much dependent upon the nature and priorities of governments, with governments of the left far more likely to be sympathetic than those of the political right. Lewis and Miller (2003) make the point that there is not a polarity between policy studies and critical traditions, as one can undertake policy-oriented analyses of cultural institutions from a critical perspective, as seen in Streeter's (1995) critique of the institutional framework which governs US broadcast media policy.

These debates are ongoing, and we will identify comparable debates emerging around the concept of creative industries (to be discussed in Chapter 5), which has many connections to cultural policy studies. Two further points could be added at this stage. The first is that, by demanding a more institutionally delineated and context-sensitive understanding of state capacities in the cultural sphere, cultural policy studies has drawn attention to the need to recognize the agency and capacity for independent initiative on the part of policy-makers. This points to the possibilities of what Yeatman (1998) termed *activism in the policy process*, or alliances between activists and policy administrators. The second is that the cultural policy studies perspective remains resolutely national, and in doing so is reflective of both its roots in cultural studies traditions that have tended to be national, and the focus of policy studies upon the nation-state as the primary locus of decision-making. In its focus upon the relationship between cultural policy and the formation of citizenship and citizen identities, to take one example, there remains an implicit assumption that both of these operate at the level of the nation-state. The rise of global media raises the question of the extent to which access to and use of cultural resources associated with the formation of citizen identities is increasingly drawn from transnational rather than national sources, through global audiovisual media and the Internet in particular (Canclini, 2000). It also raises issues concerning the micro-politics of media production, consumption and use, which are best addressed outside of the state-driven approach to understanding these relationships that remains a strong feature of the cultural policy studies approach.

Cultural and Economic Geography

The focus of geography upon the spatial dimensions of social relations, and the spatially grounded dimensions of everyday life and social interaction, provide an important perspective from which to analyse the scope, dimensions and impacts of global media. The perspectives of both cultural and economic geography have been important to understanding the distinctive relations between media, culture and space constructed within and through global media, and in this section the two will be considered together, even though in an analytical sense recent work from economic geographers will inform the analysis of media globalization developed in Chapters 3 and 4, and the significance of cultural geography perspectives will emerge primarily in Chapter 5.

There are two major 'turns' in geography that have been important to understanding the context of contemporary debates. The first, which occurred in the 1970s and is largely contemporaneous with the rise of Marxist political economy and critical theory more broadly, is the critique of positivism and the idea of geography as 'the science of the spatial' (Massey, 1985, p. 11). The observation that spatial relations were *spatial relations under capitalism*, and the resultant need to incorporate elements of the Marxist critique of capitalism – with its focus upon the dynamics of capital accumulation, the social division of labour, uneven development, and class inequality, antagonism and contradiction – generated an enormously productive moment in radical geography (see for example, Castells, 1978; Harvey, 1982; Massey, 1984; Storper and Walker, 1989; Smith, 1990). At the same time, a question that lurked around the finding that spatial relations were formed by broader social relations was whether geography mattered or whether, as Doreen Massey observed, 'geography only comes onto the scene at a later stage of analysis – that it is inherently contingent' (Massey, 1985, p. 18). While radical geographers such as Harvey (1982, 1985), Storper and Walker (1989) and Smith (1990) had sought to reconstruct political economy in explicitly spatial terms – most notably in Harvey's (1982, 1985) identification of the 'spatial fix' as a central mechanism for capital to renew itself, along with technological innovation – the question remained about the distinctive contribution of geography to critical political economy. As Massey (1985, p. 18) observed, 'if we really mean that it is impossible to conceptualise social processes and structures outside their spatial form and spatial implications, then the latter must also be incorporated into our initial formulations and definitions'. Similarly, Soja (1989) argued that the impact of critical geography had been around the reassertion of space in critical social theory.

The second major development in critical geography, which can be broadly dated from the early 1990s onwards, is the 'cultural turn'. The new cultural geography drew upon the post-structuralist critique of representation, proposing that the symbols through which 'reality' is represented could not be taken as straightforward and ideologically neutral reflections of social reality, but were modes of signification that had their own material and ideological effects, and were therefore imbued with, and embedded within, relations of power, domination and resistance (Barnes, 2003; Söderstrom, 2005). Michel Foucault's (1984, p. 252) proposition that 'Space is fundamental in any form of communal life; space is fundamental in any exercise of power', goes beyond the proposition that space matters in understanding social relations and the operations of power, which had been the argument of critical geographers in relation to political economy and critical social theory. For Foucault, it is impossible to conceive of social relations independently of their spatial dimensions:

The present epoch will perhaps be above all the epoch of space. We are in the epoch of simultaneity; we are in the epoch of juxtaposition, the epoch of the side-by-side, of the dispersed. We are at a moment, I believe, when our experience of the world is less that of a long life developing through time, than that of a network that connects points and intersects with its own skein. (Foucault, 1986, p. 22)

From a different but related perspective, Michel de Certeau proposed an explicitly spatial understanding of the operations of power in modern societies, differentiating between *space* as that which is managed and ordered by those with power towards specific strategic ends, and *place* as the site where those without power 'make do' with available resources, seeking to reorganize and reconstruct the spatial strategies of the powerful institutions and individuals towards their own ends (de Certeau, 1984).

Debate about the impact of the 'new cultural geography', the 'cultural turn' in geography and the influence of post-structuralism and postmodernism more generally, has been intense among geographers (for example, Mitchell, 2000; Smith, 2000; Thrift, 2000; Storper, 2001; Barnes, 2003). The most influential critique was that of David Harvey who, after proposing an ambitious reconstruction of Marxist political economy in a geographical frame (Harvey, 1982), undertook in *The Conditions of Postmodernity* (Harvey, 1989) a critical situating of post-structuralist and postmodernist cultural theories in the dynamics of political-economic change in the 1970s and 1980s. Harvey argued that the influence of postmodernism both within and outside of the academy – with close attention paid to postmodernist trends in architecture and urban design – could only be understood in the context of a shift in the dominant modes of capitalist production and consumption away from the 'Fordist' paradigm of mass production and mass consumption, towards transitional modes variously identified as 'flexible accumulation' and 'disorganized capitalism' (cf. Lash and Urry, 1987). For Harvey, the combined forces of 'de-massification' and globalization of both production and consumption were linked to a range of transformations in the relations of people to space and time, that have parallels in the impact of modernity upon time, space and power. The most critical element of this, for Harvey, is that it marks 'the annihilation of space through time' (Harvey, 1989, p. 293) which generates a class of skilled, geographically mobile knowledge workers attuned to the 'time-less' and 'a-spatial' cultural universe proposed by postmodernist cultural theory, and a section of the critical intelligentsia that identifies with this project of global cosmopolitanism. Critical of the rise of both locality-based politics and identity politics, Harvey argued that such 'oppositional movements become a part of the very fragmentation which a mobile capitalism and flexible accumulation can feed upon', and that political action based upon the 'aesthetics of place ... meshes only too well with the idea of spatial differentiations as lures for a peripatetic capital that values the option of mobility very highly' (Harvey, 1989, p. 303).

Critiques of Harvey's resolute defence of Marxist historical materialism against both locality-based and identity politics have come from both cultural studies (for example, Morris, 1992) and cultural geography (for example, Barnes, 2003). Rather than dwell upon these arguments, we can instead note the extent to which the rise of cultural geography has itself been linked to discourses surrounding the 'culturalization of the economy', or the degree to which the 'cultural turn' in economic geography has meant that 'we can never look at "the economic" in quite the same way' (Gertler, 2003a, p. 132; cf. Thrift, 2000).

The extent to which the contemporary global capitalist economy has been 'culturalized' has been a widely debated proposition (see, for example, Amin and Thrift, 2004). Lash and Urry (1994) argued that the interaction between the 'semiotization of consumption' and flexible production systems, and the permeation of production models with their origins in the cultural and creative industries, has meant that 'ordinary manufacturing is becoming more and more like the production of culture … It is not that commodity manufacture provides the template, and culture follows, but that the culture industries themselves have provided the template' (Lash and Urry, 1994, p. 123). Gertler (2003a) has proposed that a cultural economic geography of production draws upon three 'big ideas' that have gained common currency over the 1990s and 2000s:

1. the 'rediscovery of the social' in production, and the associated relationship between organizational culture and economic performance (cf. Clegg *et al.*, 2005);
2. the realization that knowledge and learning are interrelated, and that the most advanced forms of learning in relation to product forms are embedded in geographically specific urban and regional cultures;
3. the evolutionary dynamics of local production systems and the cumulative advantages that derive from the combination of institutional 'lock-in' and 'first mover' advantage (cf. Arthur, 1999).

From a cultural studies perspective, du Gay and Pryke (2002) have identified the 'cultural economy' as arising from:

1. arguments that the management of culture has become the key to improving organizational performance, particularly when it can align organizational goals to feelings of self-realization among those working within it;
2. the relationship between economic processes and their cultural dimension, particularly in the services sector, where economic transactions are more directly related to interpersonal relations and communicative practices;

3. the rise of the cultural or creative industries, and the adoption of practices throughout the economy that have their genesis in these industries, such as the role of cultural intermediaries in articulating design and production to the desires and values of consumers, or the role of networks in time-based and project-based forms of production.

Academic work derived from cultural and economic geography can lead to quite divergent conclusions on the nature and significance of globalization. While some geographers have drawn attention to the centrality of globalizing forces to reconstructing the geography of cities and regions (Dicken, 2003a, 2003b), others have used a geographical understanding to draw attention to the spatial limits of globalization theories (Cox, 1997; Yeung, 2002). Amin has argued that 'the distinctive contribution of ... [geography] within the congested study of globalization [lies] in the study of the spatiality – social, economic, cultural and political – of what is increasingly being seen as a single and interdependent world' (Amin, 2001, p. 6276). In particular, both cultural and economic geography question theories of globalization in their *strong* form – to be discussed below – by drawing attention to the ongoing significance of *interscalar* relationships, or the mutual interaction between the local, the national, the regional and the global (Peck, 2002). Amin has questioned the idea that globalization involves, for better or worse, a 'shift in the balance of power between different spatial scales' (Amin, 2002, p. 395), questioning claims that globalization marks the triumph of global networks over local places, or globalizing capitalism over nation-states, or the source of a conflict between global cosmopolitanism and local identities, but rather proposing that the forces of globalization point towards 'a combination of multiple spatialities of organization and praxis as action and belonging at a distance become possible' (Amin, 2002, p. 395).

Theories of 'Strong Globalization' and their Critics

The final theoretical perspectives to be considered in relation to global media are theories of *strong globalization*. By this, I refer to those theories which argue that the process of globalization has marked a shift in the economic, political and cultural dynamics of societies that is of such a scale that the analytical tools by which we understand social processes in the 21st century are fundamentally different to those which were applicable to 20th-century societies. I have elsewhere (Flew and McElhinney, 2005) referred to these as theories which propose that the interrelated trends associated with globalization have marked a *qualitative* shift in the pattern of economic, social, political and cultural relations within and between states and societies, rather than a series of extensions and intensifications of more long-standing trends, that is, part of a *quantitative* change. Examples of 'strong globalization' theories can be found in economics, sociology, political theory and cultural studies (examples include Urry, 1989; Robertson, 1991; Reich, 1992; Ohmae, 1995; Waters, 1995; Shaw, 1997; Modelski, 2000). What I wish to do here is to critically appraise the work of sociologist Manuel Castells and the academics/political activists Michael Hardt and Antonio Negri as authors who propose that globalization has marked a substantive shift in the economics, politics and cultures of the 21st century, and consider some critiques of 'strong globalization' in light of the preceding work in this chapter.

In his major three-volume work *The Information Age: Economy, Society and Culture* (Castells, 1996, 1998, 2000a), Manuel Castells has proposed that a *new economy has* emerged since the 1980s that is global, networked, and informational. While this new techno-economic framework remains capitalist in form, it is based upon what Castells describes as an *informational rather than an industrial mode of development*, where the major sources of productivity arise not from the application of social labour, but rather from the application of information technology, and 'the technology of knowledge generation, information processing, and symbol communication' that promote 'the action of knowledge upon knowledge itself as the main source of productivity' (Castells, 1996, p. 17). At the centre of the informational mode of development are networks, and Castells has termed the emergent social structure a *network society*:

> Networks constitute the new social morphology of our societies, and the diffusion of networking logic substantially modifies the operation and outcomes in processes of production, experience, power, and culture. While the networking form of social organization has existed in other times and spaces, the new information technology paradigm provides the material basis for its pervasive expansion throughout the entire social structure. (Castells, 1996, p. 469)

Castells has proposed that the rise of a network society is linked to a new regime of accumulation, or production-consumption nexus, that he terms the *information technology paradigm*, where information, networking, flexibility and convergence are inherent outcomes of the pervasive impacts of new ICTs upon all aspects of economy, politics, society and culture. Castells' metaphor of the network as the core element of the information technology paradigm is developed in explicit contrast to theories of 'Fordism', or the technological and economic systems of mass production and mass consumption, as the central metaphor of industrial society (Harvey, 1989). The new economy that is based on ICTs has three fundamental characteristics. First, it is *informational*, in the sense that 'the capacity of generating knowledge and processing/managing information determine the productivity and competitiveness of all kinds of economic units, be they firms, regions, or countries' (Castells, 2000b, p. 10). Second, it is *global*, since 'its core strategic activities have the capacity to work as a unit on a planetary scale in real time or chosen time' (Castells, 2000b, p. 10). Finally, the new economy is *networked*. It is based upon information networks such as the Internet, as well as the networked enterprise becoming the dominant form of economic organization, at whose heart is no longer the capitalist firm, but global financial markets and business projects based upon short-term strategic alliances and partnerships. For Castells, the networked enterprise is a logical corollary of electronic business, as it is based around 'the Internet-based, interactive, networked connection between producers, consumers, and service providers' (Castells, 2001, p. 75).

The corollary of a network society, and a new economy based on information, globalization, and networking, is that power is increasingly organized around the *space of flows*. These are constituted in three ways. First, they are constructed electronically through the *communications networks* themselves, and spatially through the rise of *global cities* as centres of commerce and communications. Second, *technopoles* such as Silicon Valley in California, Bangalore in India, Guangzhou Province in China, and Malaysia's Multimedia Super Corridor, provide examples of how the global space of flows is constructed through its 'nodes and hubs', and how nation-states increasingly compete to establish locations within their territorial domain as central points in this global network. Finally, for Castells, the global space of flows is constituted *culturally*, through the shared experiences and practices of geographically mobile managerial and knowledge workers, elites who, while still predominantly North American and European, are increasingly deracinated, with the rise of global elites from Asia, Latin America, the Middle East and Africa, and the increasingly multicultural nature of the metropolitan centres (Castells, 1996, pp. 410–18).

A particularly marked feature of Castells' analysis of the Information Age and the network society is the sharpness of the distinction he makes between the deterritorialized spaces through which networks of information, power, cultural forms and economic transactions flow, and the places of work, cultural experience, historical memory and everyday life. For Castells, 'the space of flows of the Information Age dominates the space of places of people's cultures', with the result being that 'the network society disembodies social relationships ... because it is made up of networks of production, power, and experience, which construct a culture of virtuality in the global flows that transcend time and space' (Castells, 2000a, pp. 369, 370). This is in contrast to the experience of modernity in the Industrial Age where 'spatio-temporal configurations were critical for the meaning of each culture and for their differential evolution' (Castells, 2000a, p. 370). Many implications follow from this in Castells' analysis, but three are particularly relevant to the study of global media. The first is that, in the Information Age, national societies are increasingly divided by a new form of class-based social cleavage, between geographically mobile workers dealing with information and symbolic communication, whose skills are highly sought after across the globe, and 'generic labour', that is particularly vulnerable to the movement of jobs offshore as a consequence of globalization and technological change. Second, Castells views the global proliferation of new forms of information and entertainment through digitally networked ICTs as meaning the 'end of mass media', and hence of the association of nationally based media with the development of national cultures. Finally, the global space of flows erodes the significance of a variety of forms of historically based and locally grounded forms of culture, to the extent that – for an ever-growing segment of the global population – their experience of culture is grounded less in a sense of place than it is by a desire on the part of a variety of social agents (corporations, governments, non-government organizations, cultural activists, and so on) to locate themselves within global networks, and to 'reinvent' institutions, traditions and places in order to more effectively do so.

In *Empire* (Hardt and Negri, 2000) and *Multitude* (Hardt and Negri, 2005), the US critical academic Michael Hardt and the Italian Marxist academic and political activist Antonio Negri have developed the proposition that Empire is the new form of imperialism in an age of globalization. They argue that sovereignty in relation to management of a global capitalist system has been selectively transferred from nation-states to a network of national and supranational entities 'united under a single form of rule ... [which] is what we call Empire' (Hardt and Negri, 2000, p. xii). Hardt and Negri argue that Empire is 'a *decentred* and *deterritorializing* apparatus of rule that ... manages hybrid identities, flexible hierarchies, and plural exchanges through modulating networks of command' (Hardt and Negri, 2000, pp. xii–xiii; authors' emphasis). For Hardt and Negri, the current phase of global capitalism is one where 'large transnational corporations have effectively surpassed the jurisdiction and authority of nation-states', to the point where 'government and politics come to be completely integrated into the system of transnational command' (Hardt and Negri, 2000, pp. 306, 307). They identify Empire as a regime for the management of populations on a global scale, that can encompass the social totality, which includes the populations of nations seen as dominating as well as those seen as dominated, that not only manages territories and populations, but the very social world that its subjects inhabit (Hardt and Negri, 2000, pp. xiv–xv).

Multitude (Hardt and Negri, 2005) is the companion volume to *Empire*, where Hardt and Negri address the question of whether they see the power of Empire to be so all-encompassing as to negate effective resistance. They instead argue that Empire produces the possibility, for the first time in human history, of global democracy. This occurs not only because globalization weakens the power of nation-states and claims to territorial sovereignty, but because the maintenance of Empire as an economic system depends upon more and more of the global population as producers, consumers, users and participants in its global network of production. Moreover, production is no longer simply economic production, or the production of material goods, but *social* production, or 'the production of communications, relationships and forms of life' (Hardt and Negri, 2005, p. xv). As a result, it creates the *multitude* as 'the living alternative that grows within Empire' (Hardt and Negri, 2005, p. xiii), that is infinitely diverse as a population, but has a capacity to act collectively as a result of the globally networked nature of social production, and the fluid, open and collaborative network form provides its primary means of acting politically. For Hardt and Negri, 'the creation of the multitude, its innovation in networks, and its decision-making ability in common make democracy possible for the first time today', and the weakening of sovereignty by globalization and Empire means that 'the autonomy of the multitude and its capacities for economic, political and social self-organization take away any role for sovereignty … When the multitude is finally able to rule itself, democracy becomes possible' (Hardt and Negri, 2005, p. 340).

Strong Globalization Theories: a Critique

Strong globalization theories generally rest upon an interrelated set of claims about the operation of markets on a world scale and the contemporary geopolitics of global capitalism, all of which can be found in a particularly marked version in Hardt and Negri's work, and in a more nuanced and complex version in the work of Manuel Castells:

1. Markets increasingly operate on a global scale, and are increasingly dominated by a diminishing number of transnational corporations (TNCs).
2. These TNCs organize their activities on a global scale, and are less and less constrained by the policies and regulations of nation-states.
3. The power of nation-states is in decline, with many of their core operations being superseded by the laws and regulations established by supra-national governmental institutions.

4. As a result, political activity that focuses upon incremental reforms within the framework of the nation-state is misplaced, as real decision-making power increasingly resides outside of its territorial boundaries.
5. Globalization generates a global cultural experience where subjective identities are defined less by the relationship of individuals to geographically defined space sand the 'imagined community' of the nation-state, and more by their relationship to complex and interconnected global media and communications flows.
6. This 21st-century global condition is unprecedented, for while capitalism has been an international system since its inception, it is only now that global networks of technology and communication enable it to function as a fully integrated global system.
7. Globalization can lead to a 'race to the bottom', where 'capital will increasingly be able to play off workers, communities and nations against one another' (Crotty *et al.*, 1998, p. 118).

The empirical validity of these claims, and their relationship to trends in global media, will be assessed in more detail in the remainder of this book. At this stage, it is important to note that the core political-economic claims associated with these arguments have been disputed, by both those whom Held and McGrew (2002, pp. 3–5) describe as *globalization sceptics*, but also by those who agree with aspects of the strong globalization argument, but question the empirical validity of some of the claims that underpin it. Aspects of these arguments that relate to global culture and subjective identity will be addressed in more detail in Chapter 5.

First, the claim that markets are increasingly global and are dominated by TNCs, and that corporations operate on an increasingly global scale, has been disputed. The detail of these debates will be addressed in Chapter 3. At the same time, economic geographers have strongly contested the claim that TNCs have risen to such a level of pre-eminence that they have flattened the complex terrain of working in different national economies, and that the expansionary dynamic of TNCs has been such as to overwhelm points of distinction between national economies. As Dicken (2003a) has pointed out, using the UNCTAD *transnationality index* (TNI – to be discussed in detail in Chapter 3), the degree of transnationality of the world's 100 largest non-financial TNCs increased from 51.6 per cent in 1993 to 52.6 per cent in 1999. This is not a significant shift in the scale of global operations of these largest corporations – who would be expected to be at the forefront of globalization – and it indicates that, on average, most of the world's largest non-financial TNCs continued to undertake 40–50 per cent of their activities in their 'home' country, with only 16 companies undertaking more than 75 per cent of their activities outside of their country of origin (Dicken, 2003a, pp. 30–1). In other words, the majority tend to be national corporations with international operations, rather than truly transnational corporations.[3]

Second, it has been argued, from the perspectives of business management, economic geography and economic sociology, that TNCs have not been able to efface the significance of their home environment in how they structure their international operations, and that international expansion invariably involves significant modifications to their general organizational culture (Hofstede, 1980; Doremus *et al.*, 1998; Dicken, 2003a; Gertler, 2003a; Clegg *et al.*, 2005). The available evidence (Doremus *et al.*, 1998) indicates that there is not a growing 'convergence' in their institutional and policy environments as a result of globalization, and that national differences in state ideology, the nature of political institutions and the nature of economic institutions continue to matter a great deal. Gertler (2003b, p. 112) has argued that 'the enduring path-dependent institutions of the nation-state retain far greater influence over the decisions and practices of corporate actors than the current prevailing wisdom would allow', while Dicken (2003a, p. 44) has concluded that 'TNCs ... remain, to a very high degree, products of the local "ecosystem" in which they were originally planted. TNCs are not placeless; "global" corporations are, indeed, a myth'.

Third, claims about the decline of the nation-state draw in part upon a statistical fallacy concerning the relative size of national economies and transnational corporations. To take one example, Steger (2003, p. 49) provides evidence that the global sales revenue of General Motors in 2000 exceeded the GDP of Denmark, Wal-Mart's global sales revenues exceeded Poland's GDP, Royal Dutch-Shell's global sales revenue exceeded Israel's GDP, IBM's global sales revenue exceeded the GDP of Ireland, and so on. Putting aside the question of what such figures might tell us about relative power in a global system – would anyone want to argue that Shell has more influence upon global events than Israel, to take one example? – these comparisons are the product of a fairly basic statistical fallacy. The fallacy is that Gross Domestic Product (GDP) is a measure of the *value-added* of a national economy, that is, the value of its outputs after subtracting the value of national inputs that went into producing those outputs, whereas gross sales figures for companies do not subtract these inputs. The problem here is one of using two very different accounting systems as the basis for making comparisons: if the data is corrected to only account for value-added in both cases, Denmark's 'economy' is about three times the size of that of General Motors (Dicken, 2003b, p. 30).

Fourth, it is argued that the assumption that supra-national governmental institutions such as the World Trade Organization (WTO), the International Monetary Fund (IMF), the World Bank and others have real power independently of those nation-states which constitute their constituent membership arises from a misunderstanding of the ongoing relationship between national governments and these supra-national governmental institutions. Joseph Stiglitz's (2002) important insider account of how a rigid adherence to neo-liberal economic orthodoxies within the IMF and the World Bank – the so-called 'Washington Consensus' – could ride roughshod over economic decision-making in countries such as Russia, Indonesia and Argentina in the 1990s, is a salutary account of how global institutions of governance could usurp and override both national sovereignty and local knowledge.[4] At the same time, the travails of the Doha Round of trade liberalization negotiations through the World Trade Organization, which commenced in 2001, reveal just how fragile and contingent the bases of supra-national institutional authority can be in the absence of consensus among leading national governments about appropriate direction for future development. Even in cases where national governments choose to adopt WTO guidelines, as China did as a condition of entry in 2001, there is evidence that this is as much to achieve domestic policy objectives – such as the desire to establish an enforceable copyright regime for the benefit of local creative producers – as it is to be a 'good global citizen' (Fewsmith, 2001; Zhu, 2003; Fitzgerald and Montgomery, 2005).

Fifth, the claim that contemporary globalization is without historical precedent has been questioned, most notably by 'globalization sceptics' such as Hirst and Thompson (1996). Hirst and Thompson argued that, while there has been a sustained and significant increase in international integration since 1970, it followed the historical period 1945–70 where international integration was relatively low, and the period 1914–45 where it actually declined. They make the point that, as measured in levels of international trade, investment, and indeed the movement of populations, the volumes of international transactions in the period from 1970 to the mid-1990s were in fact less than those of the *la belle époque* period of international capitalism from 1890 to 1914. Moreover, there is the argument that much of what is presented as globalization through raw figures on global trade and investment flows may in fact be regionalization, or expansion of corporate operations within well-established potential regions of operation. Rugman (2000) has argued that much of the empirical data that is taken as evidence of globalization in fact points to *regionalization* – the expansion of international trade and investment within defined geo-regional zones, such as the NAFTA region of North America (US/Canada/Mexico), the European Union, and the East Asian regional zone, led by Japan. There is certainly a need for caution in equating overseas expansion with globalization, as the entry of a US-based corporation into Canada, or a German corporation into Britain, does not indicate their repositioning as a fully fledged transnational corporation.

Sixth, Hirst and Thompson join other 'globalization sceptics' such as Gordon (1988), Boyer and Drache (1996) and Glyn and Sutcliffe (1999) in questioning what they see as a pre-emptive write-off of the reforming capacities of the nation-state through globalization discourse. Hardt and Negri represent a particular Marxist variant of this discourse – albeit one with a long history – but it has been put by representatives of more neo-liberal positions, such as the first Director-General of the World Trade Organization, Renato Ruggieri, who argued that 'globalization [is] a reality which overwhelms all others', or the Australian Foreign Minister, Alexander Downer, who proposed that 'whether people fear globalization or not, they cannot escape it' (quoted in Flew and McElhinney, 2005, p. 290). On both the neo-liberal and neo-Marxist ends of the political spectrum, the 'talking up' of globalization in the face of contradictory evidence can also entail 'talking down' the prospects for significant institutional and policy reform within existing liberal-capitalist political-economic frameworks.

Seventh, the proposition that globalization involves a 'race to the bottom' as geographically mobile capital relocates to low-wage economies, forcing governments around the world to 'ratchet downwards' wages, employment conditions, environmental standards and other form of regulation in order to remain globally competitive, rests upon assumptions that are open to question. First, as Glyn and Sutcliffe (1999) observe, it is far more common in the case of manufacturing than in most service industries, where the international trade-ability of goods and services is often less marked (for example, education is internationally traded, but less so than motor vehicles or children's clothing). Second, economic geographers such as Storper (1997a, 1997b) have drawn attention to the extent to which such assumptions, which are central to 'New International Division of Labour' (NIDL) and related dependency theories, rest upon some particular further assumptions about the nature of the product itself, the labour inputs required, the relevance of territory to its production, and the nature of consumer demand for that product. To summarize an argument that is considered in more detail in Chapter 3, globalization can be seen as generating two tendencies (see Table 2.1), one of which promotes cost-driven relocation of production. This is to be found in the industries and sectors where global mobility is greatly enhanced by advances in communications technology, and production has been relocating to lower-wage economies, particularly China which has arguably become the 'world's factory' from 1980 to the present (Deloitte Research, 2003). By contrast, there are other industries and sectors, and sub-branches within industries and sectors, where a range of factors related to the quality and uniqueness of both inputs and outputs sets limits to cost-driven globalization; we will refer to this as quality-driven globalization. These arguments will be considered in greater detail in Chapter 4. At this stage, they are being flagged as trends within global capitalism itself that complicate simple prognoses about the economic and geo-political implications of globalization, of the sort developed by theorists such as Hardt and Negri.

Manuel Castells' work is, I would argue, considerably more complex and nuanced than that of Hardt and Negri, who in effect present us with a world where institutions, policies, the nation-state and, indeed, place itself are becoming increasingly irrelevant as global capital has triumphed over national institutions. There are a number of critical commentaries on Castells that it is beyond the scope of this book to consider in detail (for example, Calabrese, 1999; Webster, 2002; Garnham, 2004; Hassan, 2004). What I would, however, like to focus upon are three issues raised in Castells' work: the notion of a 'space of flows' that is superseding place; the 'culture of real virtuality' driven by new media technologies; and the concept of a bifurcation between globally mobile 'information workers' and those consigned to particular localized spaces and hence to economic vulnerability in the face of globalization.

Table 2.1 Two tendencies of globalization of products and services

Factor	Cost-driven globalization	Quality-driven globalization
Nature of product	Generic and substitutable; highly price-sensitive demand	De-standardization and variety as drivers of non-price-driven demand
Labour inputs	Generic; unskilled and semi-skilled labour	Skilled and specialist; unique bundle of skills often sought
Significance of territory	Low; few location-specific resource or knowledge requirements	High; tendency for specialist knowledge to cluster in particular regions
Consumer demand	More sensitivity to price than other factors	Rising consumer expectations about product/service quality; rising average consumer incomes

Castells' theory of the global network society develops a geographical framework based upon the notion of a *space of flows*, or an organization of global space where 'the network of communication is the fundamental spatial configuration: places do not disappear, but their logic and meaning becomes absorbed in the network' (Castells, 1996, p. 412). It is an example of what Amin (2001, 2001, p. 395) identifies as an understanding of globalization in terms of 'a shift in the balance of power between different spatial scales ... [and] a deterritorialization and reterritorialization of social organization' in the associated scalar shift of places from the local and the national to the networked and the global. Amin's critique of such arguments is not based upon a defence of the local, or a *politics of place* – which he sees as the flipside of an interscalar mode of thinking about globalization – but rather proposes that places such as cities and regions are in fact 'energized networked spaces' characterized by 'multiple spatialities of organization and praxis' (Amin, 2001, p. 396). What Amin is proposing, in contrast to Castells, is that rather than seeing people as either acting within the particularisms of place or within the global space of flows, the 'energized networked spaces' that are critical to the cultural and economic geography of globalization are sites in which people engage with the local, the national, and the global simultaneously, and that what is instead challenged are the 'traditional spatial distinctions between the local as near, everyday, and "ours", and the global as distant, institutionalised, or "theirs"' (Amin, 2001, p. 395). In other words, Amin's critique of traditional concepts of spatial ontology (that is, reading the local, the national and the global as discrete spatial forms) extends Castells' notion of the network society beyond the geographical framework within which he has set it.

Castells' understanding of the cultural forms of the global network society as involving the *culture of real virtuality*, or a 'bipolar opposition between the Net and the Self' (Castells, 1996, p. 3), rests upon two related dichotomies that have proven to be less and less tenable or sustainable over time. The first is the idea that there has been both a greater global concentration of control over media distribution and at the same time a growing diversification in the tastes and preferences of media users/audiences, so that 'we are not living in a global village, but in customised cottages globally produced and locally distributed' (Castells, 1996, p. 341). The counter-trends to greater global media concentration will be discussed in later chapters, but it is important to note that arguments that we are at the end of the age of mass media may both overstate the success of broadcast television in aggregating populations around particular media consumption patterns, and at the same time greatly underestimate the continued pull of media that can reach large segments of the population simultaneously and therefore act as a magnet for associated advertising revenues. As Garnham (2004) observes, there is the real danger here of conflating arguments concerning the perceived – and often overstated – threat of imported media content and cultural imperialism, with claims that there has been a substantive *de-massification* of the media audience. Garnham finds such arguments indicative of a tendency in theories of new media and its impacts where:

> There is a failure to distinguish between the effects of new ICTs on the economy in general, which then may or may not have significant effects in the spheres of politics and culture, and the effects directly on politics and culture themselves – for instance the claims made for the Internet as an agent of democratic renewal and the 'reinvention' of government or the supposed de-massification and globalization of the media. (Garnham, 2004, p. 179)

The second set of concerns are about the relationship between the 'real' and the 'virtual'. In their detailed ethnographic study of uses of the Internet among Trinidadians, Miller and Slater (2000, p. 5) presented a compelling argument that 'we need to treat Internet media as continuous with and embedded in other social spaces', rather than identifying Internet use as happening within a 'virtual world' that is somehow disconnected from the everyday, the here and now, and interactions with pre-existing forms of community. How people engage with the multiple forms of communications associated with the Internet – which range from playing in MMOGs[5] to browsing websites and reading e-mail, and from being a consumer to a user/participant, as is promoted on blog sites and file-sharing sites such as *Flickr* and *YouTube* – is something best understood empirically and in a detailed sense, rather than read off from the intersection between particular technological developments and modish assumptions derived from recent cultural theory (Flew, 2001).

Globalization and Global Media Corporations 3

Introduction: Globalization and the Media

Globalization and its impacts have constituted one of the hot topics of our time. It is visible on the streets of the world through the global reach of the Nike running shoes brand or the McDonald's fast-food chain, in our every-day media consumption through global media coverage of events such as the war in Iraq, terrorist actions such as the video-recorded beheadings that kidnappers use to draw attention to their actions, and celebrity events such as the Michael Jackson child sex abuse trial or the relationship between Brad Pitt and Angelina Jolie. The development of the Internet as an inte-grated worldwide communications network further animates the capacity of events in distant places to have global resonance. The significance of glob-alization is seen in the ubiquitous global presence of merchandise for foot-ball teams such as Barcelona FC, Manchester United and Chelsea, and the incomes and endorsements that can be garnered by globally recognized sports people such as David Beckham, Michael Schumacher or Tiger Woods. The role played by organizations such as the World Trade Organization, the drafting of myriad international free trade agreements, and the 100-plus protests that have taken place against meetings of global political and economic organizations since the 'Battle of Seattle' that derailed the inau-gural meeting of the World Trade Organization in 1999, also draw attention to the high political and economic stakes that many identify around ques-tions of globalization. Perhaps the most potent symbol of globalization in recent times has been the attack on the World Trade Centre in New York and on the Pentagon in Washington on 11 September 2001. Anthony Giddens has observed that this was a truly global media event, with about 500 million people worldwide witnessing the second plane crash into the second World Trade Centre tower in real time, an event that took place 30 minutes after the first attack, thereby maximizing its exposure through the global media (Giddens, 2002).

David Held and Anthony McGrew have defined globalization in the follow-ing terms:

> Globalization ... denotes the expanding scale, growing magnitude, speeding up and deepening impact of transcontinental flows and patterns of social interaction. It refers to a shift or transformation in the scale of human organization that links distant communities and expands the reach of power relations across the world's regions and continents. (Held and McGrew, 2002, p. 1)

Globalization is best understood as a process rather than an outcome, and as a series of tendencies rather than an end-state. We do not have a 'one world' government or a homogeneous global culture, and the tendency towards global markets remains significantly qualified, as will be outlined in this chapter. Nonetheless, the term 'globalization' captures a series of inter-related trends that have emerged in the world since the late 1940s, and which have accelerated in scale, impact and significance since the 1980s. These include:

- the internationalization of production, trade, and finance, the rise of multi-national corporations, reductions in cross-border tariffs upon flows of goods and services, the deregulation of financial markets, and the rise of Internet-based electronic commerce;
- the international movements of people (as immigrants, guest workers, refugees, tourists, students, military personnel and expert advisers), the development of diasporic and emigrant communities, and the increasingly multicultural nature of national societies;
- international communications flows, delivered through telecommunications, information and media technologies such as broadband, cable, satellite and the Internet, which facilitate transnational circulation of cultural commodities, texts, images, and artefacts;
- the global circulation of ideas, ideologies, and 'keywords', such as the so-called export of 'Western values', democracy, the 'War on Terror', 'fundamentalism', feminism, environmentalism;
- the establishment of international regimes in intellectual property, which entrench the enforceability of ownership of knowledge and information;
- the emergence of local resistance to globalization for domestic political and cultural objectives, by both nationalist movements of the political right, and progressive and anti-colonialist movements of the left;
- the development of international organizations, including regional trading blocs such as the European Union (EU), the North American Free Trade Agreement (NAFTA), the Association of South East Asian Nations (ASEAN), and the Asia Pacific Economic Co-operation grouping (APEC);
- the emergence of cultural, professional, and standards bodies such as UNESCO, the World Trade Organization, the World Intellectual Property

Organization, the European Broadcasting Union, the Asian Broadcasting Union and the International Telecommunications Union;

- the increasingly significant role played by global non-government organizations (NGOs), such as Amnesty International, Greenpeace, Médecins Sans Frontières, and the Red Cross in domestic and international politics;
- the growing significance of international law for national policies, such as the United Nations Convention on Human Rights, or the 'Millennium Round' of the World Trade Organization;
- the globalization of war and conflict, seen in the attacks on the World Trade Centre and the Pentagon orchestrated by Al Qa'ida, the bombing of nightclubs in Bali in October 2002 by members of the Jemiah Islamiah, attacks on transport systems in Madrid in 2004 and London in 2005, and the ongoing conflicts in Iraq and Afghanistan;
- the use of overt programmes of public relations or 'spin' by governments, corporations and NGOs aimed at shaping opinion at international, national and local levels.

Evidence of economic globalization is not hard to find, although its implications are debated, and will be discussed in more detail later in this chapter. The last three decades have seen an intensification of trends promoting global capitalism. Led by the rapid globalization of financial markets in the 1970s, triggered by the breakdown of the Bretton Woods monetary system and the oil price shocks of the early 1970s (Held *et al.*, 1999, pp. 199–205), the growth in foreign trade, foreign investment and foreign exchange transactions has substantially exceeded growth in world GDP from the early 1970s on. Data from UNCTAD indicates that such globalization was particularly marked in the 1990s, with growth rates in foreign direct investment (FDI), cross-border mergers and acquisitions (M&As), and the sales, output, assets and employment rates of foreign affiliates, considerably exceeding overall growth in global Gross Domestic Product (GDP), fixed capital formation and exports. In the 2000s, there has been greater parity between rates of cross-border activity (FDI, sales and exports of foreign affiliates) and indicators of growth overall such as GDP, gross fixed capital formation and exports. Table 3.1 presents relevant data from 1982–2005:

Table 3.1 Selected indicators of foreign direct investment and international production, 1982–2005

Item	Value at current prices (US$ billion)				Annual growth rate (per cent)			
	1982	1990	2002	2005	1986–90	1991–95	1996–2000	2001–2005
FDI inflows	59	209	651	916	23.1	21.1	40.2	20.8
FDI inward stock	802	1,954	7,123	10,130	14.7	9.3	17.2	13.1
Cross-border M&As	...	151	370	644	25.9	24.0	51.5	19.5
Sales of foreign affiliates	2,737	5,675	17,685	22,171	16.0	10.1	10.9	6.3
Gross product of foreign affiliates	640	1,458	3,437	4,517	17.3	6.7	7.9	7.9
Total assets of foreign affiliates	1,091	5,899	26,543	45,564	18.8	13.9	19.2	18.6
Exports of foreign affiliates	722	1,197	2,613	4,214	13.5	7.6	9.6	13.8
Employment of foreign affiliates (thousands)	19,375	24,262	53,094	62,095	5.5	2.9	14.2	8.5
GDP (at current prices)	10,805	21,672	32,227	44,674	10.8	5.6	1.3	9.3
Gross fixed capital formation	2,286	4,819	6,422	9,420	13.4	4.2	1.0	9.1
Exports of goods and non-factor services	2,053	4,300	7,838	12,641	15.6	5.4	3.4	13.8

Source: UNCTAD (2003, 2006).

John Dunning (2001) has argued that the current phase of capitalism is properly seen as a global one since:

1. cross-border transactions are deeper, more extensive and more interconnected;
2. resources, capabilities, goods and services are more spatially mobile;
3. multinational corporations (MNCs) have become more central to wealth creation and distribution, and they originate from, and produce in, a wider range of countries;
4. there is a much greater volume of transactions, and resulting volatility, in global capital and financial markets;
5. ICTs and electronic commerce have transformed the nature of cross-border transactions, particularly in services.

Dunning identifies a series of attracting, enabling, and threatening factors that have promoted an expansion of global capitalism (see Table 3.2).

Table 3.2 Factors promoting global capitalism

Attracting	■ Liberalization of national economies (e.g. Asia, Latin America)
	■ Market liberalization in post-Communist Eastern Europe
	■ Growing markets in emerging economies
	■ Geographical dispersal of created assets
	■ Geographical dispersal of entrepreneurial activity
Enabling	■ Development of networked ICTs
	■ Lower barriers to cross-border transactions
	■ Globalization of capital and financial markets
	■ Reduced cost/improved quality of transport and communications
Threatening	■ Intensified global competition
	■ Volatility of exchange rates and financial markets
	■ Geographical dispersal of risk
	■ Accelerating rates of technological obsolescence

Source: Dunning (2001), p. 17

Media have a central place in processes of globalization for three reasons. First, media corporations have been among those corporations that have been increasingly globalizing their operations. Table 3.3 shows the media and entertainment companies listed in the *Financial Times* Global 500 for 2006.

It should be noted, however, that being a globally large corporation does not in itself make a corporation globalized. In order to identify the world's most globalized corporations, the United Nations Commission for Trade, Aid and Development (UNCTAD) has developed a *transnationality index* (TNI), whereby transnational corporations (TNCs) are ranked by the percentage of assets, sales and employees outside of a TNC's home country. The transnationality index calculates these percentages, and divides the total by three. As we will see later in this chapter, using the TNI, media and entertainment corporations are perhaps not as global in their operations as is commonly assumed, with a small number of quite notable exceptions.

The second element of media globalization, noted in Chapter 1 in relation to the development of the telegraph in the late 19th century and satellites in the 20th century, is the role played by media organizations in developing the global communications infrastructure that facilitates global information flows and cross-border commercial activity. This role became particularly imperative in the late 20th century as telecommunications companies were at the centre of developing a 'Global Information Infrastructure' (GII) to facilitate globally networked communications and commerce (Thussu, 2000, pp. 91–92; Winseck, 2002a, 2002b; Flew and McElhinney, 2005). Moreover, global commercial media are also central to the sale of products and services through their role in advertising and promotion.

Table 3.3 The world's largest media and entertainment corporations, 2004

Global rank	Company	Country	Market value US$m	Turnover US$m
2	General Electric*	US	362,526	148,019
3	Microsoft**	US	281,170	39,788
73	Time Warner	US	74,179	43,652
110	Comcast	US	57,172	22,255
120	News Corporation***	US	54,122	23,859
121	Walt Disney	US	53,711	31,994
143	Sony****	Japan	46,265	55,912
167	Vivendi Universal	France	39,560	23,632
245	Viacom	US	28,351	9,609
303	Thomson Corporation	Canada	24,192	8,703
316	Liberty Media	US	23,020	7,960
320	Reed Elsevier	Netherlands/UK	22,774	9,138
352	McGraw-Hill	US	21,157	6,003
353	DirecTV*****	US	21,017	13,164
457	CBS	US	16,962	14,536
458	British Sky Broadcasting******	UK	16,934	7,063
468	Electronic Arts	US	16,623	3,129

    * General Electric is a diversified industrial company, but is included on the bass of its 80 per cent ownership of NBC Universal.

   ** Microsoft is primarily a software and computing services company, but is included on the basis of its involvement in digital media and games.

  *** Prior to 2004, News Corporation had its corporate head office in Australia.

 **** Sony is both an electronic goods company and a media and entertainment company.

***** News Corporation acquired a 34 per cent stake in DirecTV in 2004.

****** British Sky Broadcasting was 30 per cent owned by News Corporation in 2004.

Source: Financial Times (2006).

Finally, global media are the principal means through which we make sense of events in distant places, and the information and images that they carry are central to the development of shared systems of meaning and understanding across nations, regions and cultures. It is this aspect of global media culture that has most concerned critical media theorists, who have argued that global commercial media can use their ability to transmit information and images across borders as a form of propaganda for their own corporate interests, and the interests of global corporations more generally. Critical political economists such as Edward Herman and Robert McChesney have thus described global media as the 'new missionaries' of global capitalism:

> By their essential nature the commercial media will integrate well into the global market system and tend to serve its needs. This means greater openness to foreign commerce in media products, channels and ownership. As the media are commercialized and centralized, their self-protective power within each country increases from the growing command over information flows, political influence, and ability to set the media-political agenda (which comports well with that of advertisers and the corporate community at large). (Herman and McChesney, 1997, p. 9)

There is a significant debate about the extent of globalization. In particular, there are those who present what we termed in Chapter 2 *strong globalization* arguments, which see globalization as the dominant force of our times, and *globalization sceptics*, who point to a variety of limits to globalization. It is worth noting that the radical critique of global media has tended to be associated with strong globalization arguments, seeing globalization as the dominant force in media industries today, notwithstanding counter-trends and localized forms of resistance.

Critical Political Economy and Global Media

Critical media theorists have long been concerned with tendencies towards concentration of media ownership and their impact upon politics, society and culture, and the impact of media globalization led by Western transnational media corporations. In the 1970s and 1980s, such radical critiques were associated with theories of cultural imperialism, and associated demands for the international redistribution of control over media and communications resources. In Chapter 2, the contribution of Herbert Schiller to such a radical critique was discussed. Schiller argued that the current stage of US-dominated global capitalism was one where what he termed the entertainment, communications and information (ECI) industries had achieved economic pre-eminence; their influence was enacted not only in the political-economic sphere but upon global culture and consciousness; and the result was a form of cultural imperialism, whereby the ideas and ideologies of the dominant West (and particularly the United States) exerted hegemony over the populations of the rest of the world.

The radical critique of global media associated with critical political economy has experienced a resurgence of interest in recent years. The proposition that media ownership worldwide is subject to growing concentration, leading to reduced competition and increasingly homogeneous media content worldwide, is a commonly cited one. Edward Herman and Robert McChesney have argued that 'The ... global media system is dominated by three or four dozen large transnational corporations (TNCs) with fewer than ten mostly U.S.-based media conglomerates towering over the global market' (Herman and McChesney, 1997, p. 1). This has been widely taken as a given starting point for understanding the nature of global media today, and is routinely repeated by critics of globalization. For example, Manfred Steger (2003, p. 76) argues that 'To a very large extent, the global cultural flows of our time are generated and directed by global media empires that rely on powerful communication technologies to spread their message ... During the last two decades, a small group of very large TNCs have come to dominate the global market for entertainment, news, television, and film'. Even writers who are otherwise more critical of claims about the unparalleled dominance of TNCs/MNCs, such as Held *et al.* (1999), accept it as a given where the media are concerned, observing that 'there can be little doubt that ... a group of around 20–30 very large MNCs dominate global markets for entertainment, news, television, etc., and they have acquired a very significant cultural and economic presence on nearly every continent' (Held *et al.*, 1999, p. 347).

There are three interrelated elements to the contemporary radical critique of global media:

1. The tendency towards concentration and centralization of media ownership and control now operates globally, and not simply on a national scale.
2. This is part of a wider tendency of globalization to shift the balance of political and economic power from nationally based institutions, such as governments and trade unions, towards geographically mobile multinational corporations.
3. The globalization of media production, as with foreign investment in other sectors, is reinforcing relations of economic and cultural dependency, as

seen in theories of the *new international division of labour* (NIDL) and the *new international division of cultural labour* (NICL).

The first proposition has been most clearly articulated in the *global media monopoly* thesis, presented by Herman and McChesney in *The Global Media: New Missionaries of Global Capitalism* (Herman and McChesney, 1997), and in other work by McChesney and other critical political economists (McChesney *et al.*, 1998; McChesney, 1999; 2001a; 2001b; 2003; McChesney and Foster, 2003; McChesney and Schiller, 2003).[1] The global media monopoly thesis draws upon the argument of political economists that the media industries have an innate tendency towards concentration of owner-ship and control, and that this tendency has been extended since the 1980s from the national to the global scale. Herman and McChesney (1997, p. 1) argued that 'Since the early 1980s there has been a dramatic restructuring of national media markets, along with the emergence of a genuinely global commercial media market'. The principal consequence of such developments has been, as McChesney and Schiller argue, that 'a transnational corporate-commercial communication began to be crafted and a new structural logic put in place ... [as] communications ... became subject to transnational corporate-commercial development' (McChesney and Schiller, 2003, p. 6).

Monopoly Capitalism and Dependency Theory

While the global media monopoly thesis is a relatively recent development, it has clear intellectual antecedents not only in theories of cultural imperialism, but also in the neo-Marxist theory of *monopoly capitalism* and the related theories of imperialism and dependency.

The theory of monopoly capitalism has its origins in the revisions of Marxist political economy undertaken by Hilferding (1985 [1910]) in his theory of finance capital, and Lenin (1983 [1917]) in his theory of imperial-ism as the 'highest stage' of capitalism. Both drew attention to the ways in which the transformation from competitive to monopoly capitalism occurred through the competitive process itself and that, while it marked a significant revision of aspects of Marx's political economy of capitalism, it was at the same time anticipated in Marx's analysis of the concentration and centraliza-tion of capital. Marx defined the *concentration of capital* as the expansion of the scale of production required in order to remain competitive, and the *centralization of capital* as the 'transformation of many small into few large capitals' (Marx, 1976 [1867], p. 777), greatly promoted by the emergence of large corporations and the credit system.

The monopoly capitalism thesis was further developed by neo-Marxist writers such as Paul Baran and Paul Sweezy and in academic journals such as *Monthly Review* (see for example, Baran and Sweezy, 1968; Baran, 1973; Cowling, 1982; Foster, 1987; Sweezy, 1987). The theory of monopoly capitalism was an attempt to recast Marxist political economy in an era of large corporations, which appeared to be able to 'tame' the capitalist market and insulate themselves from competitive forces through corporate planning and the management of consumer demand through marketing and advertising strategies (Baran and Sweezy, 1968). One result was that capitalism appeared less crisis-prone than traditional Marxist models had assumed, but new forms of crisis and instability emerged around how to absorb the surplus economic product that monopoly capitalism generated. In a summary of the monopoly capitalist thesis, Foster identified the resulting modifications in corporate behaviour in the context of monopoly in these terms:

> With the rise of the giant firm, price competition ceased to take place in any significant sense within mature monopolistic industries ... In this strange, semi-regulated world of monopoly capital, there is no longer a life-or-death competition threatening the survival of the mature capitalist enterprise ... Rather, the giant corporations that dominate the contemporary economy engage primarily in struggles over market share ... It remains a competitive world for corporations in many respects, but the goal is always the creation or perpetuation of monopoly power – that is, the power to generate persistent, high, economic profits through a mark-up on prime production costs. (Foster, 2000, pp. 6–7)

Hilferding and Lenin identified *imperialism*, or the territorial expansion of the dominant capitalist states into the peripheral regions through colonial annexation, as one of the mechanisms used to manage the problem of surplus capital in the dominant capitalist metropoles (Baran, 1973; cf. Brewer, 1980; Corbridge, 1986). It has been argued that the rise of MNCs marks a contemporary form of imperialism, as formally independent post-colonial states find themselves nonetheless dependent upon the capricious flows of global capital, and the forms of political power connected to these, in order to be economically viable. In the highly influential neo-Marxist theories of dependency developed by writers such as Immanuel Wallerstein, Andre Gunder Frank and Samir Amin, global capitalism is associated with the 'development of underdevelopment', whereby the nations of the 'Third World' are subject to systematic exploitation by the metropolitan 'core'. Such economic exploitation of the 'periphery' occurred through unequal terms of trade, the imposition of a primary-products-based economic structure, the development of highly exploitative and technologically retrograde systems of labour control, and the manipulation of local politics through the cultivation of political, intellectual, business and military elites who identify their interests as synonymous with those of the dominant metropolitan powers. The latter process is described as the development of a *comprador bourgeoisie*, and has the effect of rendering these nations as *client states* of the dominant core, through mechanisms of *neo-colonialism*.

While there has been political de-colonization of these states since the end of World War II, and the movement of manufacturing production from the 'First World' to the 'Third World', it is argued that such changes nonetheless perpetuate structures of dependency, as knowledge-intensive activities remain concentrated in the home country of the MNC, while it is those activities that are most cost-driven and reproducible in multiple sites that are transferred to new locations (Dos Santos, 1973). Gyorgy Ádám argued that the shift of foreign investment from agriculture and extractive industries to manufacturing simply signalled that 'banana republics are becoming pyjama republics' (Ádám, 1975, p. 102). In a recent restatement of this position, Samir Amin (2004, p. 26) has argued that 'the "globalization" thesis ... is nothing but a new way in which the inherently imperialist nature of the system asserts itself'.

Further reading: Brewer (1980); Corbridge (1986); Roberts and Hite (2000); Hoogvelt (2001); Amin (2004).

Robert McChesney's work has developed a distinctive focus upon the dynamic relationship between media globalization and the concentration and centralization of media ownership, and the interconnected nature of these two processes. McChesney has argued that, prior to the 1980s, there was a relatively stable distinction between national media systems that were predominantly domestically controlled, with film, TV, music and print media content imported predominantly from the United States overlaying these domestic systems. The trend towards a global media oligopoly developed momentum in the 1980s and 1990s out of the tendency, on the one hand, for dominant media firms to seek international expansion in order to ensure their presence in a range of media markets and, on the other, by concentration of ownership within media industries and the expansion of connections across media industries through the growth of multinational, cross-media conglomerates such as Disney, AOL-Time Warner, News Corporation, Sony, and Viacom. For McChesney, the drivers of this conglomerate-based global media system have been policies of privatization and deregulation, and the symbiotic relationship of media deregulation to the development of industries that promote the circulation of commodities, most notably the advertising and marketing communication industries (cf. McChesney and Foster, 2003). McChesney argues that the logic of such a global-commercial media system is such that 'Firms must become larger and diversified to reduce risk and enhance profit-making opportunities, and they must straddle the globe so as to never be outflanked by competitors' (McChesney, 2001a, pp. 5–6). Moreover, there is a 'feedback loop' between the concentration and conglomeration of media industries and the regime of monopoly capitalism on a global scale, since 'global media giants are the quintessential multinational firms, with shareholders, headquarters, and operations scattered across the globe' (McChesney, 2001a, p. 16). As such, they are in the front line of advocacy for globalization, and implacably opposed to interests or values that are at odds with global corporate and commercial interests. They are not only able to lobby effectively to promote their own corporate interests, but can use the media they control to present images which can in turn influence political behaviour at both elite and mass-popular levels (McChesney, 2001a, p. 11).

The global media monopoly thesis is a 'strong globalization' argument. Herman and McChesney conclude *The Global Media* by arguing that:

> Few eras in history have approached this one for tumult and rapidity of change, and key hallmarks of the era have been the spread of an increasingly unfettered global capitalism, a global commercial media and communication system, and the development of revolutionary communication technologies. For the short and medium term we expect both the global market and global commercial media to strengthen their positions worldwide. (Herman and McChesney, 1997, p. 205)

Critical political economists would be in broad agreement with theories of strong globalization that argue, for instance, that economies have become globally interdependent as a result of advances in information and communications technologies to the point where capitalism has become, as Manuel Castells describes it, 'a global economy ... with the capacity to work as a unit in real time on a planetary scale' (Castells, 1996, p. 92). At the same time, and in contrast to theorists such as Castells, they also argue that the rise of MNCs vindicates, rather than negates, the radical analysis of global capitalism derived from theories of imperialism and *dependency theory*. This is most apparent in the recent application of core concepts of dependency theory such as the *new international division of labour (NIDL)* in the recent work of Toby Miller and his colleagues on the *new international division of cultural labour (NICL)* as a core aspect of the political economy of 'Global Hollywood' (Miller *et al.*, 2001).

The concept of an NIDL was proposed by the German economists Fröbel, Heinrichs and Kreye in the late 1970s to explain the rise of foreign investment by multinational corporations in a context of stagnation in the Western industrialized economies. The theory proposed that there was a process of de-industrialization in Western Europe and the US, and a partial industrialization of the Third World, as MNCs exploited the opportunities provided by low-wage labour, advances in transport and communications technologies, and the development of 'free production zones' with minimal tax and labour regulations by the governments of various developing countries (Fröbel *et al.*, 1980). The potential outcome of such an NIDL would include a global 'race to the bottom' in labour and environmental standards (Crotty *et al.*, 1999) and a threat to democracy worldwide, as the capacity of large MNCs to rapidly shift capital and transfer production facilities around the globe could lead to wholesale shifts of production to those countries which had more 'compliant' governments and labour unions, thereby endangering democratic principles, workers' rights, environmental safeguards and human rights more generally. This has been the thesis of popular anti-globalization texts such as *The Global Trap* (Martin and Schumann, 1997) and *No Logo* (Klein, 2000). One often-cited example of the NIDL in action is the Nike Corporation, which critics have argued was able to exploit low-wage labour while globalizing its market operations through extensive global marketing strategies from the mid-1980s onwards, so that the Nike 'swoosh' has become one of the world's most recognizable symbols, while shoe production itself has shifted from countries such as South Korea and Taiwan to lower-wage economies such as those of Indonesia, China and Vietnam (Korzeniewicz, 2000).

The NIDL thesis has been applied to media globalization by Toby Miller and his co-authors in their contemporary critique of 'Global Hollywood' (Miller *et al.*, 2001). Rejecting the claim that the global popularity of US product in global film and television markets reflects the unfettered free market at work, they instead draw upon the NIDL concept to develop a theory of the *new international division of cultural labour*. The NICL concept is used to argue that the Hollywood majors are engineering a new international distribution of labour tasks and production processes, in order to both attract talent from other national media systems into their orbit (which Hollywood has done since the 1920s),[2] but also to redistribute work globally in order both to reduce costs and 'discipline' US cultural labour by demonstrating their capacity to shift large-scale media production around the globe. In such a strategy, as argued by critics of economic globalization, 'MNCs can discipline both labour and the state, such that the latter is reluctant to impose new taxes, constraints or pro-worker policies in the face of possible declining investment' (Miller *et al.*, 2001, p. 52). Miller *et al.* propose that Hollywood majors have constructed the world of audiovisual production into three zones:

(1) the US as the global centre, where knowledge, finance and decision-making remain concentrated; (2) a semi-periphery or intermediate zone of (predominantly English-language) countries – including Canada, Britain, Australia and New Zealand – where production can be transferred to take advantage of cost advantages relative to foreign exchange rates; and (3) the rest of the world, which is completely subordinate to the centre and is drawn upon opportunistically for one-off productions (Miller *et al.*, 2001, p. 54). For Miller *et al.*, the NICL marks out a stage of the development of global media which goes beyond that of the international distribution of Hollywood product that is interlocked with the trends identified by McChesney and others towards global media concentration and centralization of ownership and control:

> Shifts towards a neo-liberal, multinational investment climate over the last decade have reinforced global Hollywood's strategic power over NICL through the privatization of media ownership, a unified Western European market, openings in the former Soviet bloc, and the spread of satellite TV, the Web and the VCR, combined with deregulation of national broadcasting in Europe and Latin America. (Miller *et al.*, 2001, p. 4)

The critical political economy paradigm provides a highly integrated approach to understanding global media. In terms of the five themes outlined in Chapter 1, it has sought to address each of these systematically. It proposes that power in the global media landscape has shifted inexorably towards the transnational media conglomerates, as the concentration of global media ownership and their global reach have greatly strengthened their capacity to exercise power and influence, as compared to nationally based media corporations (including public broadcasters), national governments, and organizations of media professionals such as unions representing journalists, actors or technical personnel. It is argued that global media markets are becoming less competitive over time, as global concentration of media ownership means that these markets operate on increasingly oligopolistic rather than competitive principles. It is argued that national media policies are increasingly serving the interests of these global media corporations, particularly through policies such as privatization, deregulation of media markets and the de-funding of public broadcasters, which allows these corporations to extend their global reach, while transnational policy-makers such as the World Trade Organization pursue a neo-liberal agenda that further promotes their material and ideological interests. In cultural terms, this is seen as being linked to the growing international dominance of Western cultural values and norms worldwide, with the increasingly unfettered movement of US-based media product around the globe promoting Western economic, cultural and ideological values.

Finally, although not discussed in detail in this chapter, critical political economists have been quite clear that new media technologies such as the Internet are not reversing this process of global media concentration. They point to mergers between media, telecommunications and computing firms to demonstrate that there is a growing process of colonization of the Internet space by traditional media giants, to the point where 'to the extent that the Internet becomes part of the commercially viable media system, it seems to be under the thumb of the usual corporate suspects' (McChesney and Schiller, 2003, p 15; cf. Schiller, 1999; McChesney, 1999, pp. 119–85).

Questioning Media Globalization

In the remainder of this chapter, I wish to critically scrutinize claims made about media globalization generally, and the analysis developed through critical political economy in particular. The purpose of such an exercise is not to dismiss outright the analyses derived from critical political economy for an understanding of global media. The insights derived from this perspective have been many and considerable, and it possesses the unique virtue of developing an integrated and systematic approach to global media that can be understood by academics and activists alike. In undertaking a questioning of the critical approach to global media, my purpose is not to dismiss pre-emptively the importance of a focus upon questions of power, relations of inequality, and ongoing struggles for the right to communicate and to have one's cultural norms and values recognized by others in an increasingly interconnected world. Rather, the purpose is to indicate how the multiperspectival approach to understanding global media developed in Chapter 2 enables new insights to emerge from the analytical lens provided by different academic traditions, and how this in turn both illuminates what had been blindspots in more conventional methodologies, and challenges some previously uncontested orthodoxies.

In particular, I wish to focus upon three areas of critique that can be developed of the critical political economy paradigm as it relates to global media. The first, which derives primarily from economic theory but also from an institutionalist approach to politics, questions at an empirical level the extent to which we now operate in a global economy where there are all-powerful transnational corporations and the capacity of nation-states to intervene to shape institutional environments is weakened accordingly. The second area of critique comes from economic geography more particularly, and opens up the question of the extent to which corporations which operate internationally are best thought of as global corporations, which now operate on such a scale across multiple markets that the question of their national home base becomes less and less relevant, or whether they remain multinational corporations, who operate in multiple markets worldwide but remain closely tied to a national home base. As we will see later in this chapter, global media corporations are overwhelmingly, and with probably only one exception, multinational corporations by such criteria. Moreover, recent work in economic geography questions the assumption that low wages are the primary driver of foreign investment, and draws attention to arguments in international business theory that throw doubt upon concepts such as the NIDL. The detailed implications of such work will be discussed in this chapter, and in more detail in Chapter 4. Finally, there is the critique from the perspective of cultural studies, which has always thrown doubt upon the claims of untrammelled Western cultural dominance made in theories of cultural imperialism, from perspectives derived from audience theory, theories of multiculturalism, and the role played by language and history in generating forms of cultural proximity that cut across simple core-periphery models of the modern world-system. This will be discussed in more detail in Chapter 5.

Questioning media globalization: perspectives from institutional and economic theories

The question of whether the global media have now become concentrated to such a point that competition is being eliminated in the media sector has also been subject to some debate. As Robert McChesney has been such an influential advocate of such a position, it is worth analysing a debate that took place on the online site *Open Democracy* (www.opendemocracy.org) between McChesney and MIT media economist Benjamin Compaine (Compaine, 2001; cf. Compaine, 2000). Compaine contested McChesney's claim that 'there are now fewer and fewer companies controlling more and more' (McChesney, 2001b), instead arguing that:

- the share of the top 50 media companies over total US media revenues in 1999 was comparable to that in 1986;
- there has been significant movement within the 'league table' of major media companies in the United States;
- in the US and much of Europe – and, one could add, most of Asia and Latin America – broadcast media markets are substantially more competitive than was the case two decades before;
- the Internet has introduced new forms of competition to traditional media giants;
- the competitive advantages that are associated with conglomeration and globalization need to be weighed up against new forms of risk and possibilities to accrue losses as a result of such expansionary activities.

This debate has been joined by a number of *Open Democracy* contributors, including David Hesmondhalgh (2001), James Curran (2002), and Silvio Waisbord (2002). It has been argued that Compaine's analysis may be limited by its focus upon traditional media industry silos, rather than upon those sectors which have an increasingly important 'gatekeeper' function in a convergent media environment, such as telecommunications and computing. As we noted earlier in this chapter, the world's two largest media and entertainment corporations in 2004 were General Electric and Microsoft; these are companies that find themselves in the media business by virtue of their strategies of merger, acquisition and strategic alliance as they diversify their operations and become business conglomerates. Such dynamics are typically poorly captured within the traditional sector-specific approaches of industry economics. Nonetheless, Compaine undertakes an important service in these debates by demanding more attention to the empirical detail that underlies highly generalized claims about the concentration of media ownership and power, and I will return to this point below.

Another of Compaine's arguments is that 'there is only one truly global media corporation ... [and that is] News Corporation' (Compaine, 2001, p. 3), with the other media giants being essentially US, Japanese and European companies that operate internationally. This claim that the extent of corporate globalization and its transformative impact in recent times has been overstated receives considerable support among economists from across the political and ideological spectrum, who have been sceptical of strong claims being made about economic globalization and its purported political impacts. Political economists such as Gordon (1988) and Glyn and Sutcliffe (1999) have argued that capital is considerably less geographically 'footloose' and independent of nation-states than some key globalization theorists maintain. They also argue that 'strong globalization' arguments tend to focus upon the manufacturing sector and particularly low-value-added factory production; there has been a relative neglect of the services sector, which has been growing at a faster rate than manufacturing, but tends to be both less internationally traded, and to also have stronger public sector involvement. Rugman (2000) has argued that the concept of a single global market is an illusion; what instead exists are a series of regionalized production and market blocs, dominated by the 'triad' markets of North America, the European Union and Japan.[3] As a result, what appears as globalization, as measured by foreign investment and overseas sales, contains an element of statistical illusion, as much of the so-called 'global' expansion is regional in its focus – strengthened links between the United States, Canada and Mexico, or the economies of the European Union, or those of the East Asian region. Rugman argues that international expansion strategies generally require a greater degree of 'local knowledge' than is often accounted for, and that expansion within a region is often more straightforward and less risky than expansion across regions. In other words, the issues facing a French company seeking to expand into Eastern Europe are probably less complex than those raised by similar plans to expand into South East Asia, while a US company seeing to expand its operations in Latin America may find this less complex than expansion into China.

This turn towards demanding greater empirical detail on claims concerning globalization draws attention to some of the problematic assumptions which underpin the claim that we are moving towards media concentration and conglomeration on a global scale. One problem is the tendency to present the sheer size of figures as *prima facie* proof of trends towards greater concentration. Economists point out that growth in the size and revenue of an enterprise in a sector always needs to be considered alongside overall market growth and the entry of new competitors. If an enterprise is growing in a growing market, where there are not significant barriers to entry for new competitors, then that does not in itself provide evidence of greater concentration of ownership and control in that market. Observations that News Corporation is expanding its activities in China, or Time Warner its operations in South America, cannot in themselves be taken as evidence that by doing so they are undermining traditional local businesses and thereby reducing competition in that market. Indeed, it is very probably the case that their entry into these markets is increasing rather than decreasing competition, as they typically face well-established and highly competitive local incumbent interests in these media markets.

What often also emerges in the 'global media monopoly' thesis is a fallacy of composition. To give an example, McChesney observed that the level of mergers and acquisitions in the global media, Internet, and telecommunications industries totalled US$300 billion in the first half of 2000, which was three times the value of mergers and acquisitions (M&As) in 1999 (McChesney, 2001a, p. 3; 2003, p. 150). This is taken as evidence of the accelerating trend towards global media conglomerates and the concentration of global media ownership. Yet if we probe this figure in more detail, we can identify contextual factors which, at the very least, qualify the strong conclusions that have been attached to them. First, the overall value of M&As in 1999 was US$2.3 trillion in 1999, meaning that M&As in the media, Internet and telecommunications industries were part of a worldwide trend that saw M&As increase from 0.3 per cent of global GDP in 1980 to 2 per cent in 1990, and 8 per cent in 1999 (UNCTAD, 2000, p. 106). In other words, rapid growth in the value of M&As in the media-related sectors in the late 1990s was part of a dramatic worldwide growth in M&A activity, and not evidence in itself of the rising significance of the media-related sectors. Second, there are problems in connecting the media, Internet and telecommunications industries, for while they are all part of a broadly defined communications sector, M&As in each do not have the same implications. Two of the world's largest cross-border M&As were the US$60.3 billion merger of Vodafone (UK) with AirTouch Communications (US), and the 2000 merger of Vodafone-AirTouch with the German Mannesmann Group, which had acquired the UK-based Orange telecommunications company for US$32.6 billion in 1999. While the result has been the consolidation of Vodafone as a global telecommunications giant, it is not clear that the existence of such a global telecommunications conglomerate raises the concerns that McChesney equates with global media conglomerates since, whatever the other issues raised by concentration and global conglomeration in the telecommunications sector, they do not in themselves impact, in either a positive or a negative sense, upon questions of media content. Finally, the trebling of the value of media-related M&As in 2000 was significantly driven by the America OnLine (AOL)-Time Warner merger, valued at US$128 billion in that year. Such a large one-off M&A event will artificially inflate figures, and the subsequent travails of that merged entity, to the point where AOL was quietly subsumed back into Time Warner in 2004, suggest that there is a substantial difference between media conglomerates giving the appearance of multiheaded corporate behemoths and their abilities to effectively act upon that potential.[4]

Finally, in relation to the commonly cited claim that globalization renders national governments as compliant 'client states' of global corporations, political theorists working from an institutional perspective have drawn attention to the ongoing role of the state in managing the processes associated with economic globalization and the entry of MNCs into national economies. Linda Weiss (1997; 2003) has critiqued what she terms the *myth of the powerless state*, observing that state-led economic development strategies in East Asia have not been characterized by the notion of 'client states' beholden to multinational capital. Indeed, in many instances it has been the state itself which has orchestrated the process of internationalizing national economies. In the case of countries such as Singapore, Taiwan and South Korea, Weiss has argued that it was the state itself that promoted the international expansion of locally based enterprises, as well as opening up the economy to international competition, in order to promote competitiveness and greater efficiencies in the national economy. The accession of China to the World Trade Organization, according to such an analysis, is best understood not as a triumph of neo-liberal values or Western influence over the Chinese communist state, but rather as a pragmatic strategy to lever economic restructuring in the domestic economy, and to promote the expansion of large-scale Chinese enterprises as internationally competitive forms that have access to both markets and expertise from outside of China (Zhu, 2003).

Questioning media globalization: findings from the UNCTAD 'transnationality index'

When talking about media globalization, there is an important distinction to be made between media corporations which operate on a truly global scale, and those nationally based corporations with overseas operations. Forms of media globalization that revolve around the sale of media and creative products and services in many markets have existed at least since the expansionary strategies of the Hollywood majors into Europe and Latin America in the 1920s. They are not synonymous with the development of a geographically dispersed global assets base, arising from foreign direct investment, strategic partnerships, and mergers and acquisitions. The economic geographer John Dunning (2001) has argued that it is the accumulation of a geographically dispersed assets base in order to develop competitive advantage in multiple national and regional markets through foreign investment that enables us to speak of the current era as one of an emerging global capitalism, rather than simply marketing products and services on an international scale. Similarly, Peter Dicken (2003b, p. 30) has defined a global corporation as 'a firm that has the power to co-ordinate and control operations in a large number of countries (even if it does not own them), but whose *geographically-dispersed operations are functionally integrated*, and not merely a diverse portfolio of activities' (emphasis in original). This definition of a global corporation is contrasted to that of 'national corporations with international operations (i.e. foreign subsidiaries)' (Dicken, 2003a, p. 225).

One useful measure of the 'transnationality' of corporations on the basis of such definitions is the *transnationality index* developed by the United Nations Commission for Trade, Aid and Development (UNCTAD). The transnationality index (TNI) measures the percentage of a company's assets, sales and employees that are outside of the country's home base, and divides this figure by three. One useful feature of the TNI is that it does not rely upon a single measure of transnationality, such as foreign sales, but aligns this to other indicators of the globalization of corporate operations, such as the international deployment of assets and related international employment trends. UNCTAD's 2003 data indicated that, on the basis of the TNI, Canada's Thomson Corporation was the world's most globalized corporation, with 98.0 per cent of its combined assets, sales and employees (TNI composite) from outside of its national home base, while News Corporation was the world's third most globalized corporation, with a TNI score of 92.5 per cent (that is, the combined percentage of its combined assets, sales and employees outside of its Australian home base). Using the UNCTAD data for value of foreign assets, four media or media-related corporations were in the top 100 – Vivendi Universal (20), News Corporation (22), Thomson Corporation (65) and Bertelsmann (98). The list was otherwise dominated by electronics, telecommunications, petrochemicals, motor vehicles, utilities, pharmaceuticals and other companies in the manufacturing or resource-related industries (UNCTAD, 2005, pp. 267–9). UNCTAD's 2004 data found that Vivendi Universal and News Corporation had disappeared from the list, and in the case of News, this was because it had relocated its corporate head office from Australia to the United States (UNCTAD, 2006, pp. 280–2).

This evidence would support the arguments of some globalization sceptics, such as Glyn and Sutcliffe (1999), who argue that barriers to the international tradeability of services remain significant, and this generates a problem for 'strong globalization' arguments, as it is services industries that are growing most rapidly in terms of percentage of sales and employment worldwide. It does not provide support for the proposition that the global media and entertainment industries are increasingly controlled by an ever-smaller number of transnational media conglomerates. It indicates that there are media or media-related corporations that operate on an increasingly global scale although, with the exception of News Corporation, they are not the largest ones.[5]

If we take the world's four largest media corporations – Time Warner, Disney, Viacom and News Corporation – only one of these (News Corporation) could be said to have approached the status of a global corporation. By contrast, companies such as Time Warner, Disney and Viacom have a small share of their overall asset base outside of North America. Indeed, Time Warner does not list its assets located outside of the United States in its *Annual Report*, since the overwhelming bulk of its international revenues are derived from the sale of US copyrighted products abroad, and therefore constitute intangible assets based upon the commercial value of product titles (for this reason, in Table 3.4 there is an asterisk (*) for Time Warner's share of foreign assets and TNI measure). Moreover, even though News Corporation can be said to have pursued a globalization strategy marked by the significant role played by joint ventures and strategic partnerships in acquiring assets outside of its three 'home bases' of the United States, Australia and Britain, its transnationality comes in part from its having been listed until 2004 as an Australian company. Importantly, in 2004 News Corporation relocated its corporate head office from Adelaide, Australia – which had been something of a nominal base for many years – to Delaware in the United States, thus becoming an American corporation in order to better access US equity markets. Table 3.4 indicates that if we analyse international activity in terms of revenues acquired outside of the home country, and if we approach News Corporation as a US company, we find that Time Warner, Disney and Viacom have a comparable pattern of operations, deriving 20–25 per cent of their total operating revenues from outside of North America, with News Corporation being the significant outrider, deriving 44 per cent of its revenues from outside of North America. While all of these companies have been expanding their international operations since the 1990s, and will no doubt continue to do so, only News Corporation can lay claim to being a global corporation on the criteria used by economic geographers such as Dunning and Dicken.

Table 3.4 Transnationality of the largest global media corporations, 2005

Corporation	Total assets (US$ bn)	Foreign assets as % of total assets	TNI	Revenues earned in North America (%)	Revenues earned outside North America (%)
Time Warner	122	*	*	79	21
Disney	53	14	18.5	77.5	22.5
News Corporation	56	19	32	56	44
Viacom	19	5	10	78	22

* See explanation in text

Sources: UNCTAD (2003), p. 5; company annual reports

The evidence on how media corporations compare to other corporations in terms of global status indicates that – on average and with a few notable exceptions – media corporations are less globalized than major corporations in other sectors of the economy. In relation to the transnationality index more broadly, Dicken (2003a, 2003b) has observed that the mean TNI for the top 100 non-financial MNCs was 52.6 in 1999, compared to 51.5 in 1993, and argued from this that the movement towards the largest corporations becoming more global over time has been much slower than both advocates and critics of corporate globalization generally assume (Dicken, 2003b, pp. 28–31). Moreover, there is little correlation between the size of the corporation as measured by its foreign assets and its degree of transnationality. The TNI tends to have a bias towards Europe – perhaps due to the role of the European Union in encouraging cross-border investment within Europe – and towards countries such as Switzerland, Sweden, Belgium, Canada, Australia, and The Netherlands, which is reflective of the smaller populations of these countries, and hence their companies' greater need to establish overseas operations than US or Japanese companies. At the same time, the foreign assets measure has a bias towards the mining and extractive industries (most notably petroleum) and established manufacturing industries such as that of motor vehicles. Insofar as convergent communications services industries have had an impact in recent years, the main growth has been in the telecommunications sector, rather than media and entertainment.[6] To conclude, the

UNCTAD data reinforces the point that the globalization of the media and entertainment industries is moving more slowly than is commonly assumed, and that News Corporation is the only major media corporation with claims to be truly global, rather than a national corporation that operates in international markets, and this claim was partly conditional upon its having until recently 'home base' status in Australia rather than in the US.

News Corporation's Globalization Strategies

Of all the world's major media corporations, News Corporation has the strongest claims to be a truly global media enterprise. It has investment across five continents, in countries and regions as diverse as the US, Britain, Australia, New Zealand, China, Japan, India, Germany, Italy, Brazil, Mexico, Fiji and Papua New Guinea. From his initial involvement in running a daily newspaper in Adelaide, Australia, the Chairman and CEO, Rupert Murdoch, has established News Corporation as a complex global cross-media conglomerate, whose interests span newspapers, magazines, film, broadcast television, cable and satellite TV, music, publishing and sports. Whether revered or reviled – and Murdoch's managerial style has both fans and many detractors – News Corporation now controls many of the world's most recognizable global media brands. Herman and McChesney have observed that News Corporation 'provides the archetype for the twenty-first century global media firm … and is the best case study for understanding global media' (Herman and McChesney, 1997, p. 70).

There is debate among the many authors who have written about Rupert Murdoch and News Corporation regarding the extent to which its global expansion from a modest base in Australian newspapers to the prominence it has today has been strategic or *ad hoc* and opportunistic (Shawcross, 1992; Chenoweth, 2002). News Corporation's expansion is perhaps best understood as having four stages. The first is the expansion of newspaper interests in Britain and, later, the United States. Murdoch took over the Sunday tabloid *News of the World* in 1968, and the daily tabloid *The Sun* in 1969, and through the 1970s established these as the papers with the highest circulation in Britain. His purchase of *The Times* and *The Sunday Times* in 1981 meant that News-controlled papers had a dominant position in Britain at both the prestigious broadsheet and populist tabloid ends of the market, providing a strong platform from which Murdoch's personal support for Margaret

Thatcher's Conservative government could receive a voice. This support was reciprocated with government support for News's campaign against the print unions in 1985–86, as Murdoch moved the production headquarters for News Corporation's papers from Fleet Street to new, largely non-unionized facilities at Wapping in East London. During the 1970s, News Corporation also established a base in the United States, buying newspapers in San Antonio, Texas, and most notably, the *New York Post* in 1976. Murdoch himself became a US citizen in 1983, in order not to contravene foreign ownership limits.

The United States would be the principal focus of the second stage of News Corporation's international expansion in the 1980s, which saw News move from being primarily involved in print media to being a major player in film and television. In 1985, News Corporation bought a 50 per cent share of the Twentieth Century-Fox film group, which at that time was struggling, despite having produced the phenomenally successful *Star Wars* films. In the same year, News Corporation acquired the Metromedia chain of independent television stations. On the back of these acquisitions, the Fox Television Network was launched in 1987, with Barry Diller as CEO, and with a programming strategy that was very consciously aimed at younger audiences, who were seen as being neglected by the 'Big Three' US networks. Programmes such as *Married with Children* and *The Simpsons* attracted both the desired youth audiences and notoriety from critics. News Corporation had held interests in European satellite television since the early 1980s, but made a major move into the UK market with the launch of Sky Television in 1989. The massive investments in Fox and Sky meant that, by 1990, News Corporation was unable to meet the repayments on its rapidly growing short-term debt, which totalled US$2.3 billion and was owed to an astounding 146 financial institutions, and narrowly averted bankruptcy.

After its near-death experience, the 1990s marked the third stage of News Corporation's global expansion. Sky merged with British Satellite Broadcasting in 1990 to form BSkyB, and there was a major reversal of the floundering fortunes of British satellite TV broadcasting after BSkyB acquired exclusive rights to English Premier League soccer in 1992. By 2003, 33 per cent of British TV households were BSkyB subscribers and the service had successfully migrated its subscribers to the digital television platform. News's interest in satellite broadcasting was strengthened through its acquisition of Hong Kong-based STAR TV, a pan-Asian multichannel satellite TV service, in 1993. STAR TV struggled through its early years, partly due to its predominantly English-language programme schedule, but also because of the service being blocked in some Asian countries, most notably China, after Rupert Murdoch's various pronouncements on the threat presented by satellite broadcasting to 'totalitarian regimes'. STAR has responded through strategies of 'going local' in its programming, identifying the need to develop distinctive programming strategies for particular regional sub-markets, most notably India, where STAR has a minority stake in the Indian cable TV service ZeeTV, and 'Greater China' (China, Hong Kong and Taiwan). As a News Corporation executive commented in 1995, 'There's no money to be made in cultural imperialism' (quoted in Sinclair, 1997, p. 144). The development of STAR, and of News Corporation's ambitions in Asia more generally, has also been marked by a series of direct negotiations between Rupert Murdoch and other News Corp executives and governments in the region, most notably that of China, which have led to the Phoenix television service gaining limited 'landing rights' to broadcast into China in 2000.

The fourth stage of News Corporation's globalization strategy has been marked by the successful takeover of DirecTV, America's largest provider of satellite television, in December 2003. This enables News Corporation, which is already a strongly vertically integrated company in terms of content production and distribution, to establish Sky Global Network, and achieve the 'ring of satellites' across the globe, first prophesied by science fiction writer Arthur C. Clarke in the 1940s (Shawcross, 1992, pp. 193–5). The plan is to integrate the platforms of BSkyB in Britain, STAR TV in Asia, Sky in Latin America, and DirecTV and Fox in the US, to provide integrated transnational platforms for global media content developed through Fox film studios, Fox Television, Fox Sports and other News Corp outlets, that could be combined with enhanced services such as on-demand content, interactivity, customised news and entertainment services, and the use of digital storage devices and personal video recorders (PVRs). (Note: As this book went to press, negotiations were under way for the sale of DirecTV to Liberty Media.)

News Corporation has thus been investing heavily in the possibilities of being a globally integrated media conglomerate that exploits new possibilities to integrate content and distribution via digital platforms. The surprise decision to purchase the online social networking start-up MySpace.com in 2005 for $580 million may well mark a new development in News Corporation's corporate evolution, as Rupert Murdoch began to think out loud about the future of news and journalism for those under 25 whom he terms the 'digital natives' (Reiss, 2005). Given both the risk-taking culture and global ambitions of News Corporation, and Rupert Murdoch's strong personal instinct for popular media, its global expansion strategy is very important to watch in terms of the possibility of truly global media corporations emerging in the near future.

Further reading: Shawcross (1992); Sinclair (1997); Chenoweth (2002); Rohm (2002); Fallows (2003); Sinclair and Harrison (2004).

New Theories of Globalization and Foreign Investment: Perspectives from Economic Geography

There was an important intersection in the 1970s between neo-Marxist dependency theory and theories of foreign investment and MNC expansion which formed the basis of theories such as the New International Division of Labour (Fröbel *et al.*, 1980). At this time, the dominant theories of MNC investment activity focused upon the interrelationship between the ownership advantages of vertically integrated firms, and the cost-reducing or market-expanding opportunities presented by particular locations (Barnet and Müller, 1974; Hymer, 1975). *Ownership* advantages are those which derive from being multinational and vertically integrated across the supply chain, particularly in economies where the competition is largely nationally based. They could include the ability to produce at lower costs due to the international nature of corporate activities, superior access to financial resources, control over scarce or unique resources (both physical and human), or the uniqueness and global recognition of a particular product or brand (for example, the ability to exploit the global recognition of Coca-Cola as a brand of soft drink). It follows that the world's largest firms become MNCs, and their dominance is further extended through their decision to go global, as they can out-compete more locally based enterprises in particular national markets, and will be able to exercise power over national governments in the countries in which they invest. *Locational* advantages have been seen as in many ways complementary to ownership-based advantages, as they address the question of *where* foreign direct investment (FDI) takes place as well as *why*. Locational theory has traditionally focused upon either the availability of particular primary resources in certain markets, or access to new markets, availability of low-cost labour, or incentives offered by governments – particularly in developing countries – such as tax incentives or 'free production zones' without the usual standards of labour or environmental regulation. The implication of these theories of the rise of the multinational corporation is that it can structure its activities in ways that disadvantage governments and workers in both its home country and in those host countries in which it invests.

This model of foreign direct investment could potentially explain patterns of *horizontal* specialization, where MNCs produce and market similar products in different countries on the basis of ownership-based advantages such as global marketing and branding, as well as *vertical* specialization, where a global value chain is developed that exploits the different locational advantages of particular nations and regions. What it could not explain was *why* corporations with global ambitions would undertake foreign direct investment in other countries, with the associated risks of locating large amounts of physical assets in countries where the market was less well understood, the political risks were greater, and the capacity to recruit skilled local labour was less apparent. The benefits of new markets and/or unique resources could be accessed by other means that did not involve the investment of physical capital, such as equity investment in local producers, import/export arrangements with local distributors, or other forms of strategic partnership. In his influential OLI or 'eclectic' paradigm, John Dunning proposes that the missing element from these theories of foreign investment was an understanding of *internalization* advantages. Whereas ownership advantages (O) and location advantages (L) had been well rehearsed in theories of the MNC, Dunning argued that internalization (I) theories best explained how and why MNCs participated in foreign direct investment on the basis of advantages associated with the ability to capture more localized sources of knowledge and apply them across global markets. Such advantages included: organizational learning; cultural awareness; innovation opportunities; and opportunities to augment existing intellectual assets that arise from a direct presence as a producer and/or distributor in multiple nations.

Dunning has proposed that the principal goal of MNCs has been evolving from one focused primarily upon advancing the opportunities to exploit profit from existing assets, by reducing costs through offshore production or selling into new markets, to strategies which focus upon 'the creation, as well as the use, of resources and capabilities', and the resulting need for MNCs to 'organize their activities in order to create future assets' (Dunning, 2001, p. 100). In such a context, MNCs have an interest in being able to tap into a diverse range of knowledge and innovation systems. The drive to acquire knowledge capital from multiple sources, as well as the problem of *cultural distance* that arises from operating in multiple countries (that is, the cultural differences between nations that make it difficult to develop homogeneous 'global products'), mean that:

> Multinational enterprises are engaging in foreign direct investment specifically to tap into, and harness, country- and firm-specific resources, capabilities, and learning experiences ... MNEs may use their foreign affiliates or partners as vehicles for seeking out and monitoring new knowledge and learning experiences; and as a means of tapping into national innovatory or investment systems more conducive to their dynamic competitive advantages. (Dunning, 2000, p. 20)

The relevance of access to knowledge-based assets as primary drivers of the investment decisions of MNCs today is further enhanced by four major developments that Dunning identifies as central elements of the dynamics of contemporary global capitalism (Dunning, 2001, pp. 186–91). The first is the rise of a *knowledge economy*, or one where there is a 'growing relative importance of intangible capital in total productive wealth, and a rising relative share of GDP attributable to intangible capital' (David and Foray, 2002, p. 1). The knowledge economy places a new emphasis upon the importance of intangible assets, such as knowledge, information and creativity, that are embodied in people, organizations and processes, as compared to natural assets (land, resources, low-cost labour) and tangible physical assets (buildings, machinery, fixed infrastructure). Associated with the rise of a knowledge economy is the growing importance of innovation and the development of new products, services and processes, many of which involve new applications of 'borderless' ICTs and broadband networks (cf. Hodgson, 2000; OECD, 2001a; Flew, 2005a). The second major development is what Dunning terms *alliance capitalism*, and Manuel Castells termed *the networked enterprise model* (Castells, 1996, pp. 162–6, 170–2; cf. Castells, 2001, pp. 67–8). Alliance capitalism refers to the increased significance attached to intercorporate and other alliances (for example, with competitors, suppliers, customers, and governments) as means of achieving access to synergistic or complementary knowledge-intensive assets, learning and organizational capabilities, and markets. Third, the *liberalization of national and international markets*, arising from the combination of deregulatory government policies that have reduced barriers to trade and capital flows and the dramatic reduction in transport and communication costs, has greatly increased the capacity to move investment capital around the globe. Fourth, the *take-off of several developing economies* in Asia and Latin America in the 1990s, as well as the substantial opening up of the People's Republic of China, Russia and the postcommunist economies of Eastern Europe, have been creating major new markets and foreign investment opportunities for multinational corporations in the developed world, as well as seeing the emergence of very significant MNCs from the developing world (cf. UNCTAD, 2005).[7]

As a result, we need to see processes of economic globalization driven by MNC expansion as a multidimensional process, of which the shift of low-value-added activities to low-wage economies in order to minimize costs across the global production value chain is only one of a range of possible strategies. Michael Storper has argued that globalization can no longer be understood simply as a process of *deterritorialization*, through offshore production, the development of a global value chain or NIDL, or 'winner-take-all' global expansion of successful products, services or brands. Storper instead argues that there is a need to recognize globalization that results from the 'local, path-dependent, and highly embedded technological change' that has emerged in particular dynamic cities and regions, which is 'a strong and positive driver of globalization, ... because it supplies scarce resources to the global economy in the form of temporarily unique knowledge embedded in products or services' (Storper, 2000, p. 49). Storper argues that, in contrast to the belief that globalization of trade, communications and access to technologies would lead to product standardization, there is rather a dualistic development of technology, geographies, organization and innovation in globalizing economies, with an increased premium placed upon that which is specialized and non-standardized:

> It now appears that development ... depends, at least in part, on destandardization and the generation of variety. The increasing spatial integration of markets for standardized products bids away monopolistic rents, while automation takes away employment, and advantage accrues to low-wage, low-cost areas. The only way out of this dilemma is to recreate imperfect competition through destandardization, the source of scarcity. (Storper, 1997b, pp. 32–3)

The path from restricted local and national markets to global markets does not, therefore, mean the demise of national capitalisms, but rather a two-track relationship between globalization of specialized and standardized products and services, as discussed in Chapter 2 (see pp. 62–3). Whether an activity becomes geographically dispersed on a world scale, or concentrated in specialized industrial districts, depends upon the extent to which the resources required for that activity are geographically concentrated or dispersed, or based upon territories or flows. A purely *flow-based production model* is one where resources are perfectly substitutable across territories, and assets can therefore be distributed across multiple locations. The NIDL model, discussed earlier, is premised upon the assumption that with the rise of MNCs as the central players in the global economy, combined with improvements in transport and communication, a flow-based model of global production will become increasingly prominent, particularly when combined with global standardization of consumer tastes, product standardization and routinization of production processes. By contrast, *territorialized economic development* is defined as 'economic activity that is dependent on territorially specific resources' (Storper, 1997a, p. 170), which include specific practices, routines and relationships that have evolved over time in particular locations. These form a part of what Storper has termed *untraded interdependencies*, or 'conventions, informal rules, and habits that coordinate economic actors under conditions of uncertainty ... [and] constitute region-specific assets ... in contemporary capitalism' (Storper, 1997a, pp. 4–5).

With economic globalization and rising levels of foreign investment, what is occurring is not simply a shift from local to global production systems but differentiation within and between systems. It has been the transfer of jobs and investment associated with highly standardized, flow-based forms that has most concerned activists and critics of globalization, and which underpins the NIDL thesis. This is, however, only one of four possible scenarios, of which another is the rise of specialized and territorially based production systems, whose significance does not diminish with globalization. Figure 3.1 outlines the nature of these systems. The significant point is that economic globalization does not simply entail a shift from zone 3 to zone 2, but rather the simultaneous development of zones 1 and 2, and the 'ongoing reinvention of relational assets in the context of high levels of geographical openness in trade and communications' (Storper, 1997a, p. 184).

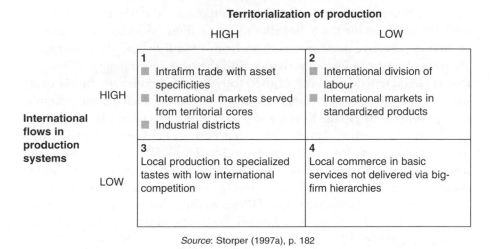

Territorialization of production

		HIGH	LOW
International flows in production systems	HIGH	**1** ■ Intrafirm trade with asset specificities ■ International markets served from territorial cores ■ Industrial districts	**2** ■ International division of labour ■ International markets in standardized products
	LOW	**3** Local production to specialized tastes with low international competition	**4** Local commerce in basic services not delivered via big-firm hierarchies

Source: Storper (1997a), p. 182

Figure 3.1 Flows and territories in global production systems

At the level of the products and services generated by the media and creative industries, there are both factors which may accentuate a new international division of cultural labour (NICL) (Miller *et al.*, 2001, pp. 49–58), and factors which promote diffusion and diversification of the global sites of cultural production. Drawing upon Storper's analysis, the extent to which an NICL will form in the global media is linked to the extent to which its products are generic, standardized, and subject to relatively low levels of 'cultural discount' in their transfer from one market to another (cf. Hoskins *et al.*, 1997). For Miller *et al.*, the capacity to transfer audiovisual media production to a range of global sites is high, but this transfer of jobs does not in any way translate into a transfer of knowledge or control. Thus, 'Global Hollywood' appears as a cost-driven process, where the compliance of local authorities in other countries enables 'runaway production' to occur.

By contrast, according to the extent to which the products and services of the media industries are unique, specialized and subject to a degree of cultural discount, and insofar as their distinctive textual and other properties derive from the unique forms of knowledge and creativity that exist in particular cultural *milieux*, there will be limits to the capacity to impose the NICL beyond the national boundaries of (mostly US-based) media MNCs. In their study of the recent global boom in studio complexes, Goldsmith and O'Regan (2003) question the extent to which both international production can be conflated with Hollywood, and the US can be seen as the natural home for audiovisual production. They point out that the term 'runaway production' and the argument that underpins it are misleading, since they continue to define production ecologies in implicitly national terms. By contrast, film production is increasingly international to the extent that it is difficult to determine the nationality of many films, as indicated by sources of finance, creative personnel both in front of and behind the camera, the location of post-production activities, and distribution strategies. Moreover, this is characteristic not only of the Hollywood blockbusters, but is being utilized as a strategy by a range of global producers such as, for example, film producers in Japan, Korea and Hong Kong producing for pan-Asian markets (cf. Curtin, 2003). The distinction between 'creative' and 'economic' reasons for determining production locations is also problematic, and assumes that workers in 'below-the-line' roles are not making creative contributions, and are largely interchangeable across global production sites. Goldsmith and O'Regan find this not to be the case, suggesting that it rests upon a limited view of creativity (Goldsmith and O'Regan, 2003, p. 12).

Drawing upon the new theories of globalization and foreign investment outlined above, we can see that, at its simplest, media globalization involves a movement from primarily locally or nationally based media systems to ones where international flows have come to be of increasing significance. At the same time, however, empirical evidence on the actual extent of 'globalization' of media corporations needs to be qualified. There is neither a strong trend towards media corporations being more internationally oriented than other branches of industry, nor is it clear that they operate as global corporations in the sense that Dicken and Dunning define them, as institutions whose geographically dispersed operations are functionally integrated into a singular global entity. Moreover, it is indicated that an increased internationalization of flows in global media is not synonymous with deterritorialization of media production nor with the standardization of media products and the homogenization of media markets. This is indeed one possibility, one whose malign impacts are explored in depth in the NICL model of Miller *et al.* The other possibility arises from the extent to which global media products and services are unique, specialized, subject to cultural discount, and have textual properties and bases of appeal which emerge from particular (non-global) forms of cultural resonance. In these instances, there may be a link between the production of non-standardized media commodities, the demand of increasingly affluent and sophisticated media consumers for variety, and the local bases of competitive advantage in a global cultural economy, which generate quite different stories to the bleak scenarios presented in radical critiques of global media and theories of global media and cultural dependency such as the NICL.

Global Media, the Knowledge Economy and the New Competition

4

Introduction

It has been argued in Chapters 2 and 3 that many contemporary accounts of global media have worked with a one-sided account of globalization, which stresses the forces of geographical dispersal and deterritorialization, while downplaying the significance of new forms of clustering and locationally specific resources for attracting international investment and developing global competitive advantage. Moreover, the ongoing legacy of dependency models found in theories of the new international division of cultural labour (NICL) has led to an overstatement of the significance of cost-based factors in foreign direct investment decisions, while underestimating both the value of knowledge assets as factors driving the expansionary strategies of MNCs, and the extent to which the recipients of such foreign investment can exercise agency in better capturing new sources of competitive capacity-building in global media markets.

In this chapter, we will turn our attention from critique to a description of what are seen as key factors shaping global media developments. In particular, five distinctive forces in early-21st-century global capitalism are identified:

1. the transition from a predominantly industrial economy to a *knowledge economy*, where ideas and intangible assets constitute the central sources of new wealth creation, and where networked ICTs provide new dynamics of the global creation, diffusion and management of knowledge and processes of innovation;
2. *new competition* theories, which draw attention to the relevance of product, service and organizational innovation, rather than simply cost advantages or economic efficiencies, as sources of sustainable competitive advantage;
3. the growing significance of *network organization* to the large, geographically dispersed global corporate enterprise;
4. the significance of *clusters* to competitive advantage, and geographical

factors more generally in promoting innovation in particular cities and regions, both within and across industrial sectors;
5. the rising importance of *global production networks* in the management of value chains by multinational corporations, and the variable consequences that can arise for nation-states in seeking to capture some of the new sources of value and economic 'rents' that are possessed by investing MNCs.

The remainder of the chapter will focus in upon two related propositions. The first is a cautionary argument that the continuing significance of nationally based media in the global media system should not be underestimated. This is in part because media markets continue to be more nationally and regionally based rather than truly global. Second, it will be argued that the forces associated with media globalization, most notably growing pressures towards competition based upon product and service innovation and intensification of pressures towards technological change and market expansion, do not involve incumbent locally based media being passive in the face of these changes. Indeed, the latter frequently possess a series of locational advantages which can be deployed effectively in the new competitive environment, whereas overseas competitors continue to face disadvantages in accessing such markets.

Knowledge Economy

It has been widely argued that the latter part of the 20th century saw a transition from a predominantly industrial economy to a knowledge economy. A *knowledge economy* is one where ideas and intangible assets rather than tangible physical assets are increasingly the central sources of new wealth creation, and where 'the economy is more strongly and more directly rooted in the production, distribution and use of knowledge than ever before' (Howells, 2000, p. 51). Such a transition has occurred not only in the so-called 'post-industrial' economies, as the 'information society' theories of the 1960s and 1970s held, but has been a global phenomenon, particularly driven by the intersection of international economic competitiveness with foreign direct investment (FDI) and the utilization of globally networked ICTs.[1]

Paul David and Dominique Foray (2002) have argued that the global nature of the knowledge economy is indicated by the extent to which:

> Disparities in the productivity and growth of different countries have far less to do with their abundance (or lack) of natural resources than with the capacity to

improve the quality of human capital and factors of production: in other words, to create new knowledge and ideas and incorporate them into equipment and people. (David and Foray, 2002, p. 9)

David and Foray observed that the rise of a knowledge economy is both a historical trend of the last 100 years, and a process which has accelerated since the early 1990s. In a historical sense, the growth in the share of *intangible capital* (devoted to knowledge production and dissemination on the one hand, and education, health and well-being on the other) had been accelerating in the US economy for the whole of the 20th century, and its share has exceeded that of tangible capital (physical infrastructure, equipment, inventories, natural resources, and so on) since the early 1970s (cf. Abramovitz and David, 2001).[2] They attributed the more recent acceleration of knowledge production to:

- the growing diversity of sources from which new knowledge is accessed (for example, users as a source of innovation);
- the role played by networked ICTs in accelerating the diffusion of new knowledge and the possibilities for collaboration;
- the ways in which ICTs enable new forms of codification of once-tacit knowledge through *knowledge management* systems;
- the importance of knowledge-sharing through cross-institutional and cross-sectoral *knowledge communities*, of which the open source software movement represents one of the most globally significant examples (cf. Benkler, 2002; Weber, 2004).

It has been argued that there has not only been an intensification of innovation in the global knowledge economy, but also a transformation of its nature. Dodgson *et al.* (2002) have referred to a *fifth-generation innovation process*, linked to the rise of *disruptive technologies* that undercut established products, management practices and industry players (Christensen, 1997), and the greater role played by both global markets and end-users in the innovation process. In contrast to ideas-push or demand-pull models of innovation, or the recent focus upon national innovation systems, fifth-generation innovation processes stress the links between suppliers and consumers, strategic integration through research and partnership networks, and technological integration through both the fusion of different technologies (for example, the linking of electrical and mechanical technologies to develop the 'hybrid' car), and the development of new ICT-based 'toolkits' that promote global collaborative knowledge networks (Dodgson *et al.*, 2002, pp. 54–7).

There is also a shift in the forms of knowledge that are most valued and which constitute the key inputs into innovation. Traditional models of innovation emphasized the role played by formalized and codified forms of scientific knowledge that constituted the 'inputs' for new products and services. In the current context, however, the distinction between knowledge and information has become increasingly important. Information refers to codified knowledge that has been translated into data and which, with developments in networked ICTs, can be reproduced cheaply and disseminated widely. By contrast, knowledge arises from a much wider process that 'involves cognitive structures which can assimilate information and put it in a wider context, allowing actions to be undertaken from it' (Howells, 2000, p. 53). Knowledge therefore necessitates processes of learning.

Moreover, the distinction between *explicit* and *tacit* knowledge – the latter defined as knowledge derived from direct experience – and the value attached to tacit knowledge as a unique source of innovation, presents major challenges for large organizations across all sectors. While large organizations are strong in the production, dissemination and use of explicit knowledge in the form of codified information, and the Internet has expanded this capability exponentially, the very factors which work to their advantage with the handling of information – large scale, ability to preserve information over time, and the capacity to distribute it across large distances – are those which make the capture of tacit knowledge so difficult. This not only presents a challenge in how to capture such knowledge and manage it by developing a *learning organization*; it also requires the ability to tap into knowledge-creating networks outside of the organization. A knowledge economy therefore not only implies a greater role for ideas and innovation, but also points to the increased knowledge-intensity of all aspects of economic and social life. Geoffrey Hodgson has observed that an economy that is 'relatively less "machine-intensive", and more and more 'knowledge-intensive"' (Hodgson, 2000, p. 93), is also characterized by growing complexity in all social activities, and economic activities relating to consumption as well as production. Such transformations have not only entailed an increased demand for specialist 'knowledge workers' as well as a variety of 'lifelong learning' opportunities, but have also pointed to the necessity of democratizing the dissemination of socially valuable forms of knowledge throughout the community (for example, ICT use at a reasonable level of sophistication). Hodgson (2000) ultimately prefers the concept of a *learning economy* to that of a knowledge economy, since the latter implies a fixed stock of knowledge to be distributed throughout a society, whereas 'in a complex and evolving, knowledge-intensive system, agents not only have to learn, they have to learn how to learn, and to adapt and create anew' (Hodgson, 2000, p. 93).

New Competition

The concept of *new competition* draws attention to both the limits of traditional conceptions of competition found in standard economics textbooks, and the need to more explicitly foreground questions of corporate strategy in environments where there is some capacity for large corporations to control market outcomes. The dominant neo-classical approach, where there is a static conception of markets and industries, and firms are conceived of as 'price-takers' in competitive markets, has been widely criticized for failing to capture the contemporary reality of large corporate organizations in capitalist economies (see, for example, Zamagni, 1987; Keen, 2001; Stilwell, 2002). Most critiques of the dominant neo-classical approach to competition tend to also argue that competition has diminished over time, as seen with the monopoly capitalism thesis discussed in Chapter 3.

It can be argued that such 'radical' conclusions about the decline of competition in advanced capitalist economies are, paradoxically, derived from a series of assumptions that are in fact rooted in the mainstream neo-classical economic tradition. In particular, the assumption that the structure of an industry (in particular the degree of concentration of control over market share by the largest firms) determines the behaviour of firms within that industry, and hence predicts the outcomes of competition in that industry in terms of prices, output and competitiveness, can be shown to rest upon the neo-classical model of competition. By contrast, Auerbach (1988) argued that a broader conception of competition – one which in fact goes back to the classical economists such as Adam Smith and David Ricardo, as well as to contemporary institutional and critical approaches – instead suggests that competition can increase over time and can in fact be greater in markets dominated by large corporations. Moreover, strategies of corporate expansion through mergers, conglomeration and internationalization can be seen as 'responses to an increasingly competitive environment ... [which] sometimes result in more, rather than less competition' (Auerbach, 1988, p. 323). Auerbach identified factors that promote greater competition in contemporary global capitalism as including:

- the role played by global capital markets in the allocation of investment funds;
- the rising investment by multinational corporations in hitherto nationally based markets dominated by a small number of local firms;

■ the expansion of markets worldwide;
■ the development of a wider range of new products and services;
■ the impact of technological innovation and technology diffusion.

From the very different perspective of business management literature, Michael Porter's theory of *competitive advantage* (Porter, 1998b) pointed out that rivalry between firms within an industry constituted only one of the five competitive forces that determine industry profitability. The other four factors were: (1) the potential for new entrants to come into the industry; (2) the bargaining power of buyers; (3) the bargaining power of suppliers; and (4) the threat of substitute products or services. Porter's work indicated that cost leadership was only one route to competitive advantage and was perhaps the least sustainable over time. Since product differentiation was as significant a factor in generating sustainable competitive advantage as cost, and competitive strategy could focus upon both broad (mass market) and narrow (niche market) segments, Porter proposed *differentiation* and *focus* as alternatives to cost leadership, arguing that innovation in the nature of the product or service and innovation in market segmentation provided alternative generic competitive strategies which may better achieve industry and market leadership. Although Porter's text was originally written in 1985, and did not explicitly address the impact of globalization, it follows that the development of global labour and product markets, and the increasing use of 'outsourcing' to lower-wage economies to achieve cost-based competitive advantage, would in turn accentuate the focus on other, non-cost-based, sources of sustainable competitive advantage.

Best (1990) drew attention to the extent to which new competition requires a focus upon the relationship between product and service innovation on the one hand, and organizational flexibility and commitment to continuous improvement in internal processes on the other. The focus on innovation can never simply be based upon the development of new products and services, nor can it simply be about technological innovation, or the development of new copyrights, patents, trademarks and designs. In order for innovation to lead to sustainable competitive advantage, Best argued that this can only take place if it is complemented by the capacity of the firm or corporation itself to engage in entrepreneurship and collective learning within its own organizational structures, and to engage in knowledge-sharing, collaborative learning and interfirm networking, in order to capture emergent knowledge forms and further develop dynamic forms of competitive advantage.

New Competition, Quality and Brand Equity in Television: HBO, *The Sopranos*, and 'TV III'

It has often been argued that the economics of limited-channel broadcast television promoted 'excessive sameness' in programming practices, whereby all channels sought to reach the largest possible audience at all times of the day (Owen *et al.*, 1974; Barwise and Ehrenberg, 1988; Neuman, 1991). A number of consequences flowed from this, including the tendency to cluster the best programming into peak viewing times ('prime time') across all of the networks, and the urge to produce 'least objectionable' programming in order to maximize audience share.

The development of subscription-based television has significantly expanded the possibilities for commercially funded television to meet the tastes and expectations of a wider cross-section of the community through its focus upon 'niche' rather than 'mass' broadcasting (see, for example, Noam, 1991). Rogers *et al.* (2002) have drawn attention to the differences between the era of limited-channel broadcast TV (or what they call 'TV I'), and the era – which is marked in the US from the 1970s to the mid-1990s – of what they term 'TV II', characterized by the competition for audiences between broadcast or free-to-air TV and subscription or pay/cable TV. This period saw substantial migration of TV audiences from the broadcast networks to the cable services, as well as the adoption – across both the broadcast and cable sectors – of comparatively lower-cost and more niche-focused television programmes. As Ted Magder (2004a) puts it, it marked 'the end of TV 101' where programming was based upon simple principles of maximizing audience share by producing non-controversial content based upon established programme genres.

The new era of television – what has been termed 'TV III' – differs from earlier periods in its emphasis upon the relationship between particular programmes on a television service and its overall *brand*. The brand of a television channel constitutes both a form of overall product differentiation from other channels, and a form of brand equity, which can both sustain audiences across the programming schedule and be sold to advertisers as a 'unique selling point' of the channel (Bellamy and Traudt, 2000, pp. 132–3). Curtin and Streeter (2001) have described this as *neo-network* TV, characterized by both globalization and fragmentation, and marked by an intensified search for programming that appeals to micro-markets in the first instance, which can then achieve 'cross-over' status to mainstream audiences. In contrast to the artificial restrictions upon programming arising in the limited-channel network environment, the neo-network context is characterized by chronic overproduction of TV content, so that branding and cross-platform synergies become the means by which some programming achieves profitability by achieving a high profile globally.

In discussing the history of the Time Warner-owned Home Box Office (HBO), from its origins as a re-broadcaster of Mohammed Ali fights to its current status as a purveyor of 'quality' and 'edgy' programmes, Rogers *et al.* (2002, p. 53) find that a programme such as *The Sopranos* (Dir. David Chase, 2000–) has been 'perfectly positioned to help HBO build its brand identity'. They argue that, in contrast to the era of TV II, where the priority of channels on cable services was to get as much content on air as cheaply as possible and appeal to niche audiences, HBO has identified a branding strategy which allows it to appeal to a range of audience demographics, while taking advantage of its freedom from the constraints of broadcast TV to depict profanity, nudity and often extreme violence. *The Sopranos* was a huge ratings hit for HBO in the United States, being, as one television executive put it, 'the first television megahit ever to be unavailable to the majority of viewers' (Thorburn, 2004, p. 2135). Moreover, the focus upon *The Sopranos* being 'quality' or 'watch again' television, arising from its scripting, acting, production values, production costs, and self-conscious cross-referencing of classic American gangster films such as *The Godfather* trilogy, lends itself well to the programme realizing further revenues by other means, such as DVD sales.

The relationship between new, edgy, programmes such as *The Sopranos*, and other HBO programmes such as *Sex and the City* and *Six Feet Under*, is well explained by the focus upon channel branding in an era of 'TV III'. The renewed focus upon branding in the television industry, which manifests itself in aspects as diverse as the use of 'water-marking' in programmes to wider scheduling practices, arises from the paradoxical need to establish more clearly the distinctiveness of one's own TV service in a multichannel, neo-network broadcasting environment, and to the ability to expand internationally on the basis of the channel/brand's reputation in other markets (Bellamy and Traudt, 2000, pp. 156–7).

Further reading: Curtin and Streeter (2001); Lavery (2002); Rogers *et al.* (2002); Cunningham (2005a).

Network Organization

The concept of networks has been identified as being central to the 'spirit of the age' of early-21st-century societies (Barney, 2004, p. 1). In his well-known discussion of the *network society*, Manuel Castells has argued that 'Networks constitute the new social morphology of our societies, and the diffusion of networking logic substantially modifies the operation and outcomes in processes of production, experience, power and culture' (Castells, 1996, p. 469). Networks, in this definition, constitute both empirically observable forms of social organization and a metaphor through which we can capture distinctive features of the current historical epoch. Networks have been defined in the following terms:

> The word 'network' describes a structural condition whereby distinct points (often called 'nodes') are related to one another by connections (often called 'ties') that are typically multiple, intersecting, and often redundant. A network exists when many nodes (people, firms, computers) are linked to many other nodes, usually by many ties which cross the ties connecting other nodes. (Barney, 2004, p. 2)

Growing interest in networked forms of organization can be attributed to three factors. First, the rapid development and diffusion of the Internet. As a digital 'network of networks' through which people, institutions and information were connected on a global scale on the basis of adoption of common computing protocols, the Internet's development has by its very existence raised issues about collaboration as an alternative mode of social organisation to institutional hierarchy. Second, the limits of the market/hierarchy distinction in economic theory, and the agency/structure dichotomy in sociological theory, promoted a new interest in networks as an explanatory factor in social behaviour (Friedland and Robertson, 1990; Polodny and Page, 1998). Mark Granovetter's work, for example, drew attention to the significance of 'weak ties' in modern societies and the continuing 'embeddedness ... of concrete personal relations and structures (or "networks") of such relations in generating trust and discouraging malfeasance' (Granovetter, 1985, p. 490). Third, the limits of bureaucratic and hierarchical forms of organization in responding effectively to emerging social and economic problems, and the limits of market-based solutions such as privatization and deregulation as applied in the 1980s and 1990s (as seen, to take one example, in policy failures such as the privatization of British Rail in the United Kingdom), have drawn new attention to networks as an alternative to hierarchical and market-based forms of organization and co-ordination.

The perceived advantages of networked forms of organization have included:

■ the capacity for collective learning across the network and the generation of innovation and new forms of knowledge;
■ the status and legitimacy acquired by small agents in a network from the presence of larger, more prestigious agents;
■ economic benefits such as improved product quality through stronger buyer–supplier relations, as well as a better capacity to adapt to risk;
■ alleviation of external constraints through better management of resource dependencies (Polodny and Page, 1998, pp. 62–6).

The conditions for effectively functioning networks have included a sense of common commitment, purpose, loyalty and trust among network members, the willingness to behave altruistically, and a commitment to co-operation and reciprocity (Thompson, 2003, pp. 39–47). Thompson (2003) identifies the differences between hierarchical, market-based and networked forms of order and organization (see Table 4.1).

Networked forms of organization have been particularly significant in the media and creative industries. Davis and Scase (2000) have argued that the growth of networked forms of organization is one of the strongest trends in the creative industries, since it best balances the dynamic interplay between explicit, formal control mechanisms which characterize bureaucratic forms, with the need in creative organizations for informal and collegial processes which facilitate creative autonomy, acknowledge flexibility and work productively with non-conformity. They identify the ascendancy of the network form as a response to the limits of bureaucratic forms of organization, as the focus upon tacit mechanisms of co-ordination and informal and collegial modes of

Table 4.1 Hierarchy, markets and networks as types of socio-economic order

Basic attributes	Hierarchical order	Market order	Network order
Type of order envisaged	Designed and consciously organized outcomes	Spontaneously generated outcomes	Negotiated outcomes
Behaviour of agents	Rule-driven and authority-driven	Private competitive decisions	Co-operation and consensus-seeking
Mechanisms of operation	Hierarchical/ bureaucratic administration	Price mechanism, competition, self-interest, self-regulation	Loyalty, reciprocity and trust
Type of overall co-ordination or governance	Overt, purposeful guidance and formal governance	Unseen 'guiding hand', minimal formal governance	Formally organized co-ordination; semi-formal governance

Source: Thompson (2003), p. 48

control address the problems of risk aversion and inflexibility seen to arise from the formal, hierarchical and explicit modes of co-ordination and control characteristic of large-scale cultural organizations.

Before claiming that we have moved to a 'network order' (Castells, 2004), however, a couple of cautionary observations need to be made. First, network arrangements inherently generate insider/outsider relationships which can not only be inequitable in their social impact (cf. McRobbie, 2005a, on 'network sociality' in the creative industries), but may cut organizations off from other well-springs of innovation by tying them too closely to pre-existing relationships. Second, as Thompson observes, the argument that networks now constitute 'the new leading-edge organizational structure' (Thompson, 2003, p. 148) nonetheless presumes their co-existence with, rather than the displacement of, other modes of organization such as those governed by bureaucratic hierarchy and arm's-length market transactions.

Clusters and the Economic Geography of Competitive Advantage

The concept of clusters has drawn attention to the relationship between the spatial agglomeration of particular activities, evidence of innovation and economic dynamism in particular cities and regions, and the importance of territorial proximity to collective learning process in increasingly knowledge-based economies. Moreover, it has been argued that such clustering arrangements become more, not less, relevant in the context of economic globalization. Cluster theories aim to capture the correlation between agglomerations of related firms and industries and sectors and the success of particular geographical places in the global economy. Storper (1997a) has argued that the interaction between new digital technologies, organizational changes such as networking, and competition among cities and regions to capture economic rents produces a global economy where:

> Certain key regions are at the heart of generating important kinds of economic rents in contemporary capitalism … [and] the image of the global economy as a sort of delocalized 'space of flows' of human, physical and financial capital controlled from major corporate headquarters manifestly fails to grasp the nature of the new competition. (Storper, 1997a, p. 218)

In a similar vein, Allen Scott has argued that economic globalization is pointing to 'the rise of a global capitalist economy characterized by … super-clusters of producers [that] come into being in the shape of dense agglomerations ... tied functionally together in a global division of labour' (Scott, 1999, pp. 89, 90).

Porter (1998a) defined clusters as 'geographical concentrations of interconnected companies and institutions in a particular field' (Porter, 1998a, p. 78), which were characterized by 'geographic concentrations of interconnected companies, specialised suppliers, service providers, firms in related industries, and associated institutions (for example, universities, standards agencies, and trade associations) in particular fields that compete but also co-operate' (Porter, 1998c, p. 197). For Porter, clusters generated sustained competitive advantage for the firms and institutions within them in three ways. First, they increased the productivity of firms within the cluster through access to specialist inputs, labour, knowledge, and technology. Second, clusters promoted innovation by making all firms within the cluster aware more quickly of new opportunities, as well as enhancing the capacity for rapid and flexible responses to new opportunities. Third, clusters promoted new business formation in related sectors, through distinctive access to necessary labour, skills, knowledge, technology, and capital (cf. Porter, 2001).

Although the cluster concept is relatively recent, the trends which lie behind it have been apparent for some time. In the global media field, Los Angeles (Hollywood) constitutes the quintessential film and television industry cluster (Scott, 2000, 2004a, 2004b; Cowen, 2002), since it is the home base of the world's largest film and television studios, a vast range of complementary firms and industries are co-located in the city-region, it is a unique repository of collective knowledge about what will be popular in global film and television markets, and it acts as a magnet to creative talent in these industries throughout the world.[3] While Hollywood's dominant global status in a particular field is unique in some respects – although the 'Silicon Valley' region of lower San Francisco County has been seen as having a comparably iconic global status – evidence of comparable *industrial districts* or 'sticky places' (Markusen, 1996) has been observed since the work of the British economist Alfred Marshall in the late 19th century (Marshall, 1961; cf. Malmberg and Maskell, 2002). Allen Scott has argued that the creative industries (or what he terms the *cultural-products industries*) demonstrate particularly strong tendencies towards both network organization and location-based clustering since:

1. The importance of specific forms of labour input, and the importance of the quality of such specialized labour and associated forms of tacit knowledge (which exists independently of the level of technology applied), requires access to particular forms of labour in particular locations at specified times.

2. Production is frequently organized in dense networks of small-to-medium-sized enterprises (SMEs), which are strongly dependent upon each other for the provision of specialized inputs and services.
3. The employment relation in creative industries is frequently characterized by intermittent, project-based work, leading to recurring job-search costs, which can be minimized for both employers and workers through co-location in particular areas.
4. Locational agglomeration (clustering) generates direct benefits in bringing labour, capital and enterprise together in ways that minimize transaction costs and search costs. At the same time, it generates indirect, synergistic benefits, which result from the considerably enhanced ability to realize the benefits of individual creativity in an environment characterized by mutual learning, strong bases of tacit knowledge and historical memory, and multiple stimuli from the co-existence of many people and enterprises engaged in interrelated activities. This is what Charles Landry has termed *soft infrastructure*, or 'the system of associative structures and social networks, connections and human interactions, that underpins and encourages the flow of ideas between individuals and institutions' (Landry, 2000, p. 133).
5. Locational agglomeration also promotes the development of associated services and institutional infrastructure which prioritizes the relevant industry sectors in the thinking of local policy-making authorities, and generates the accelerated development of critical related services, or what Landry (2000) terms *hard infrastructure*.

   The concept of clusters is not without its critics. Aside from concerns about its unproblematic embrace as a kind of universally applicable policy panacea (Martin and Sunley, 2003), there is also a concern about the apparent conflation of geographical and industrial definitions of a cluster (Malmberg and Maskell, 2002). Subsequent development of the cluster concept has revealed three issues which require further work. First, there is a need to distinguish between *horizontal clusters*, or those constituted by several firms in the same industry operating in the same city or region, and *vertical clusters*, where there are related firms operating across the value chain (suppliers, producers, buyers, providers of specialist inputs and so on) co-located in the same city or region. The capacity for clustering to promote knowledge enhancement will be quite different in these two types. In the case of horizontal clusters, such as the successful wine industries of Northern California in the United States or the Barossa Valley in Australia, collective benefits will arise from observing the outcomes of variation, making comparisons, and engaging in local rivalries, while presenting a common 'global face' for marketing and industry lobbying purposes. By contrast, vertical clusters, such as the high-quality clothing and garments clusters of Northern Italy or the ICT/electronics hub of Silicon Valley, derive enhanced knowledge and learning outcomes from the network of buyer–supplier relations, and the need for mutual adaptation in the more effective completion of complementary tasks. While the most successful clusters, such as the Hollywood film industry, or media and creative industries clusters in London or New York, combine horizontal and vertical linkages, many others will be working with one or the other, or a particular mixture, of these two ideal-types.

The second set of issues involve differentiating those forms of clusters which primarily demonstrate traditional tendencies towards industry agglomeration from those which arise in the way characterized by contemporary theories of the networked organization. It is only in the latter case that 'cluster theory also provides a way to connect theories of networks, social capital and civic engagements more tightly to business competition and economic prosperity' (Porter, 1998c, p. 227). Gordon and McCann (2001) have argued that there is a need to differentiate between at least three modes and rationales for geographically based industry clustering: (1) *pure agglomeration*, where it is cost advantages associated with geographical proximity which drive co-location in particular areas; (2) *industrial complexes*, where cost savings and economic externalities arising from geographical proximity generate both horizontal and vertical clustering; and (3) *social network models*, where cost factors are largely secondary to the benefits derived from interpersonal relationships and other forms of 'embedded' ties which promote interfirm networks, joint ventures, strategic partnerships, and other contemporary forms of network organization. Of these, the first and second are most vulnerable to cost-based competition and the development of global production networks (see below), whereas the latter tend not to be particularly sensitive to cost-related drivers of geographical relocation, as the value of the cluster is embedded in its dense interpersonal networks.[4]

The third series of issues concern the relationship between clusters and economic globalization. Porter and Sölvell (1999) have argued that knowledge embedded in physical capital is more mobile and geographically transferable than that embedded in human or social capital, since the latter are linked to value-creating networks and relationships developed within particular regions over long periods of time. As a result, they argued that the 'home base' city or nation of an MNC remains its principal site for innovation, and the scope for innovation arising from sites outside of the network 'hub' or 'home base' is limited. In contrast to the 'home base' development/global diffusion framework, Hagström and Hedlund (1999, p. 171) argued that the 'thinking and acting parts of the corporation are both geographically diffused, and the scattered "brain" proves a significant obstacle to clear hierarchical structure'. As a result, the ever more dispersed and diffuse nature of knowledge acquisition and capture increasingly act against a 'home base' bias on the part of globalizing MNCs.

Markusen (1996) has argued that two of the most internationally prominent forms of clustering – the 'hub-and-spoke' industrial district and the satellite platform – are unlikely to generate significant knowledge transfers to the host city or region if they are based around foreign direct investment. The *'hub-and-spoke' industrial district* conforms most closely on an international scale to the Porter and Sölvell model, where the 'head office' has simply outsourced aspects of its operations to external suppliers or other service providers, who remain in fundamentally unequal and dependent relationships to the core provider of knowledge capital. The *satellite platform* model is even less likely to achieve effective technology transfer and knowledge capture. As the satellite platform model emerged in both developed and developing countries through science and technology parks, enterprise zones, free-trade zones, or export production zones, it typically rested upon high levels of government incentives for large firms to invest in the city or region (tax incentives, more relaxed labour conditions and so on), combined with measures to attract locally based suppliers and others with complementary activities to co-locate within this state-derived new industry cluster. Miller *et. al.*'s (2001) critique of attempts by governments around the world to attract foreign investment in film and television production on the basis of tax incentives and lower labour costs marks a case study in the limitations of the satellite platform model as a means of generating sustainable and globally competitive clusters. It remains highly reliant upon the incentives as such, and the costs of withdrawing from a region when fixed capital investments have already been made, and is thus unlikely to promote the forms of embedded interpersonal ties, enhanced local entrepreneurship, and supportive institutional development that have characterized successful industry cluster development and new forms of product, service and process innovation (cf. Markusen, 1996, pp. 304–5).

Global Production Networks

While the hub-and-spoke and satellite platform models represent traditional models for the relationship between multinational corporations' head offices and their offshore branch operations, a very different understanding of such relationships arises with the development of *global production networks*. Ernst and Kim (2002) have argued that global production networks constitute the major organizational innovation in global corporate operations, enabling new strategies for international knowledge diffusion across national boundaries, and creating new opportunities for knowledge capture and local capability formation in hitherto lower-cost locations outside of the head office heartlands of North America, Western Europe and Japan. They argue that:

> A transition is underway from 'multinational corporations', with their focus on stand-alone overseas investment projects, to 'global network flagships' that integrate their dispersed supply, knowledge and customer bases into global (and regional) production networks. (Ernst and Kim, 2002, p. 1418)

Importantly, the benefits of global production networks for developing countries are not the result of strategic concessions from international investors. Rather, Ernst and Kim argue that they have emerged out of a highly favourable climate for foreign direct investment, which reduces the costs and risks of international transactions substantially, and hence promotes locational specialization, outsourcing and spatial mobility. The ICT revolution has increased both the opportunities and the need for international expansion, as it enables firms to disperse their resources and capabilities across national boundaries, while at the same time integrating their operations into a wider network of specialized industrial districts and industry clusters. The ability to remain globally competitive compels the largest corporations to operate in a wider range of international markets, while at the same time requiring them to more explicitly integrate and co-ordinate activities across different geographical locations and market segments. Since no firm can possess all of the resources and knowledge capabilities required for such global competitive advantage from within its own organization, 'competitive success thus critically depends on a capacity to selectively source specialised capabilities *outside* the firm ... This requires a shift from individual to increasingly collective forms of organization, from the functional hierarchy of "multinational corporations" to the networked global flagship model' (Ernst and Kim, 2002, p. 1420).

For those countries that receive these new forms of foreign direct investment, the ability to capture new forms of knowledge-based value is vitally dependent upon the capacity of local suppliers integrated into these global production networks to meet the expectations of the global flagships, while at the same time continuously upgrading their *absorptive capacity*. Absorptive capacity refers to the combination of the existing knowledge base and the intensity of commitment to acquiring new knowledge. Flagships are in a much more powerful bargaining position than local suppliers, and have considerable capacity to move activities elsewhere if not satisfied with performance. At the same time, local suppliers can capture knowledge from the flagships through processes described by Ernst and Kim as: (1) *externalization* (conversion of tacit knowledge from the flagship into explicit knowledge by the local supplier); (2) *internalization* (conversion of explicit knowledge from the flag-ship into tacit knowledge on the part of the supplier); and (3) *socialization* (sharing of tacit knowledge through joint training, relocation of key person-nel, and so on). Ernst and Kim use this framework to explain how Asian economies such as those of Singapore, Taiwan and South Korea moved up the value chain from being relatively low-cost suppliers to Western MNCs in the 1970s and 1980s to having their own leading global firms and being relatively high-wage, knowledge-intensive economies with high levels of localized inno-vation (cf. Yusuf, 2003). Similar thinking lies behind the strategy in China to develop 'national champions' in key economic sectors, whose capacity for innovation 'piggy-backs' off the knowledge acquired through partnerships with foreign investors (Nolan, 2004).

Henderson *et al.* (2002, p. 445) have identified global production networks as providing a framework that is 'capable of grasping the global, regional and local economic and social dimensions of ... globalization'. They have noted a paradox in these production networks in that, while the networks themselves are not territorially defined, they work through social, political and institutional contexts that are territorially specific, principally – although not exclusively – at the level of the nation-state. This means that the actions of local firms, governments and other economic actors, such as trade unions, 'potentially have significant implications for the economic and social outcomes of the networks in the locations they incorporate' (Henderson *et al.*, 2002, p. 446). Global production networks are thus partly deterritorialized in the sense used by Storper (1997), as they are not territorially 'bound' in the manner of firms oper-ating primarily at the level of the national economy. They are, nonetheless, spatially embedded in multiple respects. The activities of MNCs in local envi-ronments are embedded in: interpersonal networks (for example, key decision-makers in the MNC need to interact with key decision-makers in the host nation, in which there will be pre-existing social networks); the ways in which they are 'anchored' in particular national forms of governance (taxation systems, educational frameworks and so on); and institutional and cultural *milieux*, from which they can derive new forms of knowledge and draw upon distinctive well-springs of innovation. The circumstances under which host nations can enhance and capture value through FDI embedded in global production networks will depend upon factors such as: the nature and extent of technology and knowledge transfer; the sophistication and adaptive capacity of local suppliers; whether skill demands increase over time (enabling a move from low-wage, low-skill 'generic' labour to higher-skill, more specialist work); and whether local firms can begin to develop their own organizational, rela-tional and brand 'rents', or unique profit-generating attributes (Henderson *et al.*, 2002, p. 449). In all of these areas, the role played by national institutional influences, particularly those arising from government policy, is critical.

The Pie and the Crust: Globalization of Television Formats

Big Brother is the sort of television programme which attracts a wide range of comments (see van Zoonen and Aslama, 2006 for a summary). Yet one comment that you never hear is that it marks the baleful influence of Dutch cultural imperialism on the world's TV viewers. This is perhaps odd, since the *Big Brother* concept was originally developed by the Dutch production company Endemol, and it constitutes the most significant contribution to global media to come from The Netherlands.

Programmes such as *Big Brother* are part of the international trade in television formats, which has been a central driver of the globalization of television since at least the 1970s, but of growing significance since the 1990s. Moran (1998) points out that, while the concept of formats was initially linked to serial drama, the most significant growth in recent times has been of international trade in programme formats for game shows and, most spectacularly, so-called 'reality TV'. He observes that a format constitutes an internationally tradeable package of programme elements that can be sold under licensing arrangements into other television markets. What is typically sold includes information about the programme in its home country, including scheduling, target audience, ratings and audience demographics, as well as a description of the programme and its rules, and elements such as suitable artwork, graphics, catch-phrases and computer software. Collectively, these elements are known in the industry as the format 'Bible'. The sale is typically accompanied by consultancy services provided by the company owning the format, which often include the involvement of a senior producer from the original production overseeing and advising on the adaptation.

In one sense, this is a fairly prescriptive approach to programme-making, and the emergence of international programme format trade arose in part to regularize what had been a very *ad hoc* process of exchange of programme ideas in international television. Format trade also codifies the intellectual property arrangements that underpin the adoption of programme ideas from elsewhere. But Moran's point is that programme format trade that simply involves the wholesale adaptation of formats developed in one market into another is not an effective form of cultural technology transfer, and is likely to fail in purely commercial terms. It is in this sense that he uses the 'pie-and-crust' model of television programme formats: the formally traded elements of the format constitute its 'crust', which does not vary across national television markets, while the myriad local elements through which the programmes are adapted for local markets and local tastes provide the 'filling' for the programme 'pie'. As Moran puts it:

> There is a recognition that the original set of ingredients and their organization may have to be varied to fit production resources, channel image, buyer preference and so on. The original formula does not have to be slavishly imitated but rather serves as a general framework or guide within which it is possible to introduce various changes to the original formula. In other words, *there is variation within repetition.* (Moran, 1998, p. 21, my emphasis)

International format trade has regularized – at least to some extent – the terms and conditions through which the global circulation of programme ideas occurs (Moran, 2004). Its rise is recognition of the extent to which the local nature of media does not necessarily derive from ideas developed in a local context, but rather from the various adaptations made to fit imported ideas and concepts into a package that will appeal to local audiences. Koichi Iwabuchi observes, in relation to the use of American programme formats in Japanese television, that 'Who knows – and who really cares – whether the Japanese version of a popular American quiz show *The Price is Right* … was of Japanese origin or not? What audiences ultimately care about is whether the programme features a "Japanese odour", both in relation to the cast and the actual content' (Iwabuchi, 2004, p. 23).

At the same time, it is important to recognize that a format is not the same as a programme genre. While television genres are heuristic devices employed by people other than the direct producers – programmers, critics, policy-makers, academics and audiences – to classify and codify programmes in order to 'cluster' them into a common type (see Mittell, 2004), a format is a legally owned piece of intellectual property which may only be used by others through contract or some other form of permission.

This is not to say that particular programme formats do not generate 'spin-offs' that draw upon the earlier formats. Programme formats such as *Who Wants to be a Millionaire* and the *Idol* programmes have recognizable predecessors in television history; what is distinctive about them is that their particular form is an internationally tradeable commodity in which particular production companies own the copyright.

It is also not to say that programme formats do not emerge that look like those developed in other countries, without attribution or royalty payments. Keane (2004b) has noted significant parallels between the *Survivor* series and *Into Shangrila*, a highly successful reality TV programme screened in China in 2002, where young Chinese from various provinces braved the elements to scale the Himalayan foothills. Similarly, the Chinese programmes *Pink Ladies* and *Feels Like I'm Falling in Love* feature four young professional women living in the major cities (Shanghai and Beijing respectively) and looking for love; the programmes looked a lot like the HBO series *Sex in the City*, even though the latter has never been formally permitted to screen on Chinese television (Keane, 2005).

This is not necessarily direct copying, although the unacknowledged copying of programme formats developed elsewhere is certainly occurring, and the format trade can be seen in part as an attempt to regulate this. What may instead be occurring is what Braithwaite and Drahos (2000) refer to as *modelling*, which is not simply imitation, but rather actions that 'constitute a process of displaying, symbolically interpreting and copying' (Braithwaite and Drahos, 2000, p. 581). So the game show or physical challenge elements of programmes such as *Millionaire* and *Survivor* provide templates, or things to think with, in developing programme formats. Similarly, Hong Kong or Taiwanese 'Canto-pop' provide models for promoting young singers and musicians for teenage girl audiences, Hollywood blockbusters provide models for visually compelling film content which may be taken up by film-makers in South Korea or Japan, or, to extend the concept of modelling further, the high-profile actions of organizations such as Greenpeace in environmental activism provide a template for smaller local environmental campaigns.

Further reading: Moran (1998); Mathijs and Jones (2004); Moran and Keane (2004); Murray and Ouellette (2004); Roscoe (2004); van Zoonen and Aslama (2006).

Globalization and the Continuing Social Embeddedness of Market Relations

All of the elements of 21st-century global capitalism discussed above draw attention to the embeddedness of market relations in time, space and social interaction. The concept of a knowledge economy recognizes the unique well-springs of innovation that arise from ideas developed by people, and the indissolubility of individual, idiosyncratic forms of knowledge into knowledge management systems and ICT-enabled knowledge networks. The focus upon non-cost factors as the most sustainable sources of competitive advantage in 'new competition' theories also points to the significance of the innovation process, understood not simply as new products and services, but as entailing the development of a culture of learning, innovation and continuous improvement within and between organizations. The network model of organization implies a strong degree of embeddedness of interpersonal and interorganizational relations as its *sine qua non,* since successful networks cannot function without the forms of loyalty, trust and reciprocity that are their distinguishing features as distinct from bureaucratic or purely market-driven forms of organization. Cluster theories draw attention to the extent to which such successful forms of network organization are grounded in relations between people, as well as being constituted in geographical space, arising out of a complex and shifting relationship between globally mobile capital flows and territorially embedded assets that are not only resource-based or infrastructural, but also grounded in localized forms of knowledge, conventions of interaction, forms of social capital, cultural *milieux* and relational skills. Finally, work on global production networks has drawn upon such insights to emphasize the fluid, unpredictable, and non-zero-sum consequences of foreign direct investment for host nations in their dealings with multinational corporations. Importantly, the latter work draws attention to the significance of state capacity as an independent variable in determining the extent of knowledge capture and the ability of local firms to develop their own organizational, relational and brand 'rents' out of such interactions.

An emphasis upon the embeddedness of market relations has long been an argument made by institutional economists and economic sociologists about the limitations of conventional economic theory, both in its own terms and as a guide to public policy. Friedland and Robertson (1990) are among many who have pointed to the problems which arise for mainstream neo-classical economic theory due to its lack of a theory of power and of its impact upon the operation of markets, particularly in relation to 'rent-seeking behaviour', or how the use of personal power and networks for economic advantage impacts upon the operation of markets (Friedland and Robertson, 1990, pp. 24–8; cf. Flew, 2006a on rent-seeking in Australian broadcast television policy). Campbell and Lindberg (1990) have critiqued neo-classical economics for taking property rights as a given, pointing out that the allocation of differential forms of property rights by the state is central to economic power. The capacity to define the scope and domain of property rights makes state agencies both a social actor and an institutional structure in capitalist economies, through their capacity to define markets by developing particular governance regimes which create, maintain, enforce and transform property rights arrangements. Hodgson has pointed out how institutions provide relatively durable and stable mechanisms for organizing social arrangements that constitute 'both "subjective" ideas in the heads of agents and "objective" structures faced by them. The concept of institutions connects the micro-economic world of individual action, of habit and choice, with the macroeconomic sphere of seemingly detached and impersonal structures' (Hodgson, 2002, p. 220).

At the same time, these findings also provide a sting in the tail for critical theories of global media, as they suggest that market relations in contemporary global capitalist economies remain highly embedded in space and forms of social interaction, rather than becoming progressively disembedded over time through the forces of capitalism, globalization and modernity. The conception of capitalism and modernity as involving what Marx and Engels referred to as the *annihilation of space and time* by the forces of capitalism and the world market, and the associated *disembedding* of social and institutional relations over time, has been highly influential in critical social theory.[5] The idea that globalization is an inexorable consequence of capitalist modernity, which leads to disembedding and the depersonalization of economic and social relations, is one that looms large in critical academic literature, particularly where the media or 'global image industries' are concerned. Altvater and Mahnkopf (1997) interpret globalization as the final stage of disembedding of the world market and economic relations from societies grounded in time, space and sociality, to the point where 'the history of humanity for the first time runs its course ruled by a unified time regime. With this, concrete spaces also disappear; the borders between them become meaningless. Different spatial experiences get lost because they have become meaningless' (Altvater and Mahnkopf, 1997, p. 309). In only slightly less apocalyptic tones, Morley and Robins (1995) have argued that 'technological and market shifts are leading to the emergence of global image industries and world markets; we are witnessing the "deterritorialization" of audiovisual production and the elaboration of transnational systems of delivery' (Morley and Robins, 1995, pp. 1–2). For Morley and Robins, the consequences of this rise of global media corporations and markets are that 'audiovisual geographies are thus becoming detached from the symbolic spaces of national culture, and realigned on the basis of the more "universal" principles of international consumer culture', so that 'the logic of globalization [is] pushing towards the greater standardization and homogenization of output, and detaching media cultures from the particularities of place and context' (Morley and Robins, 1995, pp. 11, 17).

As we have seen in Chapter 3, and will discuss further in this chapter, the empirical evidence around which such claims are made is, at the very least, mixed. Before evaluating the empirical information further, however, it is worth considering briefly why this particular conception of globalization generally, and media globalization more particularly, has proved to be so central. Tomlinson (2003) has argued that an interest in globalization was, in the first instance, overwhelmingly an interest in the expansion of global capitalism, so that an analysis of globalizing forces was typically linked to the ways in which they were driven by multinational corporations and their supporters and ideological soul-mates in emergent global institutions such as the World Trade Organization. Tomlinson's point is that approaching globalization from the starting-point of the drivers of key economic agents, such as multinational corporations or institutions of global economic governance, is not so much incorrect as partial. In particular, Tomlinson argues that, if we instead conceive of globalization as the spread not simply of capitalism but also of modernity, then the claim that globalization is simply a metaphor for Western cultural imperialism that is destructive of other forms of identity becomes less tenable. Tomlinson argues, by contrast, that 'globalization has been perhaps the most significant force in *creating and proliferating* cultural identity' (Tomlinson, 2003, p. 16, emphasis in original).

There are also the traces of certain habits of thought which arise in the critical tradition. In his critical evaluation of radical political economy, Sayer (1995) argues that the abstractions of Marxist-derived social theory often sit oddly alongside empirically grounded 'middle-range' theories, which invariably identify that the institutional and organizational forms through which capitalist processes are meditated must qualify the assumptions of more abstract social theory. Thrift (2005) has argued that theories of capitalism have consistently underestimated the dynamism and intellectual productivity of capitalists themselves in their shaping of economic organization, which means that critical academic theory consistently lags well behind the intellectual leading edge of contemporary capitalism. A clear example of this latter tendency, which Thrift describes as 'confusing the logic of theory and the logic of practice' (Thrift, 2005, p. 76), is the assumption in critical literature on globalization that capitalist modernity has progressively moved from the local to the national to the global. This results in the claim that globalization is invariably marked by the decline of the nation-state (for example, Altvater and Mahnkopf, 1997), or that an antagonism emerges between global scalar forces and flows on the one hand and localized resistance on the other (for example, Morley and Robins, 1995; Cox, 1997). Amin (2002) has argued that such assumptions may not only generate modes of political response that are potentially regressive and reactionary (for example, a defence of the 'local' against the 'global'), but can also lose sight of the extent to which the key global networks of our time – such as the Internet or global production networks – have promoted much more innovative and dynamic ways of thinking about space and territory simultaneously (cf. Dodge and Kitchin, 2001).

Asymmetrical Interdependence and Cultural Reconversion: Different Ways of Thinking about the Global and the Local

There is a need to develop conceptual tools through which we can understand the relations between global forces and institutional responses in terms other than those of how the global media impose themselves upon national societies and cultures. In the context of Latin American media, Straubhaar (1991, 1997) developed the concept of *asymmetrical interdependence* as an alternative to the 'cultural imperialism' thesis, observing significant counter-trends to a global homogenization of television under US hegemony. Such counter-trends have included the localization over time of national broadcasting systems such as those of Brazil, South Korea, Australia and Hong Kong (cf. Ma, 1999; Cunningham and Flew, 2000; Park *et al.*, 2000), and 'the 'regionalization of television into multicountry markets linked by geography, language and culture' (Straubhaar, 1997, p. 285) or *geo-cultural markets* (Sinclair *et al.*, 1996).

The concept of asymmetrical interdependence accepts the 'impurities' of media systems. It recognizes national media policies as being not so much about the preservation of national culture against global media forms and flows, but more as about engaging in what Philip Schlesinger has termed 'communicative boundary maintenance' (Schlesinger, 1991a, p. 162), or the maintenance of some kind of dynamic equilibrium over time between locally produced media content and material sourced from overseas. As Straubhaar points out, the television systems of countries such as Brazil were developed under the close tutelage of the United States, with Time-Life being the financial backers and key advisors of TV Globo during the 1960s, a time when the military dictatorship ruling the nation enjoyed US political support (Sinclair, 1999; Waisbord, 2000). The subsequent success of TV Globo did not rest upon a nationalist media policy of *le défi américain*, but rather upon a combination of selective incorporation of international best practice and a restless search to develop programme types that tapped into local cultural desires and dynamics, such as the *telenovela*. In the Asian media context, Keane (2004c) has referred to this as *cultural technology transfer*, or the migration of techniques, practices and ideas from the major TV production centres to the recipients of foreign investment in the forms of both codified and tacit knowledge, as well as the emergence of regional production centres.

The concept of asymmetrical interdependence recognizes that, even in a multichannel and networked media environment where there is growing and seemingly limitless access to imported media content, there remains a strong attachment, which is by no means residual, to locally produced material (cf. Tracey, 1988). There are, however, no universal tendencies here, as some national media systems increase their degree of import dependency over time, while others reduce it. The extent to which localization of national media systems – and associated cultural technology transfer – actually occurs is very much dependent upon the degree of policy activism undertaken by national governments to promote local media content. Between the 1960s and the 1990s, for example, national television systems such as those of South Korea, Brazil and Hong Kong became progressively localized over time, while others, such as those of Mexico, the Dominican Republic, Lebanon, Barbados and Trinidad, became increasingly reliant upon imported media content (Straubhaar, 1997, p. 294).

What becomes the critical variable here is the adaptiveness of national media organizations as national cultural institutions in the context of global-ization. In order to understand this, we require ways of thinking about culture that do not presume a unified national culture, yet also do not lose sight of some of the advantages of national cultural institutions in an ostensibly global mediascape. The concept of *cultural reconversion*, developed in the Latin American context by Canclini (1992, 1995, 2000) provides one way of under-standing this. For Canclini, nationalist cultural projects of the sort promoted in many South American countries between the 1920s and the 1970s effec-tively collapsed in the face of the crisis of import-substituting economic devel-opment models, the external debt crises of the 1980s and 1990s, and economic deregulation. This period of economic crisis was paralleled by the decline of modernist, nation-building forms of cultural policy that sought to maximize linkages between the national and the popular through state subvention of cultural production in the name of modernization and cultural sovereignty. What resulted was a collapsing of the distinction between mass-popular modern culture and traditional 'folk' cultures, and an associated set of distinctions between what is deemed to be 'art' or 'heritage', and those media and cultural products that form a part of the 'global popular' and driven by the commercial marketplace.

The concept of cultural reconversion provides an indication why this appar-ent loss of cultural sovereignty is not synonymous with cultural loss in a wider sense. Canclini defines reconversion as strategies to 'transfer symbolic patri-mony from one site to another in order to conserve it, increase its yield, and better position those who practice it' (Canclini, 1992, p. 32). In the economic sphere, its most obvious manifestation is the transfer of investment capital across national boundaries enabled by the globalization of financial markets and the Internet. For Canclini, the complexities of cultural reconversion arise from its descriptions of how cultural capital is moved across five cultural fields (Canclini, 1992, pp. 29–34; cf. Bourdieu, 1984):

1. from a heritage-defined understanding of traditional culture to a technology-enabled fusion of high, popular, folk and mass art/culture, as national museums have reorganized their activities in order to enhance public attendance, commercial sponsorship and economic turnover;
2. from oppositional or *avant-garde* art practices to so-called 'postmodern' forms to which highly capitalized private and public sector funding institutions may be more willing to give economic support;
3. from the production of traditional forms of material culture to maintain localized or indigenous cultures over time, to indigenous cultural production which simultaneously deals with the demands of local culture and tradition, national culture through national collecting institutions, and global culture through global arts and cultural markets (e.g. auctions of Australian Aboriginal art works at Sotheby's in London);
4. from nationally based publicly owned broadcasting (PSB), or publicly regulated commercial mass media, designed to shape nationally based audiences towards an appreciation of connections between the national and the popular, towards a more promiscuous search among both commercial and public service media and cultural institutions for marketable audiences both within the national space and outside of it;
5. from global media corporations which have a 'home base' rooted in a national culture, and can view cultural exports as an additional 'layer' on the locally based 'cake', to global media corporations which seek to reconvert successful formats and genres into particular local markets, and to revise dominant operational understandings in light of the experience of operation in multiple markets.

Canclini presents cultural reconversion as a radical challenge to the precepts of cultural modernism and national cultural policy:

> Reconversion thus challenges the assumption that cultural identity is based upon a patrimony, and that this patrimony is constituted by the occupation of a territory and by collections of works and monuments ... It questions the notion that popular sectors achieve emancipation and are integrated into modernity by means of the socialization of hegemonic cultural assets through education and mass dissemination. (Canclini, 1992, p. 32)

In light of cultural reconversion, cultural fields can thus never fully operate in terms of binary oppositions between the local and the national, the global and the national, or the global and the local, since each invariably influences the other. There is a learning process which inevitably cuts across these cultural fields. It is true that neither indigenous arts nor national public service broadcasting can claim to operate independently of the global circuits of arts, media and culture that intersect with global financial flows. It also becomes the case that those media organizations which seek to operate outside of their national 'home base' need to be highly conscious of the myriad cultural complexities which arise from becoming multinational, and of the resultant forms of cultural reconversion at the very least, and of cultural technology transfer at the more advanced levels, in order to achieve their ambitions to become global media corporations.

Revising Cultural Imperialism: Cultural and Economic Perspectives

The concept of cultural imperialism has long been a central, yet highly problematic, component of critical political economy approaches to global media. As discussed in Chapter 2 through the work of Herbert Schiller, cultural imperialism referred to the ways in which the economic power of the media of dominant nations combined with the global reach of cultural commodities and media messages. The concept drew attention to the extent to which the influence of global media was never political or economic, since the media and entertainment sectors differed from other branches of commercial enterprise through their 'direct, though immeasurable impact on human consciousness', as well as their capacity 'to define and present their own role to the public' (Schiller, 1996, pp. 115, 125). The result was, as Schiller put it, 'the globalization that many find such a promising prospect can be viewed more realistically as the phenomenally successful extension of marketing and consumerism to the world community' (Schiller, 1996, p. 115).

The cultural imperialism thesis has been primarily critiqued from the perspective of cultural studies, but there are also important criticisms from within political economy. When the thesis was originally developed in the late 1960s, the United States overwhelmingly dominated world media and entertainment markets, but the intervening period has seen the rise of significant ECI corporations from Europe and East Asia. There has also been the rise of significant regional and language-based sub-markets, or what Sinclair *et al.* (1996) term *geo-linguistic regions*, particularly in East Asia, Latin America and the Middle East, as well as the contribution of media content producers such as Canada, Australia and New Zealand in the English-speaking world. While defenders of the thesis, such as Schiller (1997) and Boyd-Barrett (1998) argue that this does not affect the fundamentals of dominance by Western transnational media corporations, it does mean that, as Curran and Park (2000, p. 6) observe, there is 'a certain fuzziness in the way in which three different categories – American, Western, and capitalist – can be used almost interchangeably'. It also means, as Miller *et al.* (2001, p. 34) observe, that the concept is drawn upon for quite different strategic ends in different parts of the world. For instance, in Africa, the Middle East and Latin America, it intersects with a political debate about how to expand local democratic participation and control, whereas in Western Europe the spectre of 'Americanization' is frequently invoked as providing a case for developing pan-European audiovisual markets so that European media multinationals can compete on a more level global playing field (cf. Schlesinger, 1997).

A second, and perhaps more substantial, set of criticisms have concerned the assumptions the thesis makes about media audiences and how they use imported media content. Drawing upon reception studies of local uses of imported media content, Thompson argued that the cultural imperialism thesis remained too closely tied to mass society approaches to media reception, and that 'the composition, the global flow and the uses of media products are far more complex' than a simple equation of US media content and the promotion of Western or consumerist values allows (Thompson, 1995, p. 169). He argued that such theories fail to adequately understand the moment of consumption in the circulation of media forms, and thus 'try to infer, from an analysis of the social organization of the media industries, what the consequences of media messages are likely to be for the individuals who receive them' (Thompson, 1995, p. 171). In a similar vein, and drawing upon cross-cultural ethnographic research and reception studies, Ien Ang argued that there was a need for closer analysis of how global media content is 'actively and differentially responded to and negotiated in concrete local contexts and conditions' (Ang, 1996a, p. 153).

A third critique of cultural imperialism theories concerns the understanding of local cultures. Implicit in the analysis of cultural domination through global media is an assumption that, in the absence of such global media flows, there would be greater congruity between nation-states and a distinctive national or local culture. Tomlinson (1991) has interrogated this conception of national culture in detail, and has observed that, as well as its tendency to conflate media with culture – thereby blurring the relationship between culture as forms of symbolic representation and culture as lived experience – it also conflates the local with the national, seeing national cultures as existing prior to their constitution through social processes such as media consumption, rather than as being in ongoing construction. In their critique of the 'Global Effects Model' of media communication, Miller *et al.* argue that this forgetting of demographic complexities and internal differentiation within national media publics can have the consequence of 'valorising … unrepresentative local bourgeoisies in the name of national culture's maintenance and development' (Miller *et al.*, 2001, p. 180). This problem becomes increasingly significant as globalization develops further since, as Straubhaar has observed:

> Very few nations are ethnically homogeneous ... Most have fairly large minorities. If language is a primary characteristic of culture, then most nations are multilingual and not homogeneous nation-states. This opens up a large area of interest in media ... which address media audiences of smaller than national scope. (Straubhaar, 1997, p. 286)

Ang argued that, while the emergence of some form of 'global culture' connected to global media flows is an important element of contemporary globalization, it is never a simple process of cultural homogenization, but rather that 'it is in the particular appropriation and adaptation of such standardized rules and conventions within local contexts and according to local traditions, resources and preferences that the non-linear, fractured nature of cultural globalization displays itself' (Ang, 1996a, p. 154).

Finally, it has been argued that the cultural imperialism thesis consistently underestimates the significance of national media industries and local audience preferences for locally produced content. While it can be argued that local media industries have responded to the presence of global media by adapting to or even imitating US generic models as the exemplars of what Sinclair *et al.* (1996, p. 13) term 'international best practice', it is nonetheless the case that activist media and cultural policy can be successful in promoting viable 'national champions' which dominate local markets and achieve a level of export success. The success of the Latin American *telenovela* with audiences in the Spanish- and Portuguese-speaking worlds, Hong Kong-produced 'Canto-pop' and action/martial arts films in Chinese-speaking media markets, and Australian serial dramas or 'soaps' in English-speaking markets are commonly cited examples of such 'indigenization' or 'hybridization' of global cultural forms (cf. Lull, 1991; Straubhaar, 1991; Zha, 1995; Cunningham and Jacka, 1996).

This final point needs to be returned to, as it suggests that, in our focus upon the global nature of contemporary media, there may be a tendency to systematically underestimate the continuing significance of local advantage. Straubhaar (1991) has drawn attention to the competitive advantages enjoyed by local producers in having a greater degree of *cultural proximity* to their audiences than the producers of 'global' media content have in such local and regional markets. Moreover, the threat of 'Americanization' or cultural imperialism can be invoked to strategic advantage by incumbent media players to buy time and/or resources in order to strengthen their own competitive position in the context of emerging international threats. The first issue relates to what economists term *sunk costs*, or the capital requirements of entry into a business. These are highly variable across the media industries, with areas such as broadcast television having very high up-front capital costs, whereas newer businesses such as mobile telephony or Internet-related businesses typically have lower sunk costs. The literature on corporate strategy (for example, Johnson *et al.*, 2005) makes the point that this is not the only significant barrier to entry facing potential new entrants into an industry: access to supply or distribution channels; customer and supplier loyalty; experience in the industry and/or market; and the possibility of retaliation by incumbents (for example, price wars against a new competitor) also give potential advantages to established players. This is one reason why, in a number of expansion strategies undertaken by global media corporations (as with News Corporation, discussed in Chapter 3), a network-based model such as joint ventures with local providers is often preferred to investment to establish direct competitors to established local or national media players.[6]

This potential advantage to incumbents as established suppliers of media content within local and national media markets intersects with the complexities of demand, and particularly the relationship between local and national cultures and patterns of consumer demand and audience preference. In his well-known critique of global television as being dominated by US product, Tracey (1988) made much of the danger of equating the ubiquitous presence of US content in global broadcasting schedules with the assumption that it is the most popular content in those countries. Tracey's argument was that local audiences typically preferred local content, that local productions tended to be scheduled at the peak viewing times, and that 'where it is used U.S. television will be as a kind of televisual Polyfilla, plugging the gap in the schedule' (Tracey, 1988, p. 22). The evidence for television subsequent to Tracey's study is mixed (see e.g. Shrikhande, 2001; Freedman, 2003; Obar, 2004; Bicket, 2005; Sparks, 2005), but it remains the case that, while the US dominates global television exports, accounting for 68 per cent of the total (Freedman, 2003, p. 30), the point about local audiences having a preference for local content continues to have validity. Thomas (2005) found that, even after two decades of major take-up of satellite and cable television services in Asia and the entry of most of the world's leading transnational broadcasters, the top-rating programmes throughout the region remained local productions, even if they were in some cases local adaptations of international programme formats. This needs to be read, however, alongside film being a major counter-example, where the share of US films in total box office has continued to increase in most countries (Wasko, 2003; Wayne, 2003). A key factor has been the fast-growing increase in Hollywood film budgets, with the average cost of production growing by 119 per cent from US$26.8 million in 1990 to US$58.8 million in 2002, with a 157 per cent growth in average marketing costs during the same period, from US$11.9 million in 1990 to US$30.6 million in 2002 (Wasko, 2003, p. 33).

The focus upon global media delivery technologies as conduits for economic and cultural globalization downplays the continuing role played by national governments in relation to transnational media flows. In his study of cross-border satellite and cable television in Asia, Thomas found that while the general trend has been towards liberalization of access to transnational broadcasters over the 1990 and 2000s, the extent to which this equates to liberal access is open to question. Defining *liberal access* as 'access to all transnational media without any regulation or with explicit legal rights and protection to consumers and providers' (Thomas, 2005, p. 75), Thomas found that some countries, most notably India, Sri Lanka, Thailand, the Philippines, Indonesia, Japan, Taiwan and Hong Kong did indeed move towards liberal access models in the 1990s and early 2000s. At the same time, other countries only partially opened up their broadcasting systems, moving towards what Thomas terms *controlled access*, defined as 'access to some transnational media allowed subject to government regulation or industry self-regulation of content' (Thomas, 2005, p. 35). Notable examples of the latter have included Pakistan, Bangladesh, Singapore, Malaysia and China. In many of these cases, entry for transnational broadcasters has involved their making significant concessions in terms of both content and access to satellite broadcasters from the host country, and can be withdrawn or interrupted, as was the case with News Corporation's STAR TV service in China in the mid-1990s and Phoenix Television in the mid-2000s (Curtin, 2005).

The Globalization of Media Production Centres: 'Race to the Bottom' or Cultural Technology Transfer?

The globalization of media production, and the rise of particular centres of media production due to their capacity to attract globally 'footloose' investment capital, have generated quite different analyses. For Miller *et al.*, the emergence of such media production centres indicates the extent to which 'Hollywood's runaway trend depends on peripheral nations ... [where] there are highly-developed efficiencies available from a skilled working class in places that nonetheless continue to import what is made on "their" territory – but never under their control' (Miller *et al.*, 2001, p. 63). From this perspective, being a site for international media production involves a double loss, as both cultural sovereignty and control over intellectual property rights are conceded to the Hollywood majors, for scant economic benefit once tax breaks and other forms of pubic subsidy are factored in. By contrast, Allen Scott has argued that 'the steady opening up of global trade in cultural products is now making it possible for various audiovisual production centres around the world to establish durable competitive advantage and to attack new markets' (Scott, 2004b, p. 474). For Scott, this means that the globalization of media production through multiple production centres 'points toward a much more polycentric and polyphonic global audiovisual production system in the future than has been the case in the recent past' (Scott, 2004b, p 475). In the rise of new 'media capitals' such as Hong Kong, Michael Curtin identified the possibility that Hollywood is increasingly vulnerable, as it experiences challenges from other media capitals which constitute 'competitors who fashion products for more specific markets, using more localized labour, materials and perspectives … [for] programs [which] are not only cheaper to produce, but also more attractive to their audiences because they are more culturally relevant' (Curtin, 2003, p. 222).

In their overview of multinational corporations (MNCs) and foreign direct investment (FDI) more generally, Crotty et al. (1998) identified five views on their overall impact upon host nations:

1. the *'race to the bottom'* thesis, or the view that 'capital will increasingly be able to play workers, communities, and nations off against one another as they demand tax, regulation and wage concessions while threatening to move' (Crotty et al., 1998, p. 118);
2. the *'climb to the top'* thesis, which argued that geographically mobile capital seeks a skilled and educated workforce, good infrastructure, strong local demand, and agglomeration or clustering opportunities, which forces states competing for FDI to raise their standards in these areas, with a positive impact worldwide;
3. *neo-liberal convergence*, or the claim that free markets, maximum capital mobility, and the global movement of investment and technology are unalloyed forces for global good, particularly for economically poorer nations;
4. *uneven development*, whereby some regions of the world will experience growth as a result of their ability to attract MNCs and FDI, but that this may be at the expense of other regions (e.g. concerns that the rise of low-cost manufacturing in China is connected to the de-industrialization of Western Europe);
5. the *'much ado about nothing'* thesis, which holds that the impact of MNCs and FDI is still relatively minor, and that domestic policy settings and institutional arrangements are far more significant determinants of the economic well-being of national populations.

Crotty et al. (1998) concluded that the scenario that is most plausible will depend a great deal upon the 'rules of the game' in which foreign direct investment occurs. If economic demand is strong, governance arrangements are well understood and readily enforced, and domestic and international competition in relevant markets is robust, then more positive outcomes are likely to occur. If, however, foreign investment is sought as a desperate measure to revitalize a weak domestic economy, governance arrangements are weak, or shot through with corruption, nepotism and arbitrariness, and the consequences of foreign competition are likely to be essentially destructive upon local capital, then scenarios such as the 'race to the bottom' are far more likely to prevail. Such an analysis is consistent with the degree of uncertainty which surrounds the implications of involvement of global production networks (GPNs), and the importance of institutional arrangements to such outcomes. One could add the point made by Storper (1997) that the outcomes are also strongly linked to the types of FDI and MNC activity. Where economic operations are largely deterritorialized, and the products or services largely generic in their nature, then cost-driven capital flows will prevail. Where, by contrast, the products or services are more specialized, as are the labour, technology and other inputs required for their production, then FDI will be far more concentrated in clusters or agglomerations where the cumulative competitive advantages of co-location with both competitors and related industries and ready access to local knowledge about markets and consumers will be at a premium.

Keane (2006) has provided an analogous way of conceiving of the relationship between global media and the emergence of new production centres in East Asia. Reflecting that the moment of 'import-substitution', or promotion and protection of local media production in order to redress 'cultural imperialism' has now mostly passed in East Asia, Keane identifies five means through which regional production centres can be integrated into the global media economy:

1. the *world factory/outsourcing* model, where the attractions of a particular production location are almost exclusively cost-driven (and, in the case of film, by elements of the 'look' of an area), and where investment in the city or region is largely based upon a fly-in/fly-out model, with no retention of intellectual property rights and no reinvestment in the local sectors;
2. *isomorphism and cloning*, where imitation of global media formats becomes the sincerest form of flattery, and where predominantly US-based media formats are either directly copied without attribution of intellectual property rights, or local variants are developed with limited alteration;
3. *cultural technology transfer*, whereby the interaction between international investors and local capital, skills and talent enables the development of joint ventures which provide a springboard to local industry development through technology and – perhaps more importantly – knowledge transfer, through successful adaptation and 'modelling' (Braithwaite and Drahos, 2000);

4. *niche markets and global hits*, whereby the correlation between globalization and 'localization' is successfully exploited, so that media producers can benefit from a mix of regional sub-markets, identity-based sub-markets, an appeal to geographically dispersed diasporic communities, and niche or novelty-based markets within major global centres, such as the successful 'branding' of 'world music' (Connell and Gibson, 2003, pp. 144–59);

5. *cultural/industrial milieux* or *creative clusters*, where the value-adding associated with agglomeration emerges through the interconnections between local creativity, international finance, a growing local talent base, supportive local industries and educational and training institutions, and links to related service industries such as advertising and financial services. Such 'creative clusters' or 'media capitals' will typically service international rather than purely local or national markets, as they become a hub for media flows across geographical boundaries (Curtin, 2003).

In drawing together these competing propositions, we may conclude with two major observations. First, it is certainly the case that more media production is being outsourced, reflecting the combination of 'push' factors such as rising costs in global production centres such as Hollywood, and 'pull' factors such as competition among a range of international media production centres for foreign direct investment. In those approaches which see offshore media production as simply maintaining relations of dominance between the centre and the periphery, these international studios are basically satellite platforms, which lack the 'stickiness' to keep mobile international capital there after the low-cost productions have occurred; as a result, little or no knowledge transfer occurs. By contrast, authors such as Christopherson (2002) suggest that the emergence of such 'routine production locations' marks the early stages of development of global networks in film and television production, where such relations are less likely to be one-off and more likely to be ongoing.

While much of the talk about so-called 'runaway' production comes from local industry representatives bemoaning US job losses, there has thus far been very little evaluation of the motivations which underpin the decisions to locate film and television production in 'offshore' locations, and the extent to which this may provide sustainable foundations for audiovisual industry development in those locations which are the recipients of such foreign investment. In an important analysis of 'studio cities' worldwide, Goldsmith and O'Regan (2003) have argued that there are problems with classifying such production as inherently 'runaway', driven purely by the desire to reduce costs. They point out that, at a number of levels including those of finance, actors, directors, production crews, locations, post-production activities, and distribution, high-budget film production is increasingly 'multinational' and organized through global networks, rendering inappropriate the 'nationalist' lens through which such analysis often occurs. Moreover, they question the clear distinction drawn in these accounts between 'economic' and 'creative' factors as determinants of production location decisions. They argue that such approaches imply a limited understanding of creativity, which downplays the relevance of the creativity and skills of those working in the emergent locations. The complexity of factors which can influence production location decisions can be seen in Figure 4.1.

Australia, Canada and New Zealand as 'Second-Tier' Production Locations: Global Cities and Competition for Global Media Production

Major centres of 'offshore' production of US-developed film and television production have been Canada, Australia and, more recently, New Zealand. As English-language nations with a developed economy and well-established film production industries, these nations have been sought after as sites of offshore 'Hollywood' production. Within both Canada and Australia, there are relative 'greenfield' sites for studio development such as Vancouver in Canada and the Gold Coast in Australia, as well as more established film and television production cities, such as Sydney (Australia) and Toronto (Canada), which have undertaken significant studio redevelopment to tap into emergent global audiovisual production economics. In more recent times, a New Zealand film industry based around the city of Wellington has emerged as an aggressive competitor for international audiovisual media production opportunities, and as a would-be 'second-tier' production centre in a nation with English as its primary language.

Australia has a well-established film and television industry, which has produced internationally successful films (*Crocodile Dundee*, *Babe*) and television series (*Neighbours*, *Home and Away*). As a site for 'offshore' production, it possesses the advantages (for Hollywood) of the English language and a deep reservoir of creative personnel both in front of and behind the camera, as attested to by the very large number of Australian actors (e.g. Mel Gibson, Nicole Kidman, Toni Collette) and directors (e.g. Peter Weir, Gillian Armstrong, Philip Noyce) working primarily in Hollywood. At the same time, its geographical distance from the United States, which matters in terms of travel and transportation times and costs as well as communications issues,

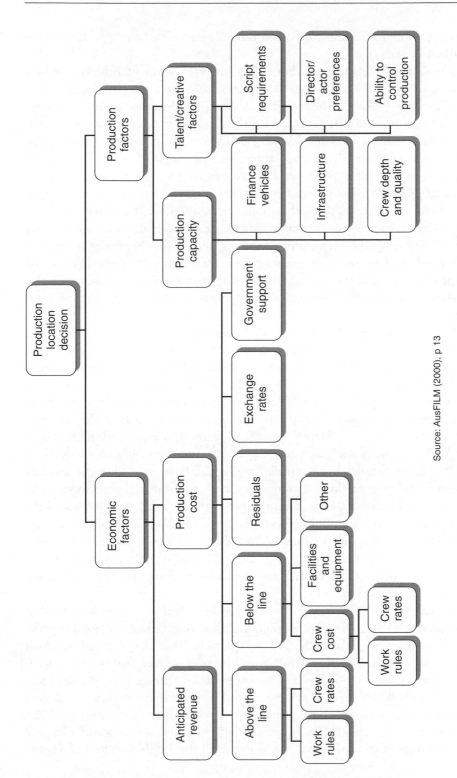

Figure 4.1 Factors behind production location decisions

Source: AusFILM (2000), p 13

will always militate against Australia becoming a 'second-tier' provider on the scale of Canada.

The Gold Coast, situated about 50 kilometres south of Brisbane, is best known for the surf beaches and theme parks that make it a popular local and international tourist destination. In 1988, considerable Queensland State government support was provided for the establishment of a film studio that came to be owned by Time Warner, which in turn incorporated the studio within a movie-based theme park. It has been the site for feature films such as the *Scooby-Doo* films and *Peter Pan*, as well as a variety of Australian and international television productions. It has always seen its role as being a commercial production site with a global orientation, and the Warners' Movie World theme park has been promoted in Australia as 'Hollywood on the Gold Coast'. The geographical location of the site outside of other major Australian film production centres sometimes works against it, partly in terms of the low regard in which it is held by the mainstream Australian film industry, but also in terms of its distance from key creative personnel and post-production facilities.

The Fox Studios in *Sydney* were an example of what Goldsmith and O'Regan (2003) refer to as a *signature development*, marking a renewed commitment on the part of Australian Federal and State governments to international film production, as well as a major investment by News Corporation in Australian film production. Since it commenced operations in 1998, it has been the site of major international film productions such as the *Mission: Impossible* films, the *Matrix* and *Star Wars* trilogies, and high-budget Australian features such as *Babe: Pig in the City* and *Moulin Rouge*. It is located in the heartland of Australian film and television production, and key international post-production companies, such as the digital animation house Animal Logic, have co-located on the site. It is not without its critics in the local film industry, who link the ownership of Fox by Rupert Murdoch with the studio's international orientation to accuse it of a cultural 'sell-out', and it is notable that the 'theme park' adjunct to the studio was a complete failure, in contrast to the Gold Coast, where the theme park has typically cross-subsidized the film studio.

As with Sydney in Australia, Toronto has historically been the heartland of Canadian film and television production, dominating English-language film production in Canada until the 1990s. It was challenged by *Vancouver*, which successfully pitched itself as 'Hollywood North', a place that is only a two-hour flight from Los Angeles and which provides access to spectacular locations, highly skilled creative personnel, and provincial governments in British Columbia that have been well disposed to foreign investment (Gasher, 2002). It was only from the 1980s, however, that it became a significant film and television production site, and it was not until the 1990s that foreign investment capital flowed into Vancouver, and facilities were developed such as The Bridge Studios (opened in 1987), Lion's Gate Studios (opened in 1989) and, most recently the Vancouver Film Studios (Goldsmith and O'Regan, 2003). Between 1995 and 2000, British Columbia's share of investment in film production grew from 8 per cent to almost 30 per cent of local film production, also attracting a growing share of foreign investment (Gasher, 2002, p. 92), requiring Toronto to develop its own large-scale studio complexes targeted at large-scale Hollywood productions.

Wellington in New Zealand has recently emerged as another prospective media capital, largely on the basis of the phenomenal success of *The Lord of the Rings* trilogy. Prior to the *Rings* films, New Zealand had been the site of a local film industry that, with a national population of 4 million, punched at or above its weight, and had produced films which had achieved moderate international success, such as *The Piano* (1993), *Once Were Warriors* (1994) and *Heavenly Creatures* (1994). Wellington film-maker Peter Jackson produced the latter, which marked his move from the producer of cult movies such as *Bad Taste* (1987), *Meet the Feebles* (1989) and *Braindead* (1992), to being one of the world's most in-demand film-makers. The three *The Lord of the Rings* films – *The Fellowship of the Ring* (2001), *The Two Towers* (2002) and *The Return of the King* (2003) – dwarfed anything previously seen in New Zealand, but their phenomenal critical and commercial success (the three films had grossed over US$2.8 billion by 2004 (Obar, 2004)) provided a massive boost to the local economy, and established Wellington, or 'Wellywood', as a site for international blockbuster film productions such as *The Last Samurai* (2003) and *King Kong* (2005). Moreover, they have been part of an international branding strategy for the city, with the national airline, Air New Zealand, promoting arrival into Wellington as 'Welcome to Middle Earth', as well as the city council's 'Creative Wellington – Innovation Capital' promotional strategy.

Further reading: AFC (2002); Gasher (2002); Goldsmith and O'Regan (2003).

The second concluding observation is that we need to note the extent to which media production is dispersed across a wide range of geographical locations, and the tendencies associated with media globalization may make it more dispersed over time. Scott (2004a) has argued that this landscape of global media production networks may be 'making it possible for various audiovisual production centres around the world to establish durable competitive advantages and to attack new markets' (Scott, 2004a, p. 474), rather than accelerating the disintegration of national media production companies and geographical centres. Demonstrating the diverse range of locations in which feature film production continues to occur (see Figure 4.2), Scott argues that:

> Although Hollywood's supremacy is unlikely to be broken at any time in the foreseeable future, at least some of these other centres will conceivably carve out stable niches for themselves in world markets, and all the more so as they develop more effective marketing and distribution capacities ... This argument, if correct, points toward a much more polycentric and polyphonic global audiovisual production system than has been the case in the recent past. (Scott, 2004a, p. 475)

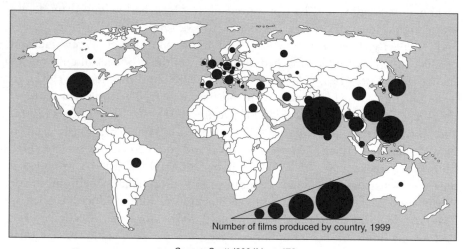

Number of films produced by country, 1999

Source: Scott (2004b), p. 476

Figure 4.2 Number of feature films produced by country, 1999

The example of television programme format trade alerts us to the complexities of considering whether cultural technology transfer actually occurs. Identifying the format as 'a cultural technology which governs the flow of programme ideas across time and space' (Moran, 1998, p. 23), Moran highlights the fact that evaluation of the impact of international programme format trade requires us to consider its legal, industrial, technological, cultural and knowledge transfer dimensions. Proposing that the concept of 'modelling' provides an important bridge between cloning or illegal copying and adaptation for local environments, Keane (2004c) and others draw attention to the extent to which the dynamic of sameness and difference inherent in the adaptation of formats is linked to wider changes in the global geo-economy, which favour flexible production networks, the development of global niche markets in parallel to national mass markets, and alternate revenue streams derived from the trade in ideas and intangibles as much as finished products. The extent to which such tendencies in global media production map across changes in culture and consumption on a global scale will be the subject of the next chapter.

Global Media Cultures 5

Introduction: Four Ways to Think about Culture

With the development of cable and satellite technologies, the Internet and World Wide Web, far more people are exposed to global media communications than ever before. It was argued in Chapter 1 that any discussion of globalization needs to give close attention to global media, since not only is globalization associated with globalizing communications technologies and with media corporations who seek to operate on a global scale, but global media are also the principal bearers of symbolic and informational content through which people make sense of their world, and their relations to distant others. At the same time, as this book has thus far indicated, claims that there has been a straightforward scalar progression of the principal locus of decision-making and action from the local/national to the global scale, or that national media systems are rapidly falling under the sway of global media corporations, need to be treated with caution for both empirical and conceptual reasons. To take one example from Chapter 4, the case of television programme format trade makes it clear that the global flow of programming ideas and media content are by no means the same thing. Formats provide 'models' of programming which are applied in multiple national media markets, and have embedded within them intellectual property that is derived from their home base, but the actual content that is made available to media audiences has typically gone through a process of cultural adaptation and localization, to remove what Iwabuchi (2002) terms the 'odours' of its country of origin, to appear as a naturalized part of the local and national culture and mediascape.

Central to all of this is the question of culture. Culture, like policy, is an inherently local filter of global media flows. In order to render the conceptually unruly beast of culture more manageable (noting Raymond Williams' definitional qualms raised in Chapter 1), I will outline in this chapter four ways in which culture has been thought about, and how the intersections between them can assist in furthering an understanding of the complexities of global media culture. These are:

1. culture as lived and shared experience;
2. culture as mediated symbolic communication;

3. culture as resource;
4. culture as policy discourse.

1. Culture as Lived and Shared Experience

One of Williams' key contributions to discussions about the meaning of culture was to insist that it was not simply an 'ideal' concept concerned principally with art and aesthetics, but that it also needed to be understood in the anthropological sense of being 'a particular way of life, whether of a people, a period [or] a group' (Williams, 1976, p. 18). This 'social' definition of culture refers to 'meanings and values not only in art and learning but also in institutions and ordinary behaviour' (Williams, 1965, p. 57). This association of culture with the everyday practices of people and social groups has certainly been a staple of cultural studies' definitions of culture. An example can be seen in Hall and Jefferson's account in *Resistance Through Rituals* of 'the "culture" of a group or class [as] the peculiar and distinctive "way of life" ... the meanings, values and ideas embodied in institutions, in social relations, in systems of belief, in mores and customs, [and] in the uses of objects and material life' (Hall and Jefferson, 1976, p. 10). In a similar vein, Frow and Morris (1996, p. 345) define culture as 'the "whole way of life" of a social group as it is structured by representation and by power'.

Certainly, if the concept of culture is taken in this anthropological sense of being a *lived and shared experience*, then global culture is a definitional impossibility. As Anthony Smith has observed:

> If by 'culture' is meant a collective mode of life, or a repertoire of beliefs, styles, values and symbols, then we can only speak of cultures, never just culture; for a collective mode of life, or a repertoire of beliefs, etc. presupposes different modes and repertoires in a universe of modes and repertoires. Hence, the idea of a 'global culture' is a practical impossibility ... Even if the concept is predicated of *homo sapiens*, as opposed to other species, the differences between segments of humanity in terms of lifestyle and belief-repertoire are too great, and the common elements too generalized, to permit us to even conceive of a globalized culture. (Smith, 1991, p. 171)

Put simply, then, if global culture needs to involve a convergence of the stuff that people do in their everyday lives, then this has clearly not happened, nor is it ever likely to happen. If the anthropological definition of culture as the lived and shared experience of social groups was sufficient, then we need not worry about global media cultures.

2. Culture as Mediated Symbolic Communication

If, however, the notion of culture as the lived and shared experience of a human social grouping is overlaid with processes of imagining and meaning-making, and the forms of communication, interaction and symbolic representation through which these processes are developed, then the question of a global media culture becomes a more pertinent one. This has also been a recurring theme of cultural studies. Taking the three authors referred to above, Williams stressed that culture could not refer simply to practices of material production, but also needed to consider 'symbolic or signifying systems' (Williams, 1976, p. 18). Similarly, Hall and Jefferson pointed out how culture also referred to the '"maps of meaning" which make things intelligible ... and through which the individual becomes a "social individual"' (Hall and Jefferson, 1976, p. 11), while Frow and Morris observed that 'every aspect of social life' is shaped by 'a network of representations – texts, images, talk, codes of behaviour, and the narrative structures organizing these' (Frow and Morris, 1996, p. 345). Such definitions obviously point in the direction of semiotics, and the insistence that 'every act of communication ... presupposes a signification system as its necessary condition' (Eco, 1976, p. 9), and that culture entails a system of social, linguistic and psychological relationship through which 'individuals' are 'produced'.

The centrality of media to any contemporary understanding of culture is usefully outlined by Douglas Kellner in these terms:

> Radio, television, film and the other products of media culture provide materials out of which we forge our very identities, our sense of selfhood; our notion of what it means to be male or female; our sense of class, of ethnicity and race, of nationality, of sexuality, of 'us' and 'them'. Media images help shape our view of the world and our deepest moral values: what we consider good or bad, positive or negative, moral or evil. Media stories provide the symbols, myths and resources through which we constitute a common culture and through the appropriation of which we insert ourselves into this culture. Media spectacles demonstrate who has power and who is powerless, who is allowed to exercise force and violence and who is not ... We are immersed from cradle to grave in a media and consumer society, and thus it is important to learn how to understand, interpret and criticize its meanings and values. (Kellner, 1995, p. 5)

Postmodernist media theory has seen the absorption of culture into global media as the *sine qua non* of the contemporary global order. At its most polemical, Jean Baudrillard's various arguments that 'the real' has collapsed into its various modes of simulation has been an ongoing provocation to those who seek to identify culture as something that exists independently of global media (see Poster, 1988). Similarly, McKenzie Wark's (1994, 1998) argument that we now exist in a 'virtual geography' where culture as everyday life is doubled by global communications vectors, so that 'we no longer have roots, we have aerials' (Wark, 1994, p. xiv), draws upon a comparable analysis of the cultural impacts of global media. In a more historical vein, John Thompson has argued that there is a strong connection between the technologies and institutions of media and communications and the globalization of modernity, when we understand culture in its 'symbolic' and communicative sense:

> If we focus in the first instance not on values, attitudes and beliefs, but rather on symbolic forms and their modes of production and circulation in the social world, then we shall see that, with the advent of modern societies … a systematic cultural transformation began to take hold. By virtue of a series of technical innovations associated with printing and, subsequently, with the electronic codification of information, symbolic forms were produced, reproduced and circulated on a scale that was unprecedented. Patterns of communication and interaction began to change in profound and irreversible ways. The changes … comprise what can loosely be called the 'mediatization of culture'. (Thompson, 1995, p. 46)

3. Culture as Resource

A third and very distinctive way of thinking about culture has been proposed by George Yúdice, with the concept of *culture as resource*. Yúdice has argued that, in the early-21st-century epoch of globalization, 'culture is increasingly wielded as a resource for both socio-political and economic amelioration, that is, for increasing participation in its era of waning political involvement, conflicts over citizenship, and the rise of … "cultural capitalism"' (Yúdice, 2003, p. 9). This has manifested itself in a number of ways which include:

- the need to develop economic rationales for arts and cultural funding;
- the growing recognition of social capital as a factor in economic development;
- the rise of the creative industries based upon wealth generation through new ideas and intangible assets;
- the uses of culture in urban promotional strategies;
- growing demands on the part of minority groups for cultural rights and recognition of cultural citizenship.

For Yúdice, the result is what he terms the *expediency of culture*, or the invocation of culture so as to constitute it as a social resource, and hence as a legitimate site for both government and private investment. Culture as a social resource is increasingly called upon to perform a variety of functions, ranging from redressing social marginalization to promoting community behaviour more conducive to economic growth, from public investment in festivals and events that promote local tourism to energizing otherwise dormant well-springs of creative energy. Such demands impact at all levels upon the conduct of contemporary cultural institutions.

Yúdice argues that 'there is an expedient relation between globalization and culture in the sense that there is a *fit* or a *suitability* between them' (Yúdice, 2003, p. 29). There are three primary reasons for this. The first is that globalization has been accompanied by both increasingly flexible production systems and differentiated consumer markets, meaning that 'under conditions of globalization, difference rather than homogenization infuses the prevailing logic of accumulation' (Yúdice, 2003, p. 28). The second is that culture can constitute the basis for what Flew (2004) has termed a *new humanism*, which can redress the historic divide between 'practical' commercial activity and the 'unworldly' arts, as it is more enmeshed with commercial popular culture and the knowledge-based economy, while revivifying humanism's traditional concerns with attributes of the 'whole person' (now described in the business literature as 'soft skills'). The boom in creativity discourses in business management literature is one clear indicator of this (Flew, 2003c). Thirdly, as globalization has placed a renewed focus upon the significance of cities and regions as the locus of economic dynamism, as distinct from nation-states, culture has become a very important signifier of distinction and difference, and has come to be seen by policy-makers as increasingly central to the *place competitiveness* of cities and regions (O'Regan, 2002; Stevenson, 2004).

A very good example of both of these tendencies was seen with the Universal Forum of Cultures, held in Barcelona, Spain, from May to September, 2004 (www.barcelona2004.org). The Forum aimed to promote 'creativity, education and the democratization of knowledge as means of transmitting values and attitudes that provide the foundation for a culture of peace and dialogue between cultures', and its programme revolved around the themes of cultural diversity, sustainable development and global peace. This UNESCO-supported Forum promoted such goals through a mix of academic conferences, public concerts by Sting, Bob Dylan and others, and public addresses by such world-renowned figures as Isabel Allende, Susan George and Mikhail Gorbachev. It also offered the Barcelona government authorities the opportunity to redevelop the run-down port district of Poblé Nou and make it more appealing to property investors and middle-class apartment buyers. It also enabled Barcelona's development agencies to demonstrate the city's unique capacity to fuse culture, world peace and urban regeneration through a spectacular range of events, to which global travellers, school children and conference delegates experienced easy access through extensions to the urban transit system, that had previously been redeveloped for the 1992 Olympic Games.

4. Culture as Policy Discourse

Culture has traditionally been employed in arts policy discourse as providing the basis for determining those intellectual and artistic forms that were most worthy of public support in order to achieve social and moral improvement in the broader population and to maintain a national cultural heritage (Williams, 1989; Lury, 1994). As governments have sought to broaden the reach of cultural policy and to align it to other policy objectives, there has been an interesting fusion between governmental and academic discourses about how to better align the study of culture with the formation and implementation of policy. This realignment between cultural theory and cultural policy, also known as the *cultural policy debate*, has focused attention on the discursive construction of culture as the object of policy, as well as the capacity to link cultural policy instruments to the pursuit of other agendas, such as citizenship, social inclusion, urban renewal and economic development (see e.g. Cunningham, 1992; McGuigan, 1996; McRobbie, 1996; Lewis and Miller, 2003). The most sustained series of arguments along these lines was developed by Tony Bennett (Bennett, 1989, 1992a, 1992b, 1995, 1998, 2003), whose work was discussed in some detail in Chapter 2.

In terms of how we are thinking here about culture, what has been particularly important about Bennett's analysis of cultural policy is that it presents culture as an object of policy discourse. It emphasizes the extent to which cultural relations are managed by governments on the basis of what Foucault referred to as a 'positive' conception of power, where governmental power acts to form and shape individual identities, rather than constrain their full development (Foucault, 1982). The concept of governmentality has also drawn attention to the ways in which *technologies of government* are used to manage populations, and their role in constructing the cultural field by defining its problems and proposing courses of action that draw upon expert knowledge of various forms (Miller and Rose, 1992; Dean, 1999; Rose, 1999; Bennett, 2003). Bennett has used the contemporary policies around multiculturalism as an illustration, arguing that the maintenance of harmony among culturally diverse populations in modern nation-states requires policy action that addresses historic and current sources of disadvantage arising from race, ethnic background or nationality, the reorganization of cultural institutions to better recognize and reflect such a culturally diverse population, and initiatives to promote cross-cultural communication and better intercultural understanding. He argues that none of this is possible without an active role being played by governmental institutions engaged with 'the management of cultural resources in ways intended to reform ways of life … [which are] very much a part of the politics and policy of culture in contemporary societies' (Bennett, 1998, p. 104; cf. Bennett, 2003).

Integrating Diverse Conceptions of Culture

Rather than thinking about the four conceptions of culture considered thus far in isolation, it is more fruitful to consider the points of intersection between these, and what they illustrate about the relationship between global media and culture (see Figure 5.1).

The four ways of thinking about culture generate six points of intersection, and it is useful to draw attention to the ways in which these intersections provide us with further insight into the nature of global media cultures.

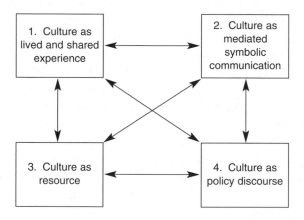

Figure 5.1 Mapping the four definitions of culture

1 and 2: Culture as lived and shared experience/culture as mediated symbolic communication

This relationship has been in many respects the heartland of cultural studies as it has evolved as a discipline. It has emerged at the intersection of concerns about understanding and engaging with culture as it is lived and experienced by those 'from below' the dominant structures of corporate and governmental power, but also understanding the implications of the massive penetration of media in their many forms into everyday life and culture for an ever-growing proportion of the global population. Many of the debates about whether we lived in a 'postmodern culture', for instance, have revolved around the extent to which collective cultural engagement through the media had displaced interpersonal dialogue and a sense of communal solidarity derived from common everyday experiences. Had watching *Neighbours* taken over from talking to our neighbours, or does *Desperate Housewives* say enough about female domesticity to make local women's groups superfluous? Similarly, debates about the cultural impact of global media raise issues as to whether the experience of global cosmopolitanism, once the preserve of elites such as political and business leaders, diplomats, military personnel, intelligence agents and senior academics, is now being democratized through mass media as well as the Internet. Have we now reached a point where access to basic communications technologies and infrastructure is so ubiquitous that, in Dick Hebdige's words, we are 'living in a world where "mundane cosmopolitanism" is part of "ordinary" experience ... [as] all culture, however remote temporally and geographically, [is] becoming accessible to us today as signs and/or commodities' (quoted in Tomlinson, 1999, p. 133).

Ien Ang's analysis of *global media/local meaning* (Ang, 1996a) sought to understand this new relationship between the 'lived' and 'mediated' aspects of culture in the context of local receptions of global media. Ang argued that 'globalization involves a chequered process of systemic desegregation in which local cultures lose their autonomous and separate existence and ... tend to reproduce themselves ... through the appropriation of global flows of mass-mediated forms and technologies' (Ang, 1996a, p. 153). For Ang, what was most significant about the global/local cultural relationship was the extent to which globalization involved the export of a cultural technology – media technologies, practices, and forms – that reorganized local media cultures around 'the commercial principle of production of culture for profit' or 'the commodification of media culture' (Ang, 1996a, p. 154). Using the example of Hong Kong action cinema, Ang concluded that 'what has emerged is a highly distinctive and economically viable hybrid cultural form in which the global and the local are inextricably intertwined ... in other words, what counts as "local" and therefore "authentic" is not a fixed content, but subject to change and modification as a result of the domestification of imported cultural goods' (Ang, 1996a, pp. 154–5). Ang's observation that the globalization of cultural forms can be observed, but that this is not synonymous with some form of global culture, also finds resonance in Simon During's theory of the *global popular* (During, 1997). During distinguishes the global popular from cultural globalization, as the global popular 'only comes into being when a particular product or star is a hit in many markets' (During, 1997, p. 810), and is therefore the outcome of particular transnational entertainment industry strategies, although it is clearly connected to other forms of cultural globalization.

1 and 3: Culture and lived and shared experience/culture as resource

The idea that cultures can constitute a resource has taken root since the 1980s. The Conservative UK governments of Margaret Thatcher and John Major fervently championed the notion that British economic renewal required the inculcation of an 'enterprise culture'. More recently, the concept of *creative cities* has placed culture at the centre of contemporary urban dynamism, pointing to the importance of *creative milieux* and 'soft infrastructure'. Such findings are supported, to take one example, by recent work on the importance of local networks to the development of a successful music industry (Brown *et al.*, 2000; Flew *et al.*, 2001; Gibson, 2003). Developing a more generally applicable argument, Richard Florida (2002) has emphasized *the power of place* for what he terms the 'creative class', arguing that creative people attach great importance to being in diverse, culturally vibrant cities with a distinctive identity and a variety of engaging experiences. His argument is that urban centres with a strong well-spring of cultural creativity will thrive, as their economic dynamism is driven, not by government incentives to attract new ICT-related industries, but by what he terms the *Three T's of technology, talent and tolerance*. This is because 'regional economic growth is powered by creative people who prefer places that are diverse, tolerant and open to new ideas. Diversity increases the odds that a place will attract different types of people with different skill sets and ideas' (Florida, 2002, p. 249).

In outlining the case for considering London to be a creative city, Landry (2005) proposed that culture constitutes a valuable resource for cities such as London in the 21st century global economy in six respects:

1. Both the historical artefacts and the contemporary practices of a city's population generate a sense of local belonging which is a source of civic pride among the population.
2. Cultural activities are linked to innovation and creativity, and it is the capacity of cities to adapt and innovate that is at the core of their longevity.
3. The cultural sectors are linked to the image of a place, which impacts upon place competitiveness through marketing and the ability to attract international capital investment and geographically mobile skilled workers.

4. Culture and tourism are inextricably linked, as tourists seek both the 'high' culture of a city (museums, galleries, historic buildings and so on) and its popular culture (clubs, bars, restaurants, street festivals etc.).
5. The growing economic significance of the creative industries in the global economy raises the significance of innovative forms of digital content for the ICT-driven knowledge economy, and the importance of networks across both the subsidized and commercial media and cultural sectors.
6. Culture may be able to promote greater social inclusion and redress economic inequality and social disadvantage, through the ability to provide places where otherwise marginalized groups can engage in collective forms of cultural activity, thereby assisting in personal development, development of life skills, and the creation of new employment and training opportunities.

While such claims about the transformative possibilities of culture certainly do not go uncontested (see e.g. Oakley, 2004, for an astute insider's analysis of the problems of such arguments in the UK context; cf. Peck, 2005, for a critique of Florida), the fact that they are made, and have such an influence upon urban and regional development policies, indicates in itself the growing extent to which often mundane aspects of the culture of a place are seen as being a valuable resource for local cities and regions in a globalizing economy.

1 and 4: Culture and lived and shared experience/culture as policy discourse

Historically, culture as everyday lived and shared experience and culture as policy discourse have been most strongly linked through the roles played by government agencies in promoting a common national culture through deliberate policies of cultural nationalism. Benedict's Anderson's pioneering work on modern nationalism has emphasized how, to the extent that such public projects of 'nationing' are successful, they transform nationalism from an ideology (or what Anderson terms 'Nationalism-with-a-big-N'), to a collective form of imagining oneself in relation to others that deeply intertwines a common language, a sense of community, a series of shared historical myths, and an amalgam of geography and destiny. The result is that a nation is 'imagined as a community, because, regardless of the actual inequality and exploitation which may prevail in each, the nation is always conceived as a deep, horizontal comradeship' (Anderson, 1991, p. 7). Antonio Gramsci's concept of the *national-popular*, as an explanatory device for identifying the conditions under which political alliances could emerge in particular national contexts that crossed class, ethnic and regional divides, and the importance of recognizing the role of popular media in speaking across political, social and cultural divides, drew attention to some of the political implications of such a connection between everyday culture and cultural policy in particular national societies (Forgacs, 1993).

The development of policies to manage increasingly multicultural societies has become an important measure of this interconnection. Bennett (1998) has observed that the pluralization of ways of life arising from increasingly culturally diverse populations generates a need to think of, and to actively support, 'cultures' in the plural, which has marked an important point of transition for arts, media and cultural policies in many nations. The *National Agenda for a Multicultural Australia*, developed in 1989, described multiculturalism as 'a policy for managing the consequences of cultural diversity', and identified its three core principles as being cultural identity, social justice and economic efficiency (quoted in Castles and Davidson, 2000, p. 166). In their commentary on multiculturalism drawing upon this policy, Castles and Davidson argued that:

> With the arrival of multi-ethnic workforces, the requirement that someone belong nationally before obtaining citizen rights has been gradually given up. The trend away from the citizen who belongs as a national has in turn spelt the emergence of new civil, political and economic rights and practices, which have had to be introduced by the state to cope with a new reality in which its inhabitants do not share common values. (Castles and Davidson, 2000, p. 166)

2 and 4: Culture as mediated symbolic communication/culture as policy discourse

The relationship between communications media and cultural policy has constituted the heartland of national media content policies, where the broadcast media as space-binding media systems are engaged with by policy-makers as an instrument for contributing to the development of a national culture, including policies that are inclusive towards cultural, ethnic and linguistic minorities. In this way, broadcast media contributed to what Ernest Gellner described as the 'striving to make culture and policy congruent' (Gellner, 1983, p. 43). They have done so in a direct sense through their capacity to engage audiences with media content that generates compelling national narratives, and in the more indirect, regulatory sense of defining the national media ecology by setting limits to the entry of imported media content. This balance between cultural promotion and cultural defence in national media policies recognizes Philip Schlesinger's point that 'in the modern world ... social spaces are also communicative spaces' (Schlesinger, 1991b, p. 299).

Citizen rights in modern societies entail forms of media citizenship, which can include access rights to information, provision of a diverse range of views and opinions on issues of national importance, and the right of all sections of society to recognition through available media representations, as well as the opportunity to participate in the shaping of such representations (Golding and Murdock, 1989; cf. Flew, 2003b, 2006b). The policy instruments through which such strategies have been pursued have included funding for national public service broadcasters, support for community or minority broadcasters, cultural diversity quotas, local-content quotas, and subsidies for local media content production.

Within this policy discourse to connect people and communities to national culture through media, there have always been tensions and ambiguities. Two in particular stand out. The first is that if media are creative industries, they are simultaneously *creative*, and thus involved in the dissemination of symbolic communication forms that use ideas and imagination to produce compelling cultural content, and *industries*, that produce cultural commodities for distribution and sale in commercial media markets. As Schlesinger has observed in relation to film and broadcast media, 'the "audiovisual" is both a symbolic arena and an economic one ... [that] allows one to make both a cultural and an economic argument at the same time' (Schlesinger, 1991a, p. 146). It has been argued by Syvertsen (2003), among others, that such a tension now pervades public service broadcasting worldwide, as audience maximization strategies driven by the need to ensure their economic survival may in turn undermine them, as they efface the distinctiveness of their 'cultural' mandate, and render them 'the target of criticism that they are not really providing an alternative to commercial television' (Syvertsen, 2003, p. 170). Second, media have a geographical reach which inherently extends beyond national territorial boundaries. The idea that they work towards a territorially defined cultural mandate has therefore been under challenge for some time, and the case for deterritorialization seems to strengthen with each new media form. For example, there is nothing about the Internet that is inherently national, just as broadcast media were never particularly local. Schlesinger has pursued this question in relation to European media content quotas, which in his view construct 'a European collective identity largely modelled on the nation' (Schlesinger, 1997, p. 371). Schlesinger argues that such arguments have involved a consistent conflation between an understanding of the audiovisual production sector as an industry that warrants policy support, and which needs expanded European markets in order to achieve the distribution economies required to better compete with the US, and the idea of audiovisual media as a critical part of a common European cultural patrimony. Such arguments seek to paper over, rather than resolve, the inherent tension between the need on the one hand to generate pan-

European media markets in order to achieve economies of scale, and the claim (which remains largely a fiction, at least as measured in media consumption patterns) that the populations of EU member states may come to identify themselves as being 'Europeans', as distinct from their current – and very much historically grounded – sense of being English, French, Welsh, German, Italian, Polish, Scottish, Dutch, Belgian and so on.[1]

2 and 3: Culture as mediated symbolic communication/culture as resource

The historical balance between 'cultural' and 'economic' rationales in media policy has been challenged since the 1990s. A raft of national information policies in the 1990s identified media as content industries that possessed new possibilities for expansion in global markets.[2] At a more global level, the OECD drew attention to advances in the distribution and marketing of media content associated with the development of the Internet, and what it termed network-based services, which enabled content to become a new growth industry (OECD, 1998). In doing so, it identified the need for a shift from traditional media policy mechanisms, designed to manage market structures and market access for established media commodities, towards regulatory strategies aimed at promoting 'open access to essential resources ... non-discrimination, innovation and competition' (OECD, 1999, p. 6). The OECD recommended, for instance, that 'governments wishing to promote cultural (and linguistic) diversity are therefore more fruitfully engaged in positively encouraging the promotion of new multimedia services than in attempting to restrict market access' (OECD, 1999, p. 7).

In the 2000s, creative industries policy statements began to displace national information policy arguments, particularly as the impact of the 2001 downturn in the IT sector revealed the vulnerability of purely ICT-driven approaches in light of the global mobility and the cost-sensitivity of investment in the sector. Examples of creative industries strategies developed at a national level over this period have included:

- United Kingdom: promotion of both national and regionally based creative industries development strategies, following from the Creative Industries Mapping Documents developed through the Department of Culture, Media and Sport in 1998 and 2001;
- Australia: adoption of a creative industries strategy by the Queensland State government in 2001, and a national Digital Content Industry Action Agenda for developing the digital media sectors (DCITA, 2004; Cunningham, 2006);

- New Zealand: identification of creative industries as one of the 'three pillars' of the 2002 Growth and Innovation Framework, along with biotechnology and information and communications technology;
- Singapore: the 'Remaking Singapore' strategy (see Leo and Lee, 2004) has drawn upon a range of policy resources developed since 2001, including the Ministry of Trade and Industry's study *Economic Contributions of Singapore's Creative Industries* (MTI, 2003);
- Sweden: the Knowledge Foundation was established by the Swedish government to examine the role and significance of what it terms the *experience industry*, defining it as 'a collective term used to describe people and businesses in creative professions whose main purpose is to create and/or supply experiences in various forms', and identifying it as now constituting 6.5 per cent of the total labour market (Nielsén, 2004, p. 48);
- Hong Kong: the *Baseline Study of Hong Kong's Creative Industries*, undertaken by the Centre for Cultural Policy Research at the University of Hong Kong (CCPR, 2003), identified the importance of creative industries to the image or branding of Hong Kong, as well as the opportunities to shift the local economy towards high-value-added services as labour-intensive manufacturing shifted to the Guangzhou (Pearl River Delta) regions of mainland China;
- European Union: the MKW study commissioned by the EU (MKW, 2001) found that employment growth rates in cultural occupations were four times the EU average, and that people working in cultural occupations were almost three times as likely to be self-employed, and twice as likely to have a tertiary qualification as those in other sectors. It also observed the conceptual difficulties in reaching a common discourse to discuss the creative industries in the EU context, oscillating between the insistence in some jurisdictions (most notably Germany) that what is cultural is by definition not part of an industry, and in others (such as Finland) that identify all activities involving 'production based upon meaning content' as cultural or creative industries (cf. Flew, 2005a, pp. 116–18).
- China: while 'creative industries' has until recently been seen as a misnomer in the Chinese context, sitting uncomfortably between the traditional focus upon state-run cultural industries (*wenhua chanye*) and an innovation agenda (*chuangxin*) focused upon the ICT sectors (Wang, 2004), there have recently been signs of change. An International Creative Industries Conference held in Beijing in July 2005 drew attention to the need to develop the creative industries (*chaungyi gongye*) in order to take advantage of opportunities in the digital content sectors, which combine knowledge economy priorities with the need for enhanced creativity. This is part of a wider set of debates about how China can move from being the 'world's factory', as a producer of low-value-added manufactured goods

('Made in China'), to a 'Created in China' agenda, which sees China as a leader in intellectual property development (Keane, 2004c; Nolan, 2004; cf. special issue of *IJCS*, 2006).

Such strategies have drawn upon the growing perception that the creative industries sectors, lying at the 'crossroads between the arts, business and technology' (UNCTAD, 2004), or at the intersection between information technology, business entrepreneurship and creative practice (Mitchell *et al.*, 2003), have become vital engines of growth in what Shalini Venturelli (2005) has termed the *global creative economy*. UNCTAD (2004) has explicitly linked expansion of the creative industries to globalization, around five trends:

1. deregulation of national cultural and media policy frameworks;
2. increasing average global incomes, which allow for more 'discretionary' expenditure on arts, cultural and entertainment products and services;
3. technological changes, particularly the role played by the Internet in the global distribution of digital media content;
4. the global rise of service industries, which place a higher premium upon intangible forms of knowledge, and are also sources of demand for creative industries outputs, particularly in areas such as design, advertising and marketing;
5. expansion of international trade generally, and trade in services in particular.

The Korean Film Boom

One of the world's most dynamic film industries in the mid-2000s was that of the Republic of Korea (South Korea). While many of the world's domestic film industries have experienced diminishing market share against imported products, most notably from the United States, the domestic market share of Korean-produced films among Korean audiences has continued to grow from the mid-1990s through the 2000s. The growth in local audience share for Korean films grew from 23.1 per cent in 1996 to 32.6 per cent in 2000, and from 45.2 per cent in 2002 to 54.2 per cent in 2004 (*European Cinema Journal*, May 2003; *Korean Film Observatory*, Winter 2004). Over the same period, Korean film exports grew from US$400,000 in 1996 to US$7 million in 2000, to over US$58 million in 2004, with over three-quarters of these exports going to Asia (of which Japan accounts for the vast majority), but with Europe and North America accounting for almost 20 per cent of exports, which would have been inconceivable only a decade ago (*Korean Film Observatory*, Winter 2004). This success has prompted international observers to 'compare the recent boom in Korean home-grown films to the burst of talent and enthusiasm that re-energized Hong Kong cinema in the late '70s and early '80s' (Smith, 2001).

The boom in Korean cinema has occurred under circumstances that would not appear particularly auspicious. The Korean language is spoken in few places outside of the Korean peninsula, the South Korean state is subject to ongoing political uncertainty in its relationship with the isolated communist state of North Korea, and there has been a strong tradition of government censorship of local film-makers. Moreover, a succession of military dictators ruled the nation from 1950 to 1993, while the United States military presence has also meant a strong, if also strongly resisted, American cultural presence in the nation. All of these factors made Korea an unlikely locale for global media production, particularly when compared to the advantages Hong Kong enjoyed as a *laissez-faire* economy with strong roots in the global Chinese cultural diaspora. In 1988, under military leader Roh Tae-Woo, two decisions were made which have continued to influence Korean cinema to this day. First, the new constitution allowed for the easing of film censorship, a trend which has been ongoing since South Korea became a democracy in 1993. Second, import restrictions on foreign films were lifted. The initial impact of this policy decision was disastrous, as films from Hollywood and Hong Kong captured local audiences, and the local industry's market share fell to a low point of 16 per cent in 1993 (Paquet, 2005).

From the mid-1990s, the situation began to change dramatically. Whereas Korean film-makers had aimed to produce films that connected to major national events and hence invoked a strong sense of local popular memory, films such as *The Contact* (1997) and *Shiri* (1999) were massive hits with Korean audiences on the basis of their combination of compelling national narratives, an eye for Western action film conventions, and production values which were both akin to the Hollywood blockbusters and informed by a strong sense of audience appeal rather than an aesthetic or political sensibility. As Anthony Leong (2002) has suggested, Korean film-makers have perhaps filled a vacuum in compelling East Asian cinema which Hong Kong vacated in the uncertainties it faced in the late 1990s, with reunification with China and the poaching of its best creative talents by Hollywood.

The success of *Shiri*, and subsequent films such as *Attack the Gas Station* (1999), *Joint Security Area* (2000), *Friend* (2001), *My Sassy Girl* (2001), *My Wife Is a Gangster* (2001), *2009 Lost Memories* (2002), *Old Boy* (2003), *Spring, Summer, Fall, Winter … and Spring* (2003), *Silmido* (2004), and *Marathon* (2005), represented an eclectic mix that clearly found favour with local audiences to the point where, by 2005, eight of Korea's ten top box-office-grossing films were Korean. The continuing strong market share of Korean films among local audiences has made it almost unique among national film cultures facing the production values and distributional clout of 'Global Hollywood'.

The factors underpinning the Korean film boom are a mix of the creative and the industrial. Leong (2002) argues that the features of the 'newest wave' of Korean cinema revolve around: unique forms of story-telling, and a readiness to mix and blur generic film elements; a culture of risk-taking and a willingness to challenge existing social mores and political orthodoxies; a level of technical sophistication that reflects not only superior production budgets, but also the extent to which this generation of film-makers were 'schooled' in Hollywood film conventions; and a cultural perspective informed by both the turbulent political history of the Korean peninsula since the Korean War of 1950–53, and the sense that Koreans remain upon a historic journey whose outcomes are by no means resolved. Leong observes that 'aficionados of Asian cinema will note that these are the same qualities that were ascribed to Hong Kong films of the late Seventies ... right up into the early Nineties' (Leong, 2002, p. 17).

Innovations in the financing of film production have also fuelled the Korean film boom. As censorship restrictions were slowly lifted in the 1990s, the big Korean industrial conglomerates (known as the *chaebol*, and including corporations such as Samsung, Hyundai, Daewoo and LG) began to invest in the film industry, but the Asian financial crisis of 1997–98 saw them largely withdraw from the sector. While this of course precipitated a crisis, it also provided a new opportunity for entrepreneurs to seek alternative sources of funding for films that were more innovative than those which the *chaebol* were prepared to support. Venture capitalists established Internet-enabled film investment funds (the 'netizen funds') to tap into small-scale investors, which were central to kick-starting the local production industry in the early 2000s (Leong, 2002, pp. 14–16).

Further reading: Leong (2002); Park and Shin (2004); Paquet (2005).

3 and 4: Culture as resource/culture as policy discourse

These two areas could be seen as synonymous, since the whole conception of culture as a 'resource' is one that certainly comes from the 'top-down' perspective of cultural administrators rather than the 'bottom-up' view of cultural producers and consumers. But the differences are nonetheless subtle and important, and relate to the dual nature of global media and culture as a part of lived everyday experience and as global informational infrastructures. For those concerned with overall cultural impact, three positive developments can be noted. First, there is little evidence that greater exposure to globally distributed media in various forms has constituted a key factor in the diminution of local cultures and identities. Global media certainly change local cultures, particularly when they are part of a package that has been described as 'global modernity' (Giddens, 1990; Tomlinson, 1999), but the idea that they exercise an acid-like corrosion of local cultures has thus far proved unsustainable. This is even more apparent when the implications of asymmetrical interdependence and cultural reconversion are acknowledged as drivers of local responses to global media and cultural flows. Second, the switch from 1990s information policy discourses to the 2000s focus upon creative industries development has also brought the creative sectors into the mainstream of policy, a position from which they have certainly been excluded in traditional approaches to national innovation systems, as well as in the IT-driven focus of information policy discourses in the 1990s (cf. Cunningham *et al.*, 2004; Cunningham, 2006). Third, the alignment of culture to 'new economy' or knowledge economy thinking enabled a move out of the hitherto dominant conceptions of culture as a 'civilizing influence' on industrial society or as a site for development of a certain type of critical mentality, towards thinking about those with a cultural training as providing generative resources for new ideas and new forms of imagining that would befit a 'new economy' (cf. Flew, 2004a). Indeed, pundits such as Daniel Pink (Pink, 2004) have gone so far as to propose that the Master in Fine Arts (MFA) degree may be the new MBA, because the fine arts constitute vital sites for counter-intuitive ideas, information and imagining.

At the same time, the 'rediscovery of culture' by policy-makers in the early 21st century has been a two-edged gift. Yúdice provides many examples of such tensions and ambivalences, ranging from the UNESCO official complaining that, as a sociologist and cultural policy specialist, she was asked to solve economic and political problems that she was not professionally trained to address, to the official from the Inter-American Development Bank (IADB) who demanded a performance metric for investments in social and cultural improvements in local communities, since he was not interested in funding 'culture for culture's sake' (Yúdice, 2003). Yúdice proposed that the 'anthropological turn' in arts, media and cultural policy – that is, a renewed interest in culture as lived and shared experience – is connected to globalization. This occurs through both an 'NGOization of social justice ... which governmentalizes counter-politics' (Yúdice, 2003, p. 37) and, by way of the joining of policy spheres that had previously been separated in modernist conceptions of policy-making, culture finding itself as 'being invoked to solve problems that previously were the province of economics and politics [and] ... resolve a range of problems for community, which seems to recognize itself in culture, which in turn has lost its specificity' (Yúdice, 2003, p. 25). Citizenship in particular has constituted itself as one of these domains in which culture as resource and culture as policy discourse are particularly likely to interact.

Culture and Citizenship

The concept of *citizenship* has been a core element of political philosophy, with debates about its nature and underpinnings ranging from the contributions of Socrates, Plato and Aristotle to the question of how to govern the Athenian city-state, to the American and French Revolutions of the late 18th century and the formation of modern liberal-democratic nation-states, to contemporary debates about the impacts of globalization and multiculturalism upon the nature of citizen identity in the 21st century. Hindess (1993) has defined citizenship as having three dimensions:

1. a *legal-political* dimension, based upon an egalitarian understanding of rights and duties, including the guarantee of legal rights of independence and equality before the law, the political rights of freedom of speech and association, and the right of citizens to participate in decisions concerning their governance, as part of their standing as independent persons;
2. a *national* dimension, or the existence of forms of exclusivity over the granting of citizen rights within a territorially defined community, and control by state authorities over formal admission into that community, including the right to deny admission, as well as requirements upon citizens to participate in the affairs of that community, including the defence of its territory;
3. a *cultural* dimension entailing, on the one hand, the sustaining of some form of moral community or 'common culture' among its citizens, as part of a binding sense of membership in a political community and, on the other, recognition and tolerance of difference, diversity and the rights of individuals to freedoms within the 'private' sphere.

Theories of citizenship emphasize the importance of its relationship to democracy, as well as questions of social inequality. T. H. Marshall's (1949) highly influential sequential conception of the historical development of citizenship saw the emergence of legal rights in the 17th and 18th centuries (such as the right to a fair trial, trial by jury, and the right to legal representation) as being reinforced in the 18th and 19th centuries by more formal political rights enshrined in liberal-democratic institutions such as the right to vote and the parliamentary system of government. Marshall proposed that the late 19th and early 20th centuries had seen a further layer of rights – economic and social rights – linked to citizenship, as the development of protective and redistributive institutions of the welfare state, provision of mass healthcare and education, as well as industrial bargaining frameworks that recognized the rights of trade unions (cf. Turner, 1997).

This framework for understanding citizenship and citizen rights has had some influence in thinking about media and communication. Using Marshall's historical typology of civil, political and social citizenship, Peter Golding and Graham Murdock (1989) proposed that communications policies that guaranteed citizenship rights would:

1. maximize access to information, particularly in areas most relevant to the rights of citizens;
2. provide all sections of the community with the broadest possible range of information, interpretation and debate of issues;
3. allow people from all sections of society to recognize themselves in the representations offered in communications media, and to be able to contribute to the development and shaping of these representations.

The necessary conditions for communications and information systems to achieve such goals are maximum possible diversity of provision, mechanisms for user feedback and participation, and universal access to services regardless of income, geographical location or social situation. In order to meet these criteria, Murdock argued that 'a communications system needs to be both diverse and open' (Murdock, 1992, p. 21).

Citizenship has long been connected to communications media. Popular media have been both the relay-points between the governing and the governed, for purposes of developing nations and citizen identities, and the places for articulating discontent with the unjust, illegitimate or unpopular uses of public authority. Modern forms of governance rest upon mediated interaction rather than direct speech and face-to-face communication, due to the size, complexity and diversity of modern nation-states. Jürgen Habermas' theory of the pubic sphere has been widely used to demonstrate the positive role that the nation-state can play in promoting citizen identities, by fostering access, diversity, pluralism and participation, either through media regulation or through directly funding public service or community-based media (Habermas, 1977; Garnham, 1990; Dahlgren, 1995). From a quite different angle, media theorists such as Hartley (1996, 1999) and McKee (2005) have presented popular media as being central to contemporary forms of citizenship, since media are the relay-point between the institutions of authority (governmental, educational and cultural institutions) and the broader population, who are increasingly constituted as readers, or users of media, as levels of literacy grow.

Debates about citizenship as understood in media and political theory intersect around the question of *cultural citizenship*, as it is the case that, whatever the significance of citizenship discourses in securing individual rights, including those of minorities, and promoting participatory democracy and an active and egalitarian sense of community, it has nonetheless been constituted within a system of nation-states. As Hindess has observed, the idea of a self-governing community 'presupposes identification in terms of a clear political demarcation of territory and population. There is an inside and an outside, and not much dispute about which is which' (Hindess, 1991, p. 176). This has meant that the category of citizen has been territorially based, it has co-existed with the fact that others are non-citizens (even within the same territorial boundaries), and that what has bound citizens into a political community is their participation in a common culture. Castles (1997) has outlined the challenge that globalization presents for the nationally based conception of citizenship:

> The concept of the nation-state usually implies a close link between ethnicity and political identity. The nation is usually seen as a group of people who belong together on the basis of shared language, culture, traditions and history – in other words an ethnic community. The state is defined as a political unit with territorial boundaries that coincide with ethnic ones. The state is meant to represent the political values of the nation. The nation-state concept implies ethno-cultural homogenization of the population. This can be achieved positively through institutions (such as schools, administration, church, national service) which transmit a common language and culture; or negatively through persecution of minorities and even 'ethnic cleansing'. This model of the nation-state finds it hard to cope with increasing migration and cultural diversity caused by globalization. (Castles, 1997, p. 5)

Cultural citizenship is one of the mechanisms for addressing this potential disconnect between political citizenship and ethno-cultural identity. In one sense, the problem is not a new one. Many nations were founded as ethnically and culturally diverse, and large-scale migration – particularly since 1945 – has greatly diversified the ethnic and cultural mix of most nations in the world. What is apparent, however, is that traditional governmental strategies for the management of culturally diverse populations, such as political exclusion of minorities, cultural assimilation, and limited tolerance of cultural diversity have increasingly proved inadequate, and have given way to more fully conceived notions of *multiculturalism*. Multiculturalism emerged in part out of the capacity of minority populations to engage in organized resistance to such strategies, but also because of the need for nations seeking to be globally competitive economically to promote the image of tolerance and cosmopolitanism in order to attract a globally mobile skilled workforce, and the extent to which apparent exclusion on ethnic, racial or cultural grounds is at odds with the formally democratic and egalitarian principles underpinning citizenship. Rosaldo (1994) has argued, in the US context, that the 'green-card phase' of multicultural citizenship, where the entry of minorities is tolerated only as long as they accept and abide by the rules of the dominant culture and its institutions, is being contested by those who believe that it is the institutions themselves that need to adapt to cultural diversity, and engage productively with plurality and difference, in order for full citizenship for all to be realized. Pakulski (1997, p. 77) has observed that 'claims for cultural citizenship involve not only tolerance of diverse identities but also – and increasingly – claims to dignified representation, normative accommodation, and active cultivation of these identities and their symbolic correlates'.

Understood in this way, three further implications of cultural citizenship follow. First, while it does entail political and resource claims at an institutional level – such as anti-discrimination legislation, strategies to promote equal employment opportunity, and provision of public resources to support cultural group identity and maintenance – it is as much about symbolic representation and ideas of the nation as an imagined community as it is about policy reform. As such, it is integrally connected to media representation and the dynamics of popular culture. Second, the ambit of cultural citizenship clearly extends beyond a concern for ethnic minorities and migrant communities, towards a spectrum of minority populations, including indigenous populations, lesbians and gay men, people with disabilities, religious minorities, and other people pursuing alternative lifestyles. If cultural citizenship involves 'the right to be "different", to re-value stigmatized identities ... [and] to embrace openly and legitimately hitherto marginalised lifestyles and to propagate them without hindrance' (Pakulski, 1997, p. 83), then it will inevitably transform 'mainstream' political and cultural institutions, and de-centre the dominant ethno-cultural identity. This may not only generate a cultural 'backlash' from hitherto dominant populations and an assertion of their own ethno-cultural rights,[3] but also can entail 'more extensive ... state interventions in the domains of cultural articulation, including the mass media and the educational institutions' (Pakulski, 1997, p. 83).

Third, and in contrast to the extension of economic and social rights associated with industrial legislation and the welfare state, it is not as clear as is sometimes presumed that the commercial market and economic globalization are at odds with the realization of minority cultural rights. There is considerable evidence that 'a global capitalism that seeks to attract new consuming publics as well as manage a diverse workforce ... should dress itself in all the trappings of multiculturalism and the empowerment of diversity' (Yúdice, 2003, p. 175). The merits of being able to trade media at a regional or global level by deracinating content, introducing cross-cultural referents or developing content which may work at different levels for local and international audiences is well known. Hollywood films such as the *Matrix* trilogy, *Kill Bill Vol. 1* and *Vol. 2*, and the *Rush Hour* films, to take a few examples, strongly foreground their influences in East Asian popular culture, thereby maximizing potential market share across geo-linguistic markets. McKee (2002) has also drawn attention to the extent to which a transnational 'Queer nation', with its own codes, signifying practices and formalities of citizenship, can be identified primarily though shared practices of consumption. At the same time, national cultural policies have in many instances been far less open to the cultural diversity of their constituent populations, giving preference to 'a conservationist vision of identity and to an integrationist view based on traditional cultural goods and institutions' (Canclini, 2000, p. 129). In considering how adequately or otherwise government policies and institutions respond to the challenge of 'rethinking citizenship to make it appropriate for a culturally diverse nation ... [in] the 21st century' (Castles, 1997, p. 21), we should lose sight neither of the productivity and innovation of the corporate sector in inserting its own commercial products into such spaces, nor of the question which has long driven citizenship discourses, namely the role for the state in addressing those communities and practices not adequately reached by capitalism and the commercial market.

East Asian Popular Culture

The rise of East Asian nations as cultural producers of global media content has been widely noted. The significance of the Hong Kong film industry and Japanese animation has long been recognized (see e.g. Bordwell, 2000; Iwabuchi, 2002; Curtin, 2003), and countries such as Taiwan and South Korea have become global production sites for animated television (famously

satirized on *The Simpsons*, which has itself outsourced production to South
Korea). Since the late 1990s, the range and depth of such East Asian cultural
production have grown immensely, ranging from the film booms in countries
such as South Korea and Thailand (Leong, 2002; Lewis, 2003), to the
phenomenal success of online gaming in South Korea (Herz, 2002), the rise of
'Canto-pop' as a global musical form, and the success of 'crossover' Chinese
cinema such as *Crouching Tiger, Hidden Dragon, Hero*, and *House of Flying
Daggers*. Even countries which have traditionally focused upon communications hardware rather than cultural software, such as Singapore, are developing their own exportable television programmes, such as the animated
children's programme *Tomato Twins* (Lim, 2004).

Beng Huat Chua (2004) has proposed that a distinctive East Asian popular
culture has been emerging around the desires and cultural consumption
patterns of a rising young urban middle class rather than state-sponsored official culture. In contrast to other attempts to assert Asian cultural distinctiveness, such as neo-Confucianism and the 'Asian values' debate, Chua observes
that 'Popular cultural products criss-cross borders everyday in East Asia [and]
East Asian popular culture has been able to carve out a significant segment of
the regional consumption economy' (Chua, 2004, p. 218). Importantly, this is
not something which happens as an alternative to flows of American and
other 'Western' popular culture, but is instead reflective of a dramatic growth
in patterns of cultural consumption among an identifiable segment of the
various East Asian national populations. This demographic are typically
under 30, based in major cities, linked into global economic and cultural
circuits as a result of their employment activities or overseas education, and
very technologically and culturally literate. This group are the beneficiaries of
rapid economic growth based upon globalization and the adoption of new
technologies, and wear a commitment to modernity and cultural hybridity like
a badge (or, perhaps more likely, like a mobile phone ring tone). With the rise
of China economically, and with this the rise of a Chinese urban middle class
that may number 100 million people by 2010, such trends can only be
expected to accelerate.

Chua argues that it is still unclear what the relationship is between intra-
Asian cultural flows, the question of an East Asian cultural identity, and the
broader political and ideological implications of such developments. He
proposes, nonetheless, five hypotheses on how the circulation of such cultural
products 'may work ... to create a discursive and imaginative space for the
emergence of such an identity' (Chua, 2004, p. 216). First, East Asian popular
television dramas strongly foreground urban identities, and hence efface
connections between the 'traditional' and the rural. Second, the focus upon
young, urban and single professionals is at odds with the focus on the family
in Confucian culture. Third, these programmes identify a comparable level of

'lifestyle consumption' among middle-class professionals, and do not draw attention to different income relativities across the region. Fourth, youth are constructed as 'beautiful', and 'pan-Asian' in their visual features, again not drawing attention to national differences. Finally, and in contrast to the project of implicit socialization seen as central to Confucian identity formation, Chua stresses that 'the construction of a pan East Asian identity is a conscious ideological product for the producers of East Asian cultural products, based on the commercial desire of capturing a larger audience and market' (Chua, 2004, p. 217).

Further reading: Ong (1999); Iwabuchi (2002); Ho *et al.* (2003); Chua (2004); Moran and Keane (2004); Tay (2005).

Global Culture, Identity and Hybridity

Given the ambivalences surrounding the relationship between globalization and culture, it is perhaps not surprising that the concept of *hybridity* has proved to be increasingly central to understandings of the relationship between global media, culture and identity. This book will not explore in depth the burgeoning literature on post-colonialism (see e.g. Spivak, 1990; Young, 1990; Bhabha, 1994; cf. McRobbie, 2005b), but will rather pursue the more modest aim of noting how the concept of hybridity in the context of globalization cuts across some of the dominant popular understandings of the impact of global media. The concept of hybridity also suggests the possibility that identity-formation in the context of globalization may not so much be suppressed as in fact proliferate, and how this can in turn be connected to its relationship to modernity. In doing so, I note Tomlinson's observation, discussed earlier, that 'far from destroying it, globalization has been perhaps the most significant force in *creating* and *proliferating* cultural identities' (Tomlinson, 2003, p. 16).

Jan Nederveen Pieterse (2004) presents the case for hybridity being the *leitmotif* of globalization. He does so by contrasting the hybridity paradigm to two other common popular understanding of the cultural impact of globalization. The first is that of cultural differentiation, most strongly developed in the work of Samuel Huntington (2000). Huntington's theory of the *clash of civilizations* foresaw a hardening of divisions between 'civilizational spheres' – defined as a loose admixture of nation-states, geographical regions, religious identities, language groups and cultural practices – between the Christian-humanist West, the Islamic Middle East, and the Confucian cultures of East Asia. Not surprisingly, Huntington's thesis received quite a kick along after the events of 11 September 2001, and the plethora of territorial conflicts (Afghanistan, Iraq, Israeli entry into Lebanon) and terrorist acts (the Bali, Madrid and London bombings) that have been subsequent to it.[4] The second perspective is that of *cultural convergence and homogenization*, or what has been termed 'McDonaldization', after the globally expansive fast-food restaurant chain (Ritzer, 1993; Barber, 2000). From this perspective, McDonaldization is synonymous with the global spread of a particular set of American values whose material and symbolic forms, values and work practices are represented by that food chain. Barber points to a global condition that increasingly will constitute 'one McWorld tied together by communications, information, entertainment, and commerce' (Barber, 2000, p. 21), and to which the only effective form of resistance has thus far been the austere, pre-modern ethos of the Jihadists, who have acquired growing influence among Muslims worldwide.

Pieterse presents cultural hybridity and cultural mixing as a more plausible point between these two perspectives. Observing that globalization simultaneously involves an 'awareness of the world "becoming smaller" and cultural difference receding' and 'a growing sensitivity to cultural difference', he argues that the notion of cultural difference has itself changed form:

> It used to take the form of national differences, as in familiar discussions of national character or identity. Now different forms of difference have come to the foreground, such as gender and identity politics, ethnic and religious movements, minority rights, and indigenous peoples. (Pieterse, 2004, pp. 41–2)

In contrast to the 'clash of civilizations' approach, which is based upon fixed and discrete understanding of cultural difference, hybridity theories draw attention to its fluidity, open-endedness and interconnectedness, of which global media flows are an important constitutive element. Similarly, while cultural homogenization arguments point to the domination of one culture over another on the basis of its economic advantages, theories of hybridity and hybridization point to the complexities and adaptation processes that occur when cultural forms derived from one place are forced to make contact with the diverse formations of identity, culture and practice that have emerged elsewhere:

> Hybridization is an antidote to the cultural differentialism of racial and nationalist doctrines because it takes as its point of departure precisely those experiences that have been banished, marginalized, tabooed in cultural differentialism. It subverts nationalism because it privileges border-crossing. It subverts identity politics such as ethnic or other claims to purity or authenticity because it starts out from the fuzzi-

ness of boundaries. If modernity stands for an ethos of order and neat separation by tight boundaries, hybridization reflects a postmodern sensibility of cut 'n' mix, transgression, subversion. (Pieterse, 2004, p. 53)

Pieterse summarizes the different paradigms for the interpretation of cultural difference as shown in Table 5.1.

Table 5.1 Three ways of seeing cultural difference

Dimension	Differentialism	Convergence	Mixing
Cosmologies	Purity	Emanation	Synthesis
Analytics	Territorial culture	Cultural centres and diffusion	Translocal culture
Lineages	Differences in religion, language, region, class or caste	Imperial and religious universalisms	Cultural mixing of technologies, languages, religions
Modern times	Romantic differentialism Race thinking, chauvinism Cultural relativism	Rational universalism Modernization Coca-colonization	Métissage, creolization, syncretism
Present	'Clash of civilizations' Ethnic cleansing	McDonaldization, Disneyfication	Postmodern culture, transnational cultural flows, cut 'n' mix
Futures	Mosaic of immutably different cultures and civilizations	Global cultural homogeneity	Open-ended ongoing mixing

Source: Pieterse (2004), p. 55

The concept of hybridity is not without its critics. Critical theorists such as Dirlik (1994) and Murdock (2004) have argued that the concept of hybridity has been constructed in overly positive terms, as affording 'a continuously productive generation of novel combinations opening new spaces for expression and identity' (Murdock, 2004, p. 28), that neglect material realities of class inequality, global capitalism and cultural dispossession. They also question the newness of phenomena such as large-scale migration and cultural mixing. Responding to such criticisms, Pieterse (2004) argues that hybridity entails three sets of claims:

1. the *empirical* claim that, with the increasingly intense global circulation of people, ideas and commodities, there is a greater degree of cultural intermixing occurring than ever before, with implications for how we think about relationships between culture, citizenship and policy;

2. the *theoretical* claim that such cultural intermixing has broader implications for how we conceive of culture more generally, in particular bringing
   a recognition that the idea of the ethnically homogeneous nation-state may
   be a particular product of European history that was never paralleled in
   those societies which were subject to colonial rule, and is of declining
   global significance today;
3. the *normative* claim that the challenging of boundaries is a positive political development, akin to the intellectual advances associated with postmodernism and deconstruction in challenging binary logics, just as
   hybridity is associated with deterritorialization and the emergence of
   cosmopolitan, post-national forms of cultural identity.

The empirical argument that cultural intermixing is a distinctive feature of
early-21st-century societies is a strong one although, as Hirst and Thompson
(1996) argue, not one without historical precedent: they note, for instance, the
large transcontinental movements in the period from 1850 to 1914. While the
level of migration of people in the period since 1945 is not historically unique,
it does nonetheless substantially outweigh previous generations of mass
migration (Held *et al.*, 1999, pp. 299–314). Moreover, large-scale migration
in the late 20th and early 21st centuries has some features that make it distinctive when compared to earlier epochs: the fact that people are now typically
moving from one state to another; their impact upon already formed nation-
states and notions of national culture; the ease with which people can move
between countries in a variety of capacities – tourist, student, advisor, professional, guest worker – using advanced air transportation systems; and the
intersections between the large-scale movement of people, and the creation of
diasporic communities worldwide, and increasing access to globally distributed media.

The concept of hybridity has also been important in de-centring a dominant
evolutionary meta-narrative around globalization, by drawing attention to the
diversity of contexts and experiences which lead different parts of the world
into globalized circuits of capitalist modernity. The Western European experience has typically been one where already established states, many of which
were formed in the late 18th and 19th centuries, have come to experience
globalization as a challenge to an already established national territorial
sovereignty, where a degree of congruity existed between polity, economy and
culture. Indeed, in some notable instances, such as Great Britain, France and,
to a lesser extent, Spain and Portugal, it comes after they have engaged in their
own exercises in exporting forms of capitalist modernity through the administration of empires. By contrast, for the post-colonial states of Asia, Africa,
the Caribbean and the Middle East, the issue was more one of attempting to
put in place the economic and cultural policy infrastructures that were seen as

markers of sovereignty for newly independent states. The final report of the 1982 UNESCO World Conference on Cultural Policies in Mexico City, for instance, referred to 'young states ... affirming their personality, building up and developing their national cultures with dignity' (UNESCO, 1982, p. 8). The Latin American case may be different again, with the inherent hybridity and instability of the various national cultural formations leading analysts such as Yúdice to suggest that 'Latin America sets the precedent of post-modernity long before the notion appears in the Euro-North American context ... the heterogeneous character of Latin American social and cultural formations made it possible for discontinuous, alternative, and hybrid forms to emerge that challenged the hegemony of the *grand récit* of modernity' (Yúdice, 1992, p. 1). Even in the so-called 'white settler' or 'dominion capitalist' states such as Australia, Canada, South Africa and New Zealand, where cultural nationalists have historically bemoaned the absence of 'the "social glue" of a shared symbolic culture, which nationalist theory insists is the *sine qua non* of political stability and legitimate political institutions' (Collins, 1990, p. xii), it may be that they are reflective of a broader historical experience where, as Tom O'Regan puts it, 'limited and shared sovereignty is nothing new' (O'Regan, 1993, p. 101). Put simply, then, the notion of *strong citizenship*, where national institutional structures have sought to bind citizens to the state through transmission of a common language, culture and national identity (a shared symbolic culture), may be more historically and geographically specific to the Western European experience than is often assumed. The concept of hybridity, taken in a historical context, is a timely reminder that, for most of the world's populations, a weaker notion of national citizenship and cultural sovereignty has long existed, and global media inserts itself into the complex cultural mosaic, rather than suddenly appearing as the 'wolf at the door', or the new and ubiquitous threat to national culture.

The claim that hybridity points to a wider tendency towards *deterritorialization*, signifying the disintegration of nationally based boundaries and binaries in a postmodern collage of thought, and the emergence of a cosmopolitan, post-national consciousness, is more problematic. Pieterse (2004) concludes his discussion of the 'global mélange' characteristic of the intersection of globalization and hybridity in terms of the necessary and inevitable decline of the nation-state:

> The nation state bonds that have exerted such great influence grew out of sedentary experiences, agriculture, urbanism, and then industry as anchors of the national economy. The nation state inherited older territorial imperatives, and 'national interest' translated them into geo-political and geo-strategic niches and projects. Together they make up a real estate vision of history ... The moment we shift lenses

from sedentary to mobile categories the whole environment and the horizon change: hunting, nomadic pastoralism, fishing, trade, transnational enterprise, and hyperspace all have deterritorialization built in. Why should identity be centred on sedentary rather than mobile categories if mobility defines the species as much as settlement does? Why should analysis privilege real estate rather than mobility? (Pieterse, 2004, p. 116)

Variants of such arguments, which associate postmodern thought with globalization, and welcome the decline of the nation-state and cultural nationalism, can be found elsewhere (see e.g. Milner, 1991; Mani, 1992). There are, I would argue, two factors driving such analyses. The first is the desire for *cosmopolitanism*, or a vision of a common humanity united by something other than nationalism. It connects to citizenship discourses since, as David Held has argued, 'there is only a historically contingent connection between the principles underpinning citizenship and the national community' (Held, 2004, p. 115). Visions of a citizenship that transcends nationhood have existed across political boundaries. Stuart Hall has observed that the perspective of the 'great discourses of modernity' such as Marxism and liberalism, 'attachments to nation, like those of tribe, region, place, religion, were thought to be archaic particularisms which capitalist modernity would, gradually or violently, dissolve or supersede' (Hall, 1993a, p. 353). The problem with cosmopolitanism when framed in this manner is that it tends to be a minority sentiment, held on the one hand by intellectuals impatient with what they see as the 'archaic particularisms' of local and national cultures, and on the other as the ideology of a geographically mobile and culturally 'modernizing' class fraction, which may be termed the 'Frequent Flyer' class of international business people, government officials and, indeed, academics. For Immanuel Wallerstein, this is the vision of 'world culture, the humanism of many sages', which can 'overcome the provincialism ... of cultural particularisms' (Wallerstein, 1991, p. 103). He is sceptical of such claims, arguing that world history has not been characterized by cultural homogenization, but rather by no less powerful trends towards cultural differentiation, with strong 'gravitational forces restraining the centrifugal tendencies and organizing them ... [and] the single most powerful such gravitational force has been the nation-state' (Wallerstein, 1991, p. 96).

The contemporary defence of cosmopolitanism identifies it less as what Bruce Robbins terms 'an ideal of detachment' from local communities and particular cultural identities, than as 'a reality of (re)attachment, multiple attachment, or attachment at a distance' (Robbins, 1998, p. 3). Aihwa Ong's (1999) work on the 'flexible citizenship' experienced by geographically mobile professionals of the Chinese diaspora draws attention to a form of 'thinking and feeling' that is not necessarily tied to the nations in which members of this professional-managerial class find themselves at particular times. At a more generalized level, Tomlinson (1999) wonders whether a cosmopolitan mode of experience is being made available to more people, both through the greatly increased opportunities to travel, and the more 'mundane cosmopolitanism' of routine exposure to cultural difference and the wider world through communications media.

The second plank of such debates concerns *deterritorialization*. The term operates in two very different intellectual registers. In the work of Gilles Deleuze and Félix Guattari where it has its origins (Deleuze and Guattari, 1987), the 'territory' refers to a space (social, psychological, environmental) that is constituted by some form of group, to which a person may routinely return. In this respect, deterritorialization in its relative sense always leaves open the possibility of reterritorialization, or a return to another group space; it is only the possibility of absolute deterritorialization, or the impossibility of ever being reterritorialized, that leaves the plane of territory altogether.[5] This is a very different usage to Néstor García Canclini's understanding of deterritorialization as 'the loss of the "natural" relation of culture to geography and social territories' (Canclini, 1995, p. 229), or to John Tomlinson's argument that:

> The idea that globalized culture is hybrid culture has a strong intuitive appeal which follows directly from the notion of deterritorialization. This is because the increasing traffic between cultures that the globalization process brings suggests that the dissolution of the link between culture and place is accompanied by an intermingling of these disembedded cultural practices producing new complex hybrid forms of culture. (Tomlinson, 1999, p. 141)

Tomlinson's approach to deterritorialization refers to the lack of congruity between particular cultures and the dominant cultural co-ordinates of the geographical spaces in which they are located. It refers, for instance, to Sikhs in London, Salvadoreans in Los Angeles, Vietnamese in Sydney, or Muslims in Paris, who live in a territorially defined location, but may struggle to belong to that place in a wider sense, since its forms of belonging as defined by genealogies of cultural meaning and history have been created independently of them. In that respect, a diasporic identity, which is neither that of a place of origin nor of a current locale, but is a new form of 'imagined community', may indeed constitute a form of deterritorialization, or a reconfiguring of the relationship between culture, place and identity. Such arguments are plausible, particularly insofar as they draw upon the contribution of theories of hybridity as a way of moving debates about global media and cultural citizenship out of a particular Western European frame where citizenship = nation/state/people. Deterritorialization is thus best understood as concerning debates about citizenship, culture and identity within nation-states, and about a non-class-specific form of cosmopolitanism, rather than as a practical application of Deleuzian thought.

The debate on nationalism and cosmopolitanism, and its implications for future understandings of citizenship, will continue to be an important one. Discussions about the crises of national culture in managing cultural diversity and emergent claims of cultural citizenship are related to the implications of theories of hybridity, and challenge a tendency towards state-centredness in the social sciences (Tomlinson, 1999, pp. 104–6; cf. Taylor, 1996). At the same time, the claim that globalization leads to a weakening of nation-states has certainly been strongly contested, particularly insofar as the claim hinges upon cultural pluralization weakening the institutional and policy frameworks of nation-states.

From Sovereignty to Software: National Media Policies in an Age of Global Media

6

Introduction: Beyond National Culture?

In the last chapter, we drew attention to the central place of culture in the defining of nations and citizenship. In a trajectory whose origins can be formally traced to the French Revolution of 1789, media and cultural policy has had a role of establishing formal and informal relationships between nation-states and people, by endowing national populations with a common national culture and national identity. Globalization in its various manifestations challenges this relationship between nation, culture and identity, although its impact is uneven globally. While globalization in its economic sense does not, for the most part, mark erasure of the significance of space, place, and identity, it does nonetheless involve the media and creative industries working productively with it, harnessing specialized resources of labour, talent and creativity across national boundaries to develop value-added cultural commodities for increasingly heterogeneous cultures and more variegated communities. Nonetheless, there continues to be a 'preference for the local' in a variety of forms of media and cultural consumption which, if met by suitably pro-active public policies, can redress trends towards 'Global Hollywood', cultural homogenization and Western cultural imperialism. Such trends have been identified in the emergence of an East Asian popular culture and, albeit more problematically, in cultural reconversion in Latin America.

This chapter will ask the question of what this means for media and cultural policy. Media and cultural policy has its origins – with some differences and nuances based upon the sectors and countries in question – in the capacities developed by the regulatory and protective state. It is this nationalist and managerial conception of policy that is in question. At the same time, there is a need for caution (as there is in the globalization literature generally) in seeing such developments as synonymous with the decline of the nation-state. It will be argued that, insofar as media and cultural policy is being increasingly oriented towards creative industries developmental strategies, there is a gradual but important shift in the *loci* of media and cultural policy. At one level, this sees local or sub-national strategies associated with creative-cities and creative-clusters initiatives becoming increasingly important as drivers of policy. At the same time, it also sees supra-national policy formations emerging, around global and regional organizations, international trade agreements, and the rise of transnational civil society organizations (international non-governmental organizations, or INGOs), as well as those of the corporate sector. This does not point to the elimination of the nation-state as a – if not still the – central site of policy and governance over media and culture in the 21st century, but rather suggests that such national agencies will see their effective political power and decision-making capacity 'shared and bartered by diverse forces and agencies at national, regional and international levels' (Held *et al.*, 1999, p. 80), as well as at local, sub-cultural and sub-national levels.

Media Policy and the Regulatory State

Media policy has been central to the development of media in all of its forms. Government policy institutions regulate the ownership, production and distribution of media, and seek to manage and shape cultural practices in order to direct media institutions towards particular policy goals. While the rhetoric of the media as the 'Fourth Estate' – the independent and impartial observers and watchdogs upon governments and other powerful interests – has prevailed in many countries, it has historically been the case that, as James Michael has observed, 'regulation of the media of communication is as old as blood feuds over insults, and ... as classic an issue as deciding whose turn it is to use the talking drum or the ram's horn' (Michael, 1990, p. 40). The freedom to communicate has been constrained by general civil and criminal law, as well as by laws and regulations specific to the media. Legal elements that are not specific to the media, but which impact upon its operations, include laws of defamation, copyright, contempt, *sub judice*, vilification, obscenity, blasphemy and sedition. Media organizations are also subject to a series of technical, marketplace and conduct regulations over elements of ownership, content and performance, both as general forms of industry regulation (for example, laws to ensure competitive markets), and regulations that are specific to the media, by virtue of their unique role as an instrument of public communication.

Print media have typically been less subject to government controls, and certainly less subject to industry-specific forms of regulation, at least in liberal-democratic societies. By contrast, broadcast media have been subject to an extensive mix of government regulations, which in most countries included the establishment of *public broadcasters*, who in many cases had monopoly control over radio and television until as late as the 1980s. Rationales for media regulation have included:

- concerns about their potential impact on children and other 'vulnerable' individuals (Hutchison, 2004);
- the ability to use such media for citizen-formation and the development of a national cultural identity (Gellner, 1983; Mattelart, 1994; Schudson, 1994);
- implied rights of public participation and involvement associated with the significance of media as forms of public communication, and possible tensions between their nature as a common cultural resource and private ownership (Horwitz, 1989; Streeter, 1995);
- 'public good' elements of the media commodity, including non-rivalrous and non-excludable elements of access and consumption, and the costs of production being largely unrelated to the costs of access or consumption (Collins *et al.*, 1988);
- 'market failure' possibilities in a purely commercial media system, including:
  - ☐ a tendency towards monopoly or oligopoly due to the prevalence of economies of scale and scope, and resulting entry barriers for potential new competitors (Picard, 1989; Litman, 1990);
  - ☐ lack of product diversity and provision to minority audiences due to the commercial benefits derived from audience maximization (Herman, 1997);
  - ☐ the potential to avoid higher-cost forms of programming – particularly that which is locally produced – where such programme genres can be imported, and local production can be focused upon low-cost programme formats (Australian Broadcasting Tribunal, 1991).

A useful distinction can be made between *input-based* forms of policy intervention, typically involving subsidizing the production of cultural activity, and *output-based* forms, involving regulations designed to encourage and manage the distribution and exhibition of media and cultural products (cf. Ham and Hill, 1993; Flew and Cunningham, 1997). The creative and performing arts, whose modes of production have characteristically been considered as artisanal, one-off, and focused upon specific forms of creative self-expression, have typically attracted a subsidy or input-based approach; sectors such as film have also attracted public subsidy insofar as their outputs have been considered to be either art and/or a significant contribution to the national cultural patrimony. By contrast, broadcast media have typically been considered to be industrial in nature, and have attracted a regulatory or output-based approach. In the latter case, this has varied across a continuum from a highly regulated free-to-air TV broadcasting industry to the virtual open market in 'media of choice' such as film, video, and the digital content industries. In the age of mass access to the Internet, such distinctions are further complicated, as the Internet is a conduit for content which ranges freely and promiscuously across the domains of print, broadcast and telecommunications media, necessitating a rethinking of domain-specific media regulation as distinct from more generic forms of regulation by convergent entities, such as the United Kingdom's Office of Communication (Ofcom) (Collins and Murroni, 1996; Tambini, 2002; Cunningham, 2005a).

Public policy principles associated with the management of media industry structure and media content relate in a broader sense to the vision of a *regulatory state* that oversees and manages the conduct and behaviour of media institutions according to 'public interest' criteria on behalf of a national citizenry. Broadcast media emerged in the period from the 1930s to the 1960s when there was a broad political consensus that the state had a central role in economic management, either as the owner of important public instrumentalities, or in extensively regulating their conduct if they were in private hands. In the wake of the Great Depression of the 1930s and World War II (1939–45), public ownership or regulation emerged alongside national economic planning, the welfare state, and Keynesian demand management for full employment as one of the central planks of liberalism and social democracy. In the US context, Horwitz (1989, pp. 25, 26) refers to a 'progressive' belief that 'democratic governmental power reconciled the tension between the needs of powerless consumers and the productive might of the corporation', and that 'the administrative process [operated] not only to protect powerless consumers, but also to effect rationality and fairness in the economy generally'. In the context of broadcast media, such regulatory processes took the form of a *social contract* between commercial broadcasters and government regulators as guardians of the 'public interest' (Flew, 2002, 2006a). The concept of the 'public interest' in broadcasting arises, as Streeter (1995) observed, from the dual nature of the airwaves (spectrum) as a public resource and as private property, meaning that access to the airwaves was seen as a 'gift' of a public resource for private uses, which broadcasters held as a form of *public trust*, and that governments could impose reciprocal 'pro-social' regulations around areas such as national content quotas, local programming requirements, children's programmes and complaints-handling procedures (cf. Flew, 2003b).

Cultural Policy and the Protective State: the State in its Ordinary Dimension

Media policy has not developed in isolation from other spheres of public policy, and in the second half of the 20th century it was increasingly linked to *cultural policy*. In its earliest incarnations, such as the establishment of the Arts Council of Great Britain in 1946, cultural policy was largely synonymous with arts policy. Lury (1994) has argued that British cultural policy in the 1950s and 1960s largely consisted of 'a series of preventative moves to preserve traditional forms of art (alternatively put, high art forms, that is opera, theatre, the visual arts, dance and literature) from market forces ... This was an explicit attempt to maintain a national cultural heritage, both for its own sake and as some kind of bulwark against the rise of consumerism and what was then called mass culture' (Lury, 1994, p. 140). While the 1960s and 1970s saw some broadening of this agenda, particularly in terms of extending access to the arts for lower-income and other disadvantaged communities, and the emergence of a more participatory community arts agenda (cf. Hawkins, 1993), it nonetheless remained the case that, for Britain and other so-called 'Anglo-Saxon' nations such as Australia and New Zealand, cultural policy was largely non-existent. What instead emerged was a demarcated realm of arts policy, based upon the largely *ad hoc* funding of individual artists and arts companies, peer assessment of quality, and an agenda of promoting artistic excellence as a bulwark of national culture (Williams, 1989).

A more dynamic and integrative conception of cultural policy emerged in Europe in the post-WWII period. The leading nation in this respect was France, with the formal creation of the *Ministre d'État chargé des affaires culturelles* (Minister of State in charge of cultural affairs) in the Gaullist Fifth Republic in 1959, and the appointment of André Malraux as head of this new Ministry. Malraux's broad trajectory for national cultural policy identified three clear tasks for such a policy: heritage, creation and democratization. The concept of *heritage* foresaw a role for the state in distributing the 'eternal products of the imagination' in the most equitable and effective manner throughout the national population: the construction, and renovation, of museums, galleries and other exhibitionary spaces both within and outside of the major cities was one of the major tasks of a national cultural policy. Further, the state had an ongoing role in promoting the *creation* of new artistic and cultural works, and needed to use public funding to provide a catalytic role in the creation of new works, with the associated need for support of artists and cultural workers. Finally, and perhaps most controversially, the objective of *democratization* constituted an activist role for cultural policy in redressing socio-economic inequalities by cultural means. Such a critique raised the issue of whether cultural policy largely entailed *action culturelle*, or cultural policy-makers identifying and supporting cultural activities and institutions in ways that bring these closer to people, communities and societies, which activists and critics saw as being essentially about the national distribution of 'great works', or *action socioculturelle*, whereby culture is understood as being principally constituted by the activities of people and communities, and cultural policy-makers need to realign their understandings of the role and purpose of cultural policy accordingly (Looseley, 1995).

The Malrauxian conception of cultural policy explicitly linked the cultural policy domain to questions of citizenship. At one level, it modernized the Republican conception of culture inaugurated with the French Revolution of 1789, particularly the idea that art treasures and monuments were understood to be the property of the nation and the responsibility of the state (*patrimoine culturel*). At the same time, it was responding to the challenge that media globalization, and particularly Hollywood cinema, presented to national cultural industries, by seeking to consolidate a national cultural infrastructure in the audiovisual industries and other sites of global cultural trade, in the spirit of *le défi américain* (Caughie, 1990; Schlesinger, 1991a). It foresaw a role for the nation-state as the *animateur*, not simply of publicly subsidized arts and 'high' culture, but of culture in what Armand Mattelart describes as its *ordinary dimension*, or what, following Michel Foucault's work on governmentality (Foucault, 1982, 1991), are 'the procedures and acts by which the government of subjects and situations becomes operational' (Mattelart, 1994, p. 193).

The vision of cultural policy as an instrument of national integration came to constitute the default setting for UNESCO strategies on how to develop a national cultural policy for the newly independent post-colonial states of Asia, Africa and the Middle East (UNESCO, 1982). With European integration and the development of the European Union, it also came to reside at the core of European cultural policy, particularly in international trade negotiations involving the United States (Galperin, 1999). It has been aligned in media and communications policy to the notion of the *protective state*, that engages in the audiovisual space through 'communicative boundary maintenance' (Schlesinger, 1991a, p. 162). This occurs in part through measures to control global media flows, that may range from banning ownership of satellite dishes to local-content quotas, to controls over foreign ownership and control of media. It may also involve more pro-active measures to stimulate local media production, ranging from subsidies and other incentives (such as tax incentives) to support local cultural production, particularly in high-cost media such as film, to support for publicly funded broadcasting which has a programming mandate to cater for national identity and community, as well as recognizing and responding to linguistic and cultural diversity within the nation (cf. Grant and Wood, 2004). It refers to measures to restrict the impact of and exposure to imported (principally American) media product among its national audiences.

There is a second dimension of cultural policy operating here, which may be better referred to as the policy of the *integrative state*, whereby the agencies and instruments of media and cultural policy are engaged in 'nationing' a people, or generating a common national culture that provides a repertoire of images, symbols, concepts and popular imaginings that enable diverse populations to conceive of themselves as part of a nation. In the Latin American context, Martín-Barbero (1993) has drawn attention to the nation-building mission of some Latin American states from the 1930s onward, where the state financially supported local cultural production, particularly national cinema, so that the people would receive images of themselves, their imaginings, and their history. Where it was successful, as in Mexico until the 1970s, 'film formed [the people] into a national body; not in the sense of giving them a nationality but in the way they experienced being a single nation' (Martín-Barbero, 1993, p. 166).

The Limits of Cultural Policy in the Contemporary Global Media Context

Craik *et al.* define cultural policy as 'the range of cultural practices, products and forms of circulation and consumption that are organised and subject to domains of policy' (Craik *et al.*, 2002, p. 159). To this end, they identify the four critical domains of cultural policy as being:

- *arts and culture*, including direct funding to cultural producers, and funding of cultural institutions, such as libraries, museums, galleries and performing arts centres, and the funding of cultural agencies responsible for such funding administration;
- *communications and media*, including policy mechanisms to fund and support broadcast media (both publicly funded and commercial), and policies related to new media technologies, multimedia, publishing, design, and digital rights management in a convergent media environment;
- *citizenship and identity*, including language policy, cultural development policy, multiculturalism, diasporic identities, cultural tourism, and questions of national symbolic identity;

■ *spatial culture*, including urban and regional culture and heritage, urban and regional planning, cultural heritage management, cultural tourism, leisure and recreation.

Any cultural policy presents two questions for policy-makers, and these questions have become increasingly urgent over time. The first concerns the breadth and reach of cultural policy, or the question of where culture as an object of government begins and ends. The debate in French cultural policy between *action culturelle*, or the use of public resources to make available to citizens those forms which the state deems to be cultural, and *action socio-culturelle*, or culture that is defined through the actions and activities of the people that are facilitated through state cultural policies, is one manifestation of this. The second question for cultural policy is the relationship between publicly funded and supported cultural forms and cultural commodities produced and distributed through the commercial market. In work undertaken for UNESCO in the early 1980s, Augustin Girard observed that national cultural policies had promoted state-funded cultural activities with limited impact, while largely ignoring and often condemning the commercial sector, and that 'far more is done to democratise and decentralise culture with the industrial products available on the market than with the "products" subsidised by the public authorities' (Girard, 1982, p. 25). In the context of local government cultural policy initiatives in 1980s Britain, Nicholas Garnham reached a similar conclusion, that 'Most people's cultural needs and aspirations are being, for better or worse, supplied by the market as goods and services. If one turns one's back on an analysis of that dominant cultural process, one cannot understand either the culture of our time or the challenges and opportunities which that dominant culture offers to public policy makers' (Garnham, 1987, pp. 24–5).

We can identify three points of dispersal of cultural policy as it has been traditionally conceived (cf. Flew, 2005c). In the first instance, there is the

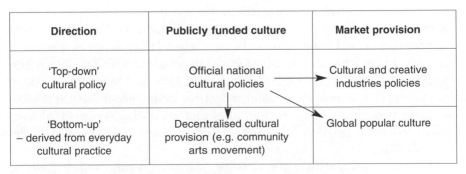

Direction	Publicly funded culture	Market provision
'Top-down' cultural policy	Official national cultural policies	Cultural and creative industries policies
'Bottom-up' – derived from everyday cultural practice	Decentralised cultural provision (e.g. community arts movement)	Global popular culture

Figure 6.1 The dispersal of cultural policy

demand for decentralization and a 'bottom-up' approach drawn from the consumption practices of the people, rather than the definitional edicts of the state. Second, there is the demand for a more explicit recognition of the importance of the market – particularly for media-related cultural goods and services – that would come to be central to cultural industries and creative industries policies. Finally, with the spread of global popular media, there is a move in demand away from the cultural forms underwritten by the nation-state through cultural policy towards global cultural commodities. This state of affairs can be represented graphically as shown in Figure 6.1.

Creative Industries Policy and the Enabling State

The 1990s were a key decade for cultural policy development. The signing of the General Agreement on Trade in Services (GATS) in Marrakesh in 1994 – after the famous stand-off between the United States and the European Union on the question of trade liberalization in audiovisual media policy – seemed to many to signal the gradual demise of national cultural policies that incorporated a protectionist approach towards the inexorable rise of global media and creative industries. Moreover, the tide of media production, consumption and corporate strategy seemed to be pointing towards the rapid expansion of 'Global Hollywood' and a global popular culture based upon the deracinated products of US film and television. At the same time, there was a surge of interest in developing national policies for ICT development, as the implications of the Internet's take-off as a mass global communications medium became more apparent to governments worldwide. As the convergence of computing, telecommunications and media content became more an issue requiring government stewardship, media policy in particular came to be increasingly seen as an element of *national information policy*. As a result, there was greater attention being paid to the use of public policy to promote technological change by incubating the 'content industries' as 'new growth industries', and establishing national media and ICT industries as 'players at the table' of the emergent global information economy (OECD, 1998, 1999; cf. Mattelart, 2003, pp. 99–127; Flew, 2005a; Flew and McElhinney, 2005). This came at a time when cultural industries development initiatives were gradually percolating upwards from local and regional government authorities to the policy platforms of national governments (Hesmondhalgh and Pratt, 2005).

The Australian government's *Creative Nation: Commonwealth Cultural Policy* statement, released in 1994, is in many respects an emblematic transitional document. Arising in the latter stages of the centre-left Australian Labor Party's control over national government, and coming out of at least five years of rethinking of Federal government cultural funding and how to better integrate arts, media and communications policies, the statement constituted a fascinating mix of the traditional concerns of national cultural policy to foster national cultural citizenship and identity, and strategies to harness the media and cultural sectors as industries able to generate competitive advantage in the global economy. Its statement about the importance of a national cultural policy – in a nation which had traditionally eschewed such grand cultural gestures – could easily have been taken from a speech by André Malraux, or a UNESCO policy handbook of the 1970s:

> To speak of Australian culture is to recognise our common heritage. It is to say that we share ideas, values, sentiments and traditions, and that we see in all the various manifestations ... what it means to be Australian. Culture ... concerns identity – the identity of the nation, communities, and individuals. We seek to preserve our culture because it is fundamental to our understanding of who we are. It is the name we go by, the house in which we live. Culture is that which gives us a sense of ourselves ... With a cultural policy we recognise our responsibility to foster and preserve such an environment. We recognise that the ownership of a heritage and identity, and the means of self-expression and creativity, are essential human needs and essential to the needs of society. (DoCA, 1994, p. 5)

Alongside such concerns for the maintenance of a common national patrimony in the face of globalization was a considerably more pragmatic assessment of why investment in a national cultural policy was good not just for the nation's collective soul, but for its economic bottom-line:

> This cultural policy is also an economic policy. Culture creates wealth ... [and] adds value, it makes an essential contribution to innovation, marketing and design. It is a badge of our industry. The level of our creativity substantially determines our ability to adapt to new economic imperatives. It is a valuable export in itself and an essential accompaniment to the export of other commodities. It attracts tourists and students. It is essential to our economic success. (DoCA, 1994, p. 7)

In its focus upon the cultural industries value chain, strategies to stimulate demand and consumption as well as supply, its interest in promoting cultural exports, and its focus upon the capacity of ICTs to enable new forms of cultural practice, *Creative Nation* was exemplary in its move from the traditional concerns of arts policy towards a cultural industries framework, along the lines advocated by Garnham, Girard and others. At the same time, it is apparent that its case as a policy priority needed to be built around the traditionally nationalist precepts of cultural policy, which not only teach a population 'what it means to be Australian' (DoCA, 1994, p. 5), but also operate – as stated elsewhere in the document – to protect this national population from the 'wave of global mass culture', in order to ensure that the nation does not become 'a sea of globalised and homogenised mediocrity' (DoCA, 1994, pp. 6, 7).

The rise of creative industries policies was linked to the policy strategies of the 'New Labour' government headed by Tony Blair when it came to power in the United Kingdom in 1997. It has been noted in previous chapters that a range of conceptual and definitional issues surround this new concept, with some writers preferring to retain the term 'cultural industries', seeing the term 'creative industries' as involving an unduly optimistic take on more long-standing problems and issues in the arts and cultural sectors, in order to link arts and cultural policy to the 'sexier' domain of information policy (see e.g. Garnham, 2005; Hesmondhalgh and Pratt, 2005). Others have seen the move from cultural to creative industries as marking out a new domain for the cultural sectors, that focuses upon their relationship to national research and development strategies, the rise of the consumer as co-creator of content in digital environments, and the growing significance of entrepreneurship and small-to-medium-sized enterprises (SMEs) as compared to the large corporations and publicly funded flagships that have been the traditional focus of arts and media policy (see e.g. Cunningham, 2002; Cunningham *et al.*, 2004; Hartley, 2005).

It is worth noting that a growing international uptake of creative industries as a policy discourse has been linked to a shift away from national information society or information economy strategies since their heyday in the late 1990s. The Asian economic downturn of 1997–98 exposed significant problems with state-led *dirigiste* approaches to developing a national ICT sector in industries that are inherently globally mobile. Shortly after, the crash of the US NASDAQ stock exchange in April 2001 left many countries, particularly in the Asia-Pacific region, exposed in terms of the extent to which they had hitched their global economic star to the ICT bandwagon (Flew and McElhinney, 2005). Creative industries strategies, with their focus upon building linkages between the arts, media, intellectual property and ICT industries, have been seen by many governments – as discussed in Chapter 5 – as presenting a more inclusive and holistic approach to policy development. Creative industries strategies are based upon the premise that, in an age of globally mobile capital, commodities and information, it is the 'cultural' or 'software' side of ICTs that can generate distinctive forms of intellectual property and sustainable competitive advantage. The flip side is a view that the core activities related to the technologies themselves, such as programming, are highly exportable to emergent economies that combine high skills and comparatively low wages, such as China and India. Such strategies also implicitly share John Howkins' observation that, 'If I was a bit of data, I would be proud of living in an information society. But as a thinking, emotional, creative being – on a good day, anyway – I want something better' (Howkins, 2005, p. 117).

Beyond definitional questions, the rise of creative industries policy discourse foreshadows, I would argue, a significant rethinking of cultural policy for the 21st century. Media policy in the 20th century was linked to the regulatory state, and cultural policy – including media policy insofar as it went beyond the arts to culture more generally – to the protective state. Creative industries policy, by contrast, points in the direction of what has been variously termed the *enabling state* (Mulgan and Wilkinson, 1992; Botsman and Latham, 2001), the *new regulatory state* (Braithwaite, 2000), the *new cultural state* (Redhead, 2004a), the *promotional state* (Abramson, 2001), and *network governance* (Thompson, 2003; Barney, 2004). In contrast to those approaches which see the role of the state as being one of 'taming' the commercial market, it envisages the issue as being not one of more or less regulation, but rather of how to develop policy frameworks that promote both regulation *of* the market (to minimize consumer or worker exploitation, to maintain basic standards of service, or to ensure universal access to basic services), and regulation *through* the market (to achieve greater diversity through promoting competition, or enhance technological change or industry responsiveness to consumers). It identifies interconnections between innovation, entrepreneurship and competition as part of what the 20th-century Austrian economist Joseph Schumpeter termed *creative destruction* (cf. Garnham, 2005), and the need for media and cultural policies which do not simply protect the *ancien régime* of existing institutional privileges and *quid pro quos*, but create an environment in which new initiatives can flourish, in a context of rapid technological, organizational and socio-cultural change (cf. Flew, 2005c).

Big Media from Small Nations: Al Jazeera in the Middle East

While the Middle East – taken to be those nations between the eastern Mediterranean, the Persian Gulf, the Red Sea and the Indian Ocean – has historically been a site of heavy media consumption, it has been less notable as a site of significant media production. Arab broadcasting institutions have, until very recently, been government-run, and most have avoided political content for purposes other than supporting the programmes of the government. While there has been some trade in Arab media, particularly in film, where Cairo has been described as 'the Hollywood of the Arab world' (Boyd, 1999, p. 50), governments have also tended to control the flows of media from other countries, and Dajani (2005, p. 599) has observed that 'the processes of media regulation in all states are not transparent and their media systems are politically charged'.

The Arab media landscape changed dramatically from 1990, with the Iraqi invasion of Kuwait, and the Second Gulf War of 1991.[1] In particular, the fact that the Cable News Network (CNN) was able to broadcast continuous, free and uncensored coverage of the war throughout the Arab world from its base in Egypt, greatly stimulated both the demand for satellite television and the expectation that news services should provide something other than the traditional, predictable and highly censored content of the state-run television services. The realization that there was considerable demand in the region for uncensored satellite broadcasting acted as a catalyst for the development of a variety of pan-Arab satellite channels and services, of which the most internationally famous has been Al Jazeera, which commenced broadcasting as an all-news satellite channel out of Doha, Qatar in 1997.

The name 'Al Jazeera' means 'the island' or 'the peninsula', drawing attention to its location on the tiny Gulf state of Qatar. Qatar has a population of about 750,000, of whom only about 200,000 would be citizens, with the rest being guest workers of various forms. As well as meeting the large unmet demand in the Arab world for uncensored satellite news channels that CNN had first tapped into in 1991, Al Jazeera owed its emergence to two other factors. First, a contract between the Rome-based but Saudi-owned Orbit Radio and Television Service and the Arabic TV division of the BBC News Service, which had been signed in 1994 with the intention of establishing the region's largest satellite news service, was terminated in 1996 amidst Saudi discontent with the new network's content. Al Jazeera executives, seeking media professionals for their fledgling service, quickly hired the staff formerly employed by the BBC Arabic News Service, and relocated them from London to Doha. The second factor has been the commitment of the Emir of Qatar, Sheikh Hamad bin Khalifi Al-Thani, to providing financial support to Al Jazeera as an independent network free of government control. Sheikh Hamad gained power from his father in a bloodless coup in 1995 and has promoted a modernizing agenda for Qatar, including parliamentary elections, giving women the right to vote, and lifting government censorship and controls over the flow of information.

The relationship between Al Jazeera and the Qatari government is an unusual one in the Arab world. Al Jazeera is neither financially nor personally independent of the government (members of the Qatari royal family are on its board), but it has benefited from the aspirations of Qatar as a small Gulf state to assert its difference from Saudi Arabia, and for its government to gain wider influence in the Arab world by promoting a media service free of state controls as a flagship for wider modernizing and democratizing aspirations among the people of the Middle East.

Al Jazeera has come to fill not only a media void in the Middle East, through its lack of censorship and willingness to address controversial issues. It has also been filling a political void, as an outlet for dissenting and opposi-tional voices in a region where tolerance of political opposition is in most countries highly limited. Its positioning as a pan-Arab channel, that addresses issues that are pressing in the Arab and Muslim world, and which approaches global issues from an Arab perspective, has led some to see the network as generating the possibility of an autonomous public sphere in the Arab world, and constituting a voice for those elements of civil society and popular opinion not represented by the governments or the state-run media channels (El-Nawawy and Iskandar, 2002, pp. 68–9; El Oifi, 2005). With the estab-lishment of a high-profile English-language broadcasting and online news service in 2006, Al-Jazeera is also seeking a wider international profile and influence.

Such a position is of course highly contentious, particularly in the context of the Middle East's volatile political environment, with seemingly intractable problems such as the Israel–Palestine question, the rise of militant Islamic movements, and the future of Iraq. It has frequently angered Arab govern-ments, not used to public criticism or have opposing views broadcast, and it is not currently recognized by the Arab States Broadcasting Union (Zayani, 2005, p. 3). The fact that the network remains dependent upon funding from the Qatari government points to the continuing difficulties it faces in attracting advertisers, many of whom are cautious about having their products associated with a network that other governments in the region, most notably the Saudi government, are highly critical of. Western perceptions of the role played by the network in Middle East politics are even more fraught. Best known in the West as the network that broadcast Osama bin Laden's statement after the 11 September 2001 attacks, it is routinely criticized in the US in particular as providing an outlet for anti-American, anti-Israeli sentiment, and promoting political extremism in the Arab world. Its journalists were expelled from the New York Stock Exchange in 2003, and its offices in both Kabul and Baghdad have been hit by US missiles and one of its journalists killed, although US authorities have claimed this was an accident. These tensions are featured in the 2004 documentary *Control Room* (Dir. Jehane Noujaim).

Whether the rise of Al Jazeera is a portent for wider change in Arab media, and indeed political change in the Arab world, remains to be seen. It has many competitors in the region, most notably the Al Arabiya network based in Dubai in the United Arab Emirates, and elements of the 'Al Jazeera news style' have been adopted widely in the region. Indeed, the US has funded its own satellite channel, Al Hurra, partly in order to redress its poor image in the region. How Al Jazeera's English language service fares against the likes of CNN and the BBC in international news markets also remains a question of great interest. What is notable from the rise of Al Jazeera, however, is the extent to which, given the right set of influences, highly influential media organizations can emerge from states that would seem to be relative minnows in the wider regional political, cultural and economic landscape.

Further reading: Boyd (1999); Sakr (2001, 2005); El-Nawawy and Iskandar (2002); Dajani (2005); El Oifi (2005); Zayani (2005).

Sub-national Cultural Policy: Creative Cities and Creative Clusters

The US cultural policy analyst J. Mark Schuster has posed the question of whether the *sub-national* levels of government – cities, states and provinces – have increasingly become the most dynamic sites of cultural policy formation and implementation (Schuster, 2002). He notes that, in countries with a federal government structure, such as the United States, Germany and Australia, cultural policy funding must occur on a co-operative basis between different levels of government, but also argues that, even in countries with a more centralized system of government, 'programs of delegation, devolution, decentralization, and *désétatization* have been taking hold', making the shift towards sub-national cultural policy more generalized (Schuster, 2002, p. 184). Schuster has also argued that the growing significance of sub-national cultural policy accelerates other trends in the field, such as a stronger focus upon popular cultural practices than upon the 'high arts', a greater role for public–private partnerships and other more entrepreneurial forms of arts and cultural management, and a greater enmeshing of cultural policy with policy fields such as tourism, economic development, education, youth policy, multi-culturalism and social policy (Schuster, 2002, pp. 14–16; cf. Rentschler, 2002; Stevenson, 2004). A growing role for sub-national forms of cultural policy is consistent with Cunningham's (2002, 2005b) proposition that national cultural policy fundamentals are being squeezed from both ends, by global-ization of the creative industries and international trade agreements on the one hand, and the growing significance attached to SMEs and geographically situated knowledge to contemporary forms of cultural entrepreneurship.

A focus upon the sub-national dimensions of cultural policy draws attention to its links to the burgeoning literature on *creative cities* and *creative clusters*. The creative-cities literature has highlighted both the reassertion of place in the context of globalization and seemingly 'weightless' new media, and the positive agglomeration effects that arise from the development of urban sites, or what Charles Landry terms *creative milieux* (Landry, 2000; cf. Hall, 2000), which bring together complementary practices of cultural production and consumption for further creativity and innovation spin-offs (Pratt, 2000, 2002; O'Connor, 2004, 2005; Tay, 2005). At one level, creative cities may be simply global cities by another name. *Global cities* are those cities which, by virtue of their dominant place within the key global service industries, constitute critical nodes for all global transactions, and whose relative significance grows the more that economic activity moves from predominantly national to increasingly global circuits (Sassen, 2000, 2001, 2002; Taylor *et al.*, 2002). On this basis, cities such as New York, London, Tokyo, Paris, Los Angeles, Hong Kong, Singapore and Sydney emerge as creative cities on the basis of their dominant place in such key global service industries as accountancy, advertising, banking and finance, insurance and law, as well as being at central hubs in communications and transportation networks. Such cities inexorably draw in, or have embedded within them, the other key components of creative cities, such as investment capital, highly skilled and ambitious people, culturally diverse populations, an arts, cultural and entertainment infrastructure, ancillary service industries (such as media post-production, fashion, tourism), and key educational institutions. On this register, it would be hard to know whether a city is global because it is creative or creative because it is global.

The 'creative cities' debate has tended to have the strongest resonance among so-called *second-tier* cities, as it raises the issue of whether pro-active public policy can either capture creative activities from the first-tier global cities, or generate new forms of competitive advantage in the global cultural economy. It raises questions about the conditions through which, for example, cities such as Boston and San Francisco can be leaders in the US new-media sectors on the basis of their cultural amenities and diverse populations (Florida, 2002), whether cities such as Manchester and Glasgow can challenge the hegemony of London in the British cultural economy (O'Connor, 1999, 2004), or whether cities such as Melbourne, Brisbane and Wellington can constitute alternative points of attraction for global investment capital to the lead Australian and New Zealand cities, Sydney and Auckland. Such place-based competition for being 'lead site' for creativity has become increasingly intense in the East Asian context, as the realization that IT-based jobs are highly geographically mobile has seen cities such as Shanghai, Beijing, Seoul and Shenzhen challenging traditional leaders such as Hong Kong, Singapore and Tokyo for being the hubs for creative work which fuels East Asian popular culture, particularly in the digital media content industries (Keane, 2006). In all of these forms of place-based competition for global investment in the creative industries, there is a strong emphasis upon building the *soft infrastructure*, or the 'system of associative structures and social networks, connections and human interactions, that underpins and encourages the flow of ideas between individuals and institutions' (Landry, 2000, p. 133), alongside the *hard infrastructure* of buildings, transport systems, communications infrastructure and public institutions. As such 'soft infrastructure' invariably develops best outside of the direct purview of the state, it points to the need for 'enabling state' policy strategies that work in new forms of partnership and mutuality with non-governmental, 'third-sector' or civil-society-based networks and social infrastructures.

More direct attempts to manage urban space in order to promote the creative industries through cultural policy have been seen with strategies to promote *creative clusters*. Drawing upon a variety of experiences in the new-media sectors, such as rise of the South-of-Market Area (SoMA) in San Francisco, 'Silicon Alley' in New York, and the Cardiff Bay region in Wales (Cooke, 2002; Pratt, 2002), as well as the literature from economic geography and business studies on cluster dynamics and agglomeration effects, there has been a growing focus in cultural planning upon the capacity of local governments to facilitate the creation of new urban sites able to stimulate and integrate cultural creativity and economic innovation. In an analysis of creative-cluster formation in The Netherlands in cities such as Amsterdam, Rotterdam, Tilburg and Utrecht, Mommaas (2004) has observed that creative cluster strategies have been driven by a heterogeneous range of policy priorities including:

- attracting globally mobile capital and skilled labour to particular locations;
- stimulating a more entrepreneurial and demand-oriented approach to arts and cultural policy;
- promoting innovation and creativity more generally, through the perceived interaction between culturally vibrant locales and innovation in other economic sectors;
- finding new uses for derelict industrial-era sites in post-industrial economies;
- promoting cultural diversity and cultural democratization, and being more inclusive of the cultural practices of otherwise marginalized social groups.

Mommaas describes the resulting policy strategies as exhibiting *ad-hocracy*, whereby different arguments are drawn upon in different situations on a contingent, highly localized, case-by-case basis. He observes that this is not only a consequence of the relatively recent development of such new cultural policies, but is also a reaction against earlier, top-down models of arts policy and cultural planning. While he broadly welcomes such reflexivity and 'enabling' in the policy process, he goes on to note that there is also an 'art of tightrope walking' on display in these cases, which could easily lapse into essentially a 'high arts' policy by new means on the one hand, and a subsumption of progressive cultural policy initiatives into speculative real estate strategies which drive out non-commercialized forms of cultural expression on the other (Mommaas, 2004, pp. 525, 528, 530).

A stocktake of creative-cities and creative-clusters initiatives indicates the extent to which, in the face of the impasses of 20th-century national cultural policy in terms of its attachment to the 'high arts' and cultural citizenship defined through national identity, local and regional authorities are taking up the baton with more entrepreneurial and *ad hoc* forms of sub-national cultural policy. In this sense, they adopt a 'Third Way' approach of engaging with globalization (Giddens, 2000; Stevenson, 2004), that maintains the need for a positive role for the state in managing and directing market forces, but which also rejects the dichotomy between national culture and global commerce that animated cultural policy for much of the second half of the 20th century.

Recognition of such innovation and dynamism in the local cultural policy sphere does not, however, entail an uncritical endorsement of what Stevenson (2004) has termed the new 'civic gold rush' in urban cultural policy and cultural planning. One concern that Stevenson identifies is that there is often a slippage in such strategies around the concepts of cultural or creative capital, which is held to be both the actually existing local and vernacular cultural resources and practices which successful urban cultural policies will be able to tap into, and the expectation that one of the outcomes of such policies will be the development of new forms of cultural or creative capital, particularly among marginalized and socially excluded populations. The danger is that such policies may set up false hopes of addressing conflicting policy objectives, such as being able to simultaneously promote expansion of the local cultural economy and address social exclusion and marginalization. In particular, tensions emerge between the promotion of those creative-industries sectors whose products and services circulate in largely global circuits of cultural production and consumption, and where returns to the local economy are likely to be minimal, and those sectors where cultural products and practices remain strongly grounded in a sense of locality and place, which remain highly vulnerable to the broader tendencies associated with economic and cultural globalization.[2] Moreover, there is the danger of overly genericized creative-industries policies – such as creative-clusters models – adopting a 'cookie-cutter' approach grounded in excessive sameness. Oakley (2004) has expressed concern in the UK context that creative industries strategies too often 'seem hellbent on trying to replicate a single creative industries model', characterized by 'a university, some incubators, and a "creative hub", with or without a café, galleries and fancy shops' (Oakley, 2004, p. 73). As Oakley notes, such strategies cannot simultaneously work in all places, and it would be better to try and understand and work with local and regional differences rather than apply this model to all places, in the vain hope that, for instance, the British advertising industry may move *en masse* from London to Sheffield or Huddersfield. On an international scale, it would be one thing to observe that Beijing has aspirations to be a creative city, but another to then assume that Richard Florida's emphasis on San Francisco's large gay population as a factor in its creative dynamism will find enthusiastic acceptance with Beijing's local political authorities.

Cities, Festivals and Events: Performing Creativity in the City

The relationship between large-scale events and urban regeneration has a long history. The 1851 Great Exhibition in London and the 1855 World Fair (*Exhibition universelle*) in Paris perhaps provide the two most famous historical examples of such events being used to fundamentally reconstruct a city in order to make it more public and 'on display'. The massive investment in architecture, design, transport and communication in these two cities at that time has legacies which remain apparent today (Hobsbawm, 1990; Hall, 1998; Tay, 2005). It has been the case, however, that large-scale events that have focused upon urban regeneration and developing a global profile, such as major sporting events (like the Olympics, World Cups) or trade and technological showcases (Expos, World Fairs), have not tended to attach much significance to arts and cultural activities as an important element of the urban mix that authorities have sought to promote to the rest of the world. This is despite the extensive literature on the role of the arts in the marketing of cities and cultural tourism, suggesting that considerable scope for establishing such linkages existed (García, 2004; cf. Landry et al., 1996; Landry, 2000).

There has been a very sharp and significant change of thinking on the relationship between cultural activities and major events in cities since the early
1990s. Two developments seem to have been critical to this. The first was the
European Cities of Culture (now European Capitals of Culture) initiative,
initially developed by the European Community (now the European Union) in
1985. While the initial successful bidders, such as Athens, Amsterdam,
Florence and Paris, largely used the event to showcase existing cultural activities and institutions, the cities of Glasgow (European City of Culture, 1990)
and Dublin (1991) approached the event as part of a wider transformation of
their cities' infrastructure, image, amenity and appeal, to both local residents
and the wider European and global community. In the case of Glasgow, it
provided an opportunity to reposition the city from an image that was associated with unemployment, de-industrialization, drug and alcohol problems,
and sectarian violence, to being seen as a vibrant artistic and cultural centre.
For Dublin, the 1991 European City of Culture award provided the opportunity, not only for urban renewal in the city centre – particularly the redevelopment of the Temple Bar area – but also for promoting its emergent image
as a European city, rather than an impoverished backwater dependent upon
EU subsidies. Dublin's success as European City of Culture in 1991 was linked
to its economic boom in the 1990s as the 'Celtic Tiger', just as Glasgow's
successful initiative was a factor in promoting a resurgent Scottish national
identity in the 1990s.

The other major development which drew attention to the links between
major events, culture and the development of global creative cities was the
1992 Barcelona Olympics. While most Olympics hosts had given little attention to the potential of the event to trigger wider urban regeneration, and the
Olympic Games of the 1970s and 1980s had mostly been mired in controversy
(terrorism in Munich, 1972, boycotts in Moscow, 1980 and Los Angeles,
1984), or had been financial disasters (Montreal, 1976), the Barcelona Games
were universally hailed as a success, that had put Spain's second largest city –
a city which had suffered significant deprivation under the Franco dictatorship as the centre of the Catalan minority population – onto the global map.
It continues to be seen as an emblematic European and global city for the 21st
century, as shown by Barcelona now being identified as Europe's sixth most
desirable city in which to locate a business by leading CEOs in 2002, as
compared to 11th in 1990 (Landry and Wood, 2003, p. 36).

Balibrea has noted that Barcelona's successful Olympics bid acted as a
galvanizing influence for a range of key urban constituencies in the post-
Franco 1980s, as it was 'a sporting, cultural and ideological event all in one
… [that] succeeded totally in generating local patriotism and consensus, as
well as introducing the city to the world at large' (Balibrea, 2001, p. 198).
Balibrea has, however, contested the claim that the 'Barcelona model' is an

unequivocal success story which other aspirant creative cities should emulate. More recent events such as the UNESCO-endorsed Universal Forum of Cultures (Fòrum Universal de les Cultures), held in May–September 2004, have had the potential to endanger the sustainability of the lower-income communities in the coastal areas where the major Forum events were held (Balibrea, 2001; cf. García, 2004).

The ambition to link the arts and culture to global profile and economic competitiveness in 21st-century cities is now apparent from multiple perspectives. Landry and Wood (2003) have asserted the importance of cultural factors to the competitive advantage of cities in the global economy through their notion of the *drawing power* of cities. The concept of drawing power refers to 'the dynamics of attraction, retention and leakage', or 'the contributing factors which encourage outsiders to come in [to cities] or existing populations to stay' (Landry and Wood, 2003, p. 23). They argue that the drawing power of globally successful cities is linked to three factors:

1. the successful branding of the city as comprising a unique combination of cultural resources, heritage, and symbolic assets;
2. the ability of a city to act as both an attractor of new talent and as an incubator of its own talented people and creative resources;
3. the existence of a range of activities and opportunities in a city that can lift the everyday lives of its residents, and generate new forms of self-expression, civic pride and community identification.

The renewed focus upon creativity and cultural activity as drivers of the success of cities in the global economy can be seen in one sense as a return to classical understandings of the nature of the city. Critical urban theorists of the 20th century, such as Lewis Mumford and Jane Jacobs, saw the integration of both art and community as central to a human-centred vision of the modern city as part of 'good city planning ... [that] promotes the full participation of citizens, both as performers in the urban drama and as spectators of it' (Makeham, 2005, p. 3). At the same time, this focus upon the city as a 'theatre of social action' (Makeham, 2005, p. 1) also draws attention to George Yúdice's arguments that globalization demands an increasingly *performative* role for culture, which becomes a resource for social and economic development and 'a generator of value in its own right' (Yúdice, 2003, p. 336) in the location-based competitive advantage of cities in the global economy.

Further reading: Hall (1998); Landry (2000); Landry and Wood (2003); García (2004); Stevenson (2004); Makeham (2005); Tay (2005).

Supra-national Media and Cultural Policy: Trade Agreements, Cultural Diversity and Global Civil Society

Just as there is a growing momentum and dynamism in sub-national forms of media and cultural policy, the 21st century is also seeing a continuation of the growth in international associations, and *supra-national forms of media and cultural policy*. This is part of a trend where the number of intergovernmental organizations (IGOs) grew from 37 in 1909 to 260 in 1996, and the number of international non-governmental organizations (INGOs) grew from 176 in 1909 to 5,472 by 1996 (Held *et al.*, 1999, p. 53). Moreover, the number of international treaties in force between governments grew from 6,351 to 14,061 between 1946 and 1975. Held *et al.* (1999, p. 55) see such trends as evidence of the extent to which 'national government is locked into an array of global, regional and multilateral systems of governance'. The website of the Union of International Associations (www.uia.org) demonstrates the extent to which this trend has accelerated in the 21st century, as it now has listings for 50,000 international organizations and INGOs including:

- 5,900 intergovernmental organizations and networks;
- 38,000 international NGO associations;
- 529 universal membership organizations;
- 1,050 intercontinental organizations;
- 4,100 regional (sub-continental) organizations and networks;
- 850 transnational religious orders;
- 2,700 semi-autonomous international bodies;
- 4,500 internationally oriented national organizations.

Raboy (2002) has also drawn attention to the significance of global media policy, and 'the question of how to transpose the issues that have occupied national agendas at least since the invention of the telegraph to the transnational level where, to all intents and purposes, the most important issues are henceforth being played out' (Raboy, 2002, p. 5). In mapping out this 'complex ecology of interdependent structures ... [and] vast array of formal and informal mechanisms working across a multiplicity of sites' (Raboy, 2002, p. 7), he develops the following institutional typology:

1. *global organizations*, such as those which have been traditionally a part of the United Nations structures, such as UNESCO and the International Telecommunications Union (ITU), as well as newer, more commercially

focused entities such as the WTO and the World Intellectual Property Organization (WIPO);

2. *multilateral exclusive 'clubs'*, such as the Organization for Economic Co-operation and Development and the Group of Eight (G8), which are collective groupings of the world's most powerful nations;

3. *regional multistate groupings*, such as the European Union (EU) and the Asia Pacific Economic Co-operation (APEC) group, as well as multilateral trade agreements such as the North American Free Trade Agreement (NAFTA) between the United States, Canada and Mexico, and the MERCOSUR trading zone between Brazil, Argentina, Uruguay and Paraguay;

4. *transnational private sector organizations* which have gained recognition in official *fora*, including the Global Business Dialogue for e-commerce (GBDe), the World Business Council for Sustainable Development, and the International Intellectual Property Alliance;

5. *transnational civil society organizations*, such as the World Association of Community Radio Broadcasters (AMARC), Vidéazimut (film and video), the Association for Progressive Communication, the World Association for Christian Communication, the Cultural Environment Movement, the People's Communications Charter, and Computer Professionals for Social Responsibility;

6. *'transversal' regulatory sites* (Raboy, 2002, p. 8) which operate across institutional and categorical jurisdictions, such as the Internet Corporation for Assigned Names and Numbers (ICANN), which is a loose federation of parties – principally business interests – that regulates online domain-name registration.

The finalizing of the General Agreement on Trade in Services (GATS) in Marrakesh in 1994, and the establishment of the World Trade Organization (WTO) the following year, were the two major catalysts for thinking about global media policy in terms of trade liberalization strategies for the audiovisual services sector. The GATS has the potential to impact upon national media and cultural policies in its Articles concerned with Most-Favoured-Nation Treatment (Article II), Market Access (Article XIV), and National Treatment (Article XVII).[3] All of these Articles of the GATS throw into question the capacity of national governments to undertake policies which favour local service providers (Footer and Graber, 2000; Grant and Wood, 2004). It was the case, however, that at the conclusion of the Uruguay Round of General Agreement on Tariffs and Trade (GATT) negotiations, which led to the GATS in 1994, 40 WTO member countries (including the European Union as a single entity) had taken exemptions from the Most-Favoured-Nation clause of the GATS (Article II) and the National Treatment clause (Article XVII), and there has been little movement in the area of audiovisual services in the 'Millennium Round' or 'Doha Round' of WTO negotiations.

As Dwayne Winseck (2002a, 2002b) has argued, however, the real significance of the WTO for global media and cultural policy lay less in its capacity to override national legislation than in the discursive shift it promoted. It was part of a wider trend towards thinking about media and communications as being essentially service industries, subject to generic forms of law such as competition policy, with a primary remit of delivering low-cost, innovative media and communications services to consumers worldwide, as distinct from adhering to traditional communications policy values such as freedom of expression, diversity, pluralism and the promotion of national culture and cultural identity.

It is very important to observe that the emergence of supra-national media and cultural policy agendas is not simply the imposition of a global neo-liberal policy regime upon these sectors, although that has been a vital animating concern of critics of the GATS and WTO policy initiatives. It also refers to the impact of bilateral and regional trade agreements, of which the most notable have been the European Union's 'Television Without Frontiers' directive of 1989, which set a 'European Works' programme-content quota of 50 per cent binding upon all EU members, as well as NAFTA and MERCOSUR. In his survey of media and cultural policy initiatives in regional trade agreements, Hernan Galperin (1999) found that variations in treatment of audiovisual industries within the regional trading agreement were shaped by:

- their *industrial profile*, or the distribution of economic and political resources among the trading partners' audiovisual industries;
- their *domestic communications policies*, or the regulatory framework governing communications industries, and including audiovisual, telecommunications and cultural policies;
- the degree of *'cultural distance'* among member states, including similarities and differences in language, audiovisual consumption habits, and genre preferences. A relevant issue is also the degree of cultural distance between those nations and other nations, most notably the United States as the world's leading audiovisual services exporter.

Galperin's framework enables us to understand some important practical dynamics of such regional trade agreements. In the case of NAFTA, it is apparent why Canada successfully sought a 'cultural exemption', on the basis that it is not only geographically proximate to the United States, but also shares (at least in English-speaking Canada) cultural and linguistic proximity, and hence feels culturally threatened by its big neighbour to the south. By contrast, Mexico has been less concerned about this aspect of NAFTA, because its cultural and linguistic differences provide some 'natural protection' from US dominance and, insofar as it shares cultural features with the US – such as the large and growing Hispanic population in the US – this presents new opportunities for media and cultural exports into a large and prosperous market.[4]

Within the European Union, Great Britain has tended to be less concerned about the possible impact of US audiovisual and other cultural imports than France, since Britain has significance linguistic, cultural, diplomatic and other affinities to the United States, whereas French concern about the 'hegemony of Hollywood', and its potential to dilute the significance of French language and culture, has a long and widespread intellectual and political history. In a review of the media, cultural and communications policies of the European Parliament (EP), Sarikakis (2005) has provided a mixed report card. She argues that the EP has been an effective entity in developing policy initiatives that define and delineate a distinctive European audiovisual space, such as the 'Television Without Frontiers' initiative, support funds for EU media and cultural production, and a defence of public service broadcasting (PSB) that is conceptual and philosophical as well as practical. At the same time, Sarikakis (2004, p. 169) observes that the EP's 'angst over the domination of American culture in the European space reveals a "blind spot" as far as internal processes of domination are concerned', that 'has served to legitimize a status quo, that supports "European" expression in order for it to compete in a market system'. For Sarikakis, two instances of this stand out. The first is the difficulty of allowing legitimate cultural expression for racial and ethnic minorities within the EU member states, partly in relation to the 'historic' minorities, such as the Welsh in Great Britain, the Bretons in France or the Walloons in Belgium, but more so in relation to the more recently arrived migrant populations, many of whom have no citizenship rights.[5] The other issue that has proved unmanageable on the part of the EP is the concentration of media ownership within national media markets, as it is here that the alliances between national representatives and dominant media industry interests are at their most powerful, with the most obvious example being Italy, where Silvio Berlusconi was from 1994 to 1995 and from 2001 to 2006 both Italy's Prime Minister and its most powerful media owner.

Another important set of trends that run counter to understanding media as simply cultural commodities for trade in the global market has been the movement that has developed through UNESCO for a Convention on Cultural Diversity. UNESCO argued that cultures could be understood as akin to ecosystems 'made up of a rich and complex mosaic of cultures, more or less powerful [that] need diversity to preserve and pass on their valuable heritage to others'. Drawing a parallel with the Convention on Biodiversity, UNESCO argued that 'Only adequate cultural policies can ensure the preservation of the creative diversity against the risks of a single homogenizing culture. Cultural diversity is the positive expression of the overarching imperative to prevent the development of a uniform world by promoting and supporting all world cultures' (UNESCO, 2003). The Convention on Cultural Diversity emerged as an initiative of the International Network on Cultural Policy (INCP), an association of over 50 ministers of culture from throughout the world, with Canada playing a key facilitating role (Goldsmith, 2002). The INCP sought to develop a new legally binding instrument that would give signatory states the option of taking measures to protect and enhance cultural diversity, even if these were at odds with the guiding principles of the GATS and the WTO (Grant and Wood, 2004, pp. 381–90; Smeers, 2004).

This initiative was positively embraced by UNESCO, which in 2001 circulated a *UNESCO Declaration on Cultural Diversity* (UNESCO, 2001). Among the key principles of the *Declaration* were:

- the proposition that, as 'commodities of a unique kind', there was a need to pay particular attention to 'the diversity of the supply of creative work', and to recognize 'the specificity of cultural goods and services which, as vectors of identity, values, and meaning must not be treated as mere commodities or consumer goods' (Article 8);
- the proposition that, since cultural policies are 'catalysts of creativity', it is therefore the role of 'each State, with due regard to its international obligations, to define its cultural policy and to implement it through the means it considers fit, whether by operational support or appropriate regulations' (Article 9);
- the proposition that 'Market forces alone cannot guarantee the preservation and promotion of cultural diversity. Therefore, in promoting sustainable human development, the key role of public policy, in partnership with the private sector and civil society, must be reaffirmed' (Article 11).

Smeers (2004, p. 86) has observed that a Convention on Cultural Diversity has the dual role of both preserving a diversity of existing forms of cultural heritage and cultural practice and promoting new forms of diverse cultural forms and practices. As one of a number of subsequent initiatives to preserve and promote cultural diversity that have been initiated by UNESCO since 2001, the Convention on the Protection and Promotion of the Diversity of Cultural Expressions (UNESCO, 2005b) affirms the sovereign right of signatory nations to 'formulate and implement their cultural policies and to adopt measures to protect and promote the diversity of cultural expressions and to strengthen international co-operation to achieve the purposes of this Convention' (UNESCO, 2005b, Article 5), including regulations to limit the flow of imported cultural goods and services and measures to subsidize and promote domestic cultural production and distribution. This Convention was supported by 148 UNESCO member states, with only the United States and Israel voting against it, and with four members (including Australia) abstaining.

As the significance of such Conventions on Cultural Diversity plays itself out, and the related question of whether non-binding instruments such as a Declaration have real legal weight alongside the rules-based framework of the WTO – which is in part an issue about the significance and influence of UNESCO and the United Nations more generally in world affairs – four issues stand out as critical. First, there is the obvious point that the United States, as the world's largest economic and military power and the world's largest exporter of cultural goods and services, is opposed to such Conventions and will no doubt seek to influence attempts to implement them as elements of the cultural policy of other nation-states. The US approach receives some intellectual support from trade economists and cultural theorists. One example is Cowen (2002), who argues that dynamic cultures are by their nature syncretic, cosmopolitan and forward-looking, and that the processes of 'creative destruction' associated with cultural globalization stimulate new cultural forms. Cowen argues that attempts to enshrine 'cultural diversity' through international law are simply attempts to preserve the nationally based cultural *status quo*, whereas cultural production and consumption practices are in fact already increasingly global and multicultural, and this should be welcomed by people of a progressive and cosmopolitan-minded nature, even if it has been the expansion of global cultural markets that has been its principal conduit.

The second point is that the UNESCO Conventions, and policy discourse more generally in this realm, run up against the familiar definitional tension between culture as the totality of lived experience and forms of human expression, and culture as media, which was discussed in Chapter 5. Magder (2004b) has noted that references to the audiovisual sectors (film and television) are relatively few in the primary UNESCO documents or related statements on the need for a Convention on Cultural Diversity, yet they are the principal animators of supra-national initiatives in terms of cultural policy, as they are the cultural goods and services that are most widely produced, consumed and internationally traded, particularly if ancillary sectors such as advertising are included (UNESCO, 2005a).

Third, there is the question of the relationship between state and non-state actors in the promotion of cultural diversity. Magder has observed that the *UNESCO Declaration on Cultural Diversity* tended to prioritize cultures as collectivities over individual rights to freedom of opinion and expression, as clearly enshrined in Article 19 of the United Nations Universal Declaration of Human Rights (Magder, 2004b, p. 392). This has been a long-standing problem with UNESCO-supported campaigns for the democratization of communications that goes back to the New World Information and Communications Order of the 1970s and 1980s (see below). The tensions that can result from governments being the arbiters of culture at the UNESCO level, and how this squares with individual rights and questions of cultural diversity and dissent within nation-states, is discussed in more detail later in this chapter.

Fourth, from a more legal standpoint, the adoption of the UNESCO Convention on Cultural Diversity, and related agreements such as the Convention on the Protection and Promotion of the Diversity of Cultural Expression, raises the question of the appropriate authority through which to adopt such Conventions. In particular, it raises the issue of the capacity of those involved in negotiations in international *fora* such as UNESCO to ratify supra-national agreements on behalf of national governments which, where they are democratically elected, are understood to be custodians of the national patrimony on behalf of those citizens within the nation-state who elected them to public office. The former Chief Justice of the High Court of Australia, Sir Anthony Mason, drew attention to this issue in relation to the Australian Government's decision to sign on to the GATS in 1994, even though the government of the day had not sought any form of direct or indirect democratic mandate for this decision, and the implications of such a decision had never been promulgated or made open for debate and deliberation among Australia's citizens (Mason, 1996). While the commitment to be a signatory to a Convention that is not legally binding may differ from legally binding agreements such as the laws, codes and conventions of the GATS and the WTO, it nonetheless remains the case that international negotiators and domestic policy-makers are making decisions on issues that potentially impact upon their national citizenry in the absence of well-thought-through mechanisms by which those citizens are engaged in the decision-making process.

The World Summit on the Information Society (WSIS)

The First World Summit on the Information Society (WSIS) was held in Geneva in December 2003, and the Second World Summit was held in Tunis in November 2005. The WSIS events, organized through the United Nations by the International Telecommunications Union (ITU), brought together representatives of government, international organizations, the private sector, and NGOs or civil society organizations from 175 countries. The aim has been to develop an agenda, as the Geneva WSIS Declaration of Principles statement described it, for building:

> a people-centred, inclusive and development-oriented Information Society, where everyone can create, access, utilize and share information and knowledge, enabling individuals, communities and peoples to achieve their full potential in promoting their sustainable development and improving their quality of life, premised on the purposes and principles of the Charter of the United Nations and respecting fully and upholding the Universal Declaration of Human Rights. (WSIS, 2003)

The summit model of international negotiations has been a feature of United Nations conferences since the end of the Cold War, with the Earth Summit (Rio de Janeiro, 1992) the Word Food Summit (Rome, 1996), the World Summit Against Racism (Durban, 2001), and the World Summit on Sustainable Development (Johannesburg, 2002) being among the most prominent (Klein, 2003). Summits are a distinctive UN activity as they explicitly seek the active participation of civil society organizations such as NGOs in the decision-making process, and the WSIS was developed and conducted very much within this spirit, although civil society organizations have notably contested its outcomes. They are an example of a tripartite approach to global governance that the UN has sought to fashion in recent years, where both the private sector and NGOs are seen as legitimate stakeholders alongside national governments in processes of global decision-making (Klein, 2003; Ó Siochrú, 2004; Raboy, 2004).

In its Declaration of Principles, the final text of the 2003 Geneva WSIS identified the following as some of the key principles of an 'Information Society for All':

1. a *multi-stakeholder approach*, with the private sector, civil society, international organizations and the UN all having a role, along with national governments, in promoting ICTs for development through co-operation and partnerships;
2. developing a comprehensive and affordable ICT *network infrastructure*;
3. *universal access to knowledge* that is in the public domain;
4. *capacity-building*, and extended ICT knowledge and literacy throughout the population, particularly among disadvantaged and marginalized groups;
5. strengthening *information and network security*, including provisions for authentication, privacy and consumer protection, that increase user trust and promote cyber-security;

6. an *enabling national and international policy and regulatory framework*, that promotes transparency, competition, development of international standards, and intellectual property protection;
7. promoting the *benefits of ICTs in all aspects of life*, including e-government, e-health, e-learning, and other ICT applications for economic and social progress and well-being;
8. *promotion of cultural diversity and identity, linguistic diversity and local content.*

As is commonly the case with such documents that arise from multigovernmental and multistakeholder negotiations, the Declaration of Principles is reflective of a series of political compromises. Raboy (2004) observed that major points of disagreement that are largely papered over in the final text concerned: the declaration of the right to communicate as a universal human right (opposed by China, Russia, Pakistan and Iran, among others); transformation of intellectual property rights regimes from the approach adopted by the WIPO (unsuccessfully sought by Brazil and India); establishment of a 'Digital Solidarity Fund' to be levied from governments of developed nations and heavy users of telecommunications infrastructure, in order to fund projects in the least developed nations; and the proposal to shift responsibility for Internet governance from the US-dominated Internet Corporation for the Assignment of Names and Numbers (ICANN) to the more multilateral ITU (on ICANN, see Paré, 2003; Flew, 2005a, pp. 194–5).

In its critique of the WSIS final documents, circulated at the conclusion of the 2003 Geneva WSIS, the Civil Society Declaration to the WSIS, titled *Shaping Information Societies for Human Needs* (Civil Society WSIS, 2003), proposed an alternative wording of the vision of the WSIS:

> At the heart of our vision of information and communication societies is the human being. The dignity and rights of all peoples and each person must be promoted, respected, protected and affirmed. Redressing the inexcusable gulf between levels of development and between opulence and extreme poverty must therefore be our prime concern. (Civil Society WSIS, 2003)

The Civil Society Declaration focused its critique of the official WSIS documents around four key themes. First, it was argued that communications rights must be linked to questions of social justice on both a local and a global scale, and that this required the transfer of funds to the least developed nations for poverty eradication, the broadening of access to the means of communication (particularly among local communities, minority groups, and vulnerable people such as refugees, those displaced by war, and asylum seekers), and sustainable, community-based models for ICT development and use. Second, the civil society groups asserted the centrality of individual human rights, as first promulgated in the UN Charter and the Universal Declaration of Human Rights in 1948, such as the right to freedom of expression, the right to privacy, and the right to participate in public affairs, and that these must not be subordinated to government censorship, monitoring and surveillance by governments or the private sector, and questions of national security. Third, it was argued that cultural and linguistic diversity can only be guaranteed by measures to inhibit the rise of media monopolies and by safeguards of media pluralism, ensuring access to both information and software on 'public domain' and 'open content' principles, and by a review of intellectual property rights and patent rights to see if current regimes are inhibiting creativity, innovation, and promotion of the public good. Finally, the civil society groups argued for more democratic and accountable forms of governance, questioning what they saw as the undue faith of the WSIS leaders in technological solutions to social, cultural and political problems, and for ensuring that the institutions of global governance work within frameworks that take as a primary goal the more equitable distribution of the benefits of ICT development across nations and social groups.

Reviews of civil society participation in the 2003 Geneva WSIS (for example, Burch, 2004; Ó Siochrú, 2004; Raboy, 2004) have argued that the achievements of civil society groups in relation to WSIS may lie less in their influence upon the final Declaration of Principles and the associated Action Plan – both of which are seen as being deeply flawed – than in their capacity to move beyond a very delimited role of contributing their 'hands-on experience' to the 'real' decision-makers, towards an enhanced capacity to broaden the decision-making agenda to include such themes as human rights, open access to information and knowledge, and the relationship between cultural and linguistic diversity and media diversity and pluralism. Moreover, through their enhanced capacity to organize among themselves towards common goals and self-governing collective action, and to promote these in ways that influence negotiations by both official and more informal means and mechanisms, Raboy (2004, p. 355) has argued that 'the WSIS process has shaken the status quo of global governance', and sees it as 'a laboratory experimenting with a new distribution of power involving emerging as well as established social forces'.

The 2005 Tunis WSIS Summit demonstrated that the civil society agenda had made progress in some areas, particularly in the development of an Internet Governance Forum (IGF) as a basis for identifying more multilateral and inclusive mechanisms than that of ICANN. However, on the question of linking communications rights and human rights, particularly around the right to privacy, freedom of expression, freedom of association, and freedom of information, the WSIS Tunis Agenda (WSIS, 2005) is arguably more opaque in its statements than was the 2003 Geneva WSIS. This may be indicative of the declining centrality of the United States to such processes, and the rise of China and Russia as key global players, as well as the very different perspectives that exist among governments of Africa and the Middle East on such questions.

The WSIS and the NWICO: Comparing and Contrasting Two UN Approaches to Global Media and Communication

The United Nations Educational, Scientific and Cultural Organization (UNESCO) was established as one of the original United Nations agencies in 1945. UNESCO has since its inception understood questions of cultural diversity and their relationship to communications media as being central to its organizational remit. While its thinking in these areas was initially very much focused upon artistic production, the importance of questions of cultural identity to newly independent states led it over the course of the 1960s to focus more upon the role of mass media and, with that, questions of international trade in cultural products (UNESCO, 2004). In the 1970s, as the relationship between culture, development and international power relations became increasingly central to the demands of nations of the 'Third World' or the 'Global South' for reform to power asymmetries in the global system, demands for a New World Information and Communications Order (NWICO) rose to prominence. The 20th General Conference of UNESCO affirmed a need to 'end the dependence of the developing world as regards information and communication', and to 'establish a new, more equitable and effective information and communication order' (quoted in Pasquali, 2005, p. 292). These actions can be seen in the wider context of the formation of the 'Non-Aligned Movement' of states that were not a part of the US-led Western alliance or the Soviet-led states, who had self-identified as the 'Third World', and had commenced a campaign in 1973–74, through the United Nations, for the establishment of a 'New International Economic Order'.

In 1980, the International Commission for the Study of Communications Problems, established by UNESCO and chaired by Sean MacBride, the Irish-born founder of Amnesty International, released its final report on global communications, *Many Voices, One World*, also known as the MacBride Report (1980). The Report was highly critical of what it saw as the 'one-way flow' of information from the developed Western nations to the Third World, that arose from the control of multinational corporations over information technologies and resources. It saw arguments promoting the global 'free flow' of information as needing to be weighed up against the rights of national governments, particularly in the developing world, to manage such flows in order to maintain national sovereignty, build cultural identity, and harness communication resources more effectively to developmental goals. The recommendations of the MacBride Report were adopted by UNESCO at its 21st General Conference held in Belgrade (then in Yugoslavia) in 1980.

The UNESCO campaign for a NWICO suffered a slow and painful death over the course of the 1980s and early 1990s. Three factors were critical. The first was the unequivocal hostility of the United States to this agenda, which was strengthened when the Reagan administration came to power, to the point where the US government, along with the governments of Great Britain and Singapore, withdrew all financial support from UNESCO in 1984, and it was not until in 2004 that the US rejoined UNESCO. The US position saw the NWICO as an attempt to impose state regulation on the media that was fundamentally at odds with liberal Western values, as seen in the First Amendment to the US Constitution guaranteeing freedom of speech, and the global doctrine of the 'free flow of information'. Critics also argued quite effectively that many of the governments that were demanding reform of international communications were at the same time engaging in political censorship and suppressing media freedom in their own countries, an argument which had support from some Third World media-owners and news editors, as well as many of the international associations of professional journalists and communications specialists. This drew attention to the second problem, which was that the NWICO was the product of a dialogue between nation-states, which could be criticized for being overly nationalistic and state-centred, downplaying the suppression of media freedoms within many of the participating nation-states. This was in part a by-product of the 'Cold War' between the US and the Soviet Union and their respective allies, where a degree of silence about the undemocratic nature of internal arrangements was often a condition for support in multinational *fora* such as the UN (Tomlinson, 1991, pp. 70–3; Mattelart, 1994, pp. 182–4; Roach, 1997). Finally, the NWICO agenda withered away not only as a result of direct political and financial pressure from the US government, or indeed the end of the Cold War, but also because the growth of the Internet was linked to strong trends in international communications policy towards the promotion of free trade, deregulation of national communications systems, and the development of a Global Information Infrastructure (GII) led by private sector investment. There was alongside this a process of 'forum-shifting' of communications policy debates away from UNESCO, towards more economics-oriented, pro-market agencies such as the International Telecommunications Union (ITU), as well as towards the Uruguay Round of trade negotiations that led to the General Agreement on Trade in Services (GATS) in 1994, and the formation of the World Trade Organization in 1995 (Ó Siochrú and Girard, 2003; Mastrini and de Charras, 2005).

The WSIS differed from earlier *fora*, such as the debates within UNESCO about the NWICO, in several key structural and institutional respects. First, and most importantly, it has been from the outset committed to a multi-stakeholder approach to agenda formation, deliberation, and implementation, that identifies a key role for NGOs as representatives of civil society. While the extent to which such NGOs can 'represent' civil society is a widely debated point, it is nonetheless the case that the WSIS has been explicitly constructed as less of a state-to-state dialogue than was either possible or actively sought during the NWICO negotiations. Second, as Klein (2003) has noted, such summits have taken advantage of the greater diplomatic fluidity of the post-Cold War world, and that summits which have global jurisdiction, topical jurisdiction, broad legitimacy, and timeliness in relation to topical global issues have a greater chance of substantial governmental sign-on than was the case in the pre-1991 global political order, as there is less 'block voting' than was the case in the UN pre-1991. Third, the belated discovery by the ITU of the value of summits and multistakeholder approaches to decision-making and governance may have been advantageous to civil society organizations, as their distance from previous UN approaches enabled them to avoid the pitfalls of previous models, such as a tendency to view NGOs as essentially the advisors and implementers of decisions reached by official agencies (Ó Siochrú, 2004). Finally, the relatively open-ended and multiperspectival nature of the 'information society' as a concept allows for wider debates than does a more straightforward 'political' or 'policy' issue. As Raboy has observed, the WSIS has been 'an encounter between ... opposing views of the information society ... the stakes of the WSIS were conceptual, philosophical and discursive as well as political in the narrow sense' (Raboy, 2004, p. 355).

Padovani (2005) has undertaken a discourse analysis of the WSIS Official Declaration, the WSIS Civil Society Declaration and the recommendations of the MacBride Report to identify continuities and differences over time (cf. Padovani and Tuzzi, 2004 on the WSIS texts). Padovani found that, while all three documents referred extensively to 'development', the differences between the three were quite substantial. Comparing the WSIS Official Declaration and the WSIS Civil Society Declaration, it was observed that while the former referred extensively to building an information society through technology, connectivity and infrastructure, and to the importance of economic growth, productivity, job creation and competitiveness, the latter referred much more to democracy, participation, human rights, communication rights, openness, power and plurality. Both WSIS documents take a quite different focus to the earlier MacBride Report, where a focus on mass media, journalists, transnational corporations, concentration of ownership, self-reliance and national priorities was much more prominent.

One interpretation of Padovani's findings is that, whereas the NWICO was very much concerned with global media as print and broadcast media, and the distribution of control over outlets and images, the WSIS has developed in an environment of media convergence and global digital networks, with ICTs now clearly embedded in all aspects of economic relations, social life and global power relations. The other important point is of course the extent to which NGOs have been central to the WSIS process in a way that was for the most part not true with the NWICO. At the same time, continuities have been identified between the WSIS Civil Society Declaration and the MacBride Report that are absent from the WSIS Official Declaration, such as an insistence upon looking at all media and not just the Internet, a questioning of technological solutions that are isolated from political and socio-cultural processes, and a willingness to talk about the real consequences of imbalances in global power and the distribution of resources between wealthy and poorer nations (Padovani, 2005; cf. Mastrini and de Charras, 2005).

Further reading: On the NWICO, see MacBride Report (1980); Roach (1987, 1997); Nordenstreng and Schiller (1993); Mattelart (1994), pp. 167–86; Hamelink (1997); MacBride and Roach (2000). On the WSIS, see special issues of *Continuum: Journal of Media and Cultural Studies* 18 (3), 2004; *Media Development* 1, 2004; *Global Media and Communication* 1 (3), 2005.

Conclusion: Theories of Global Media Revisited

It has been argued in *Understanding Global Media* that communications media have been central to globalizing processes in modern societies, and that media globalization challenges some long-standing assumptions about the relationship between territory, identity and culture, as well as presenting new challenges to those agencies that seek to manage and regulate media flows, media power and media control. Digital media technologies have further destabilized these relationships by promoting the borderless flow of media content, enabling users to become producers through the new tools of digital content creation and networked distribution, furthering the convergence and hybridization of media forms, and generating media content that is increasingly less identifiable as being produced and regulated within specific nation-states. While these are not unique products of the development and popularization of the Internet, as the rise of cable and satellite broadcasting and 'big media from small nations' such as the Qatar-based Al Jazeera indicates, they nonetheless point to media that are considerably more deterritorialized in the early 21st century than was the case for the 20th century, where one-to-many broadcast communication was in many respects hegemonic.

At the same time, *Understanding Global Media* has also sought to sound a considerable note of caution about theories of strong globalization in relation to the media. It was observed that of the two most influential paradigms in media and communications studies – critical political economy and cultural studies – it has been the *critical political economy* tradition that has developed the most long-standing and coherent approach to global media. It has always strongly foregrounded the relationship of media to power, and the interconnectedness of regimes of economic, political and cultural power. Drawing upon the pioneering work of authors such as Herbert Schiller, critical political economists have argued that the dynamics of large-scale media have extended the tendencies originally identified in Marxism from the national to the global scale, including the concentration of ownership and control, the commodification of social and cultural relations, the weakening of the nation-state as a source of countervailing influence, the development of a global division of cultural labour, and the promotion of ideologies of consumerism and global emulation of Western values that, as Herman and McChesney put it, 'grease the wheels of the global market' (Herman and McChesney, 1997, p. 189). New media are seen from this perspective as reinforcing these social and cultural relations of dominance and subordination, through the rise of transnational cross-platform media conglomerates, the promotion of neo-liberalism as a hegemonic popular and policy discourse, and the shift in the locus of regulatory power and authority from nation-states to supra-national – and decidedly pro-market – institutional agencies such as the World Trade Organization and the World Intellectual Property Organization.

While *cultural studies* has sought to strongly problematize some of the key assumptions of the critical political economy tradition, particularly around questions of media power as it relates to audiences, it has been criticized for implicitly working within a national frame of reference, that limits its capacity to understand global media as related to a set of international social and cultural processes. Its focus upon questions of ideology, reception and audience decoding of media messages has also been seen as a problem, since it is taken by critics as having little to say about actual processes of media production and distribution. At the same time, by questioning claims that global media generate a globalized, hegemonic and homogenized form of mass popular culture, it has linked up with influential theories of cultural hybridity in relation to the movements of people, technologies, media, capital and culture, that have been generated in cognate disciplines such as sociology and anthropology.

This book has sought to move beyond the impasse that has existed between critical political economy and cultural studies in relation to global media. In Chapter 2, it introduced three other ways of thinking about the relationship between media, economics, culture and power. The first of these was *institutionalism*, as it has developed in a variety of branches of the social sciences. Institutionalism has long stressed the social embeddedness of markets and economic agents, the interconnectedness and path dependency of decision-making processes, the relationship between institutions and identity, and the autonomous capacity of decision-making agents. There is an ongoing debate about the relationship between institutions and networked forms of organization, that is discussed in Chapter 4, but it is the case that institutionalism provides the basis for a coherent middle-range theorization of global media that moves beyond debates conducted at a high level of abstraction that are not grounded in particular places, sites of decision-making and social and cultural practices.

Second, *cultural policy studies* is important in linking an understanding of the relationship between political and cultural power to frameworks that stress the decision-making capacities of state institutions and their ability to shape decision-making environments, rather than simply being the puppets of corporate power. Cultural policy studies also develops a distinctive under- standing of the 'government of culture', that questions claims that the media and other cultural forms emerge out of spontaneous action that is subse- quently regulated, but rather proposes that government involvement in the media and cultural spheres has been linked historically to wider projects related to modernity, state-formation and citizenship.

Finally, *cultural and economic geography* is vitally important to the argu- ments developed in this book. By stressing the spatial dimensions of social, economic, cultural and political relations, cultural and economic geography often provides a necessary corrective to highly generalized understandings of globalization and its implications, found in theories of *strong globalization* such as those to be found in the work of Hardt and Negri (2000, 2005) and, to a lesser extent, in the work of Manuel Castells (1996, 1998, 2000a, 2001). It also points to a different understanding of globalization that is very relevant to theories of global media, that questions a *scalar* understanding of how media develop over time (that is, from the local to the national to the global), by drawing attention to the importance of *interscalar* relationships as a central element of contemporary globalization, or the mutual and cross-cutting inter- actions between the local, the national, the regional and the global.

How Significant Is Media Globalization?

The usefulness of such a multiperspectival approach to understanding global media was demonstrated in Chapter 3. The general literature on globalization identifies some of the key economic factors promoting global capitalism as being: the greater volume and intensity of cross-border transactions; enhanced spatial mobility of goods, services and resources, including specialized labour; the general rise of multinational corporations (MNCs); the greater volume and volatility of transactions in global capital and financial markets; and the rising significance of ICTs and electronic commerce.

In their understanding of the implications of such trends, contemporary political economists have drawn upon the insights of neo-Marxist political economy to develop four propositions. The first is that there is growing media concentration on a global scale, and that this is associated with a reduction in competition in the media sector. Second, this leads to the dominance of global media product in domestic media markets to the detriment of local media and cultural forms, and a weakening of the capacity of nationally based governments to regulate media flows in order to promote national cultural policy objectives. Third, the globalization of media production and investment is reinforcing centre–periphery relations between predominantly US-based media corporations and the rest of the world, whether this be through notions of cultural dependency linked to the 'cultural imperialism' thesis, or through economic ties arising from the emergence of a new international division of cultural labour (NICL). Finally, media globalization is seen as reinforcing the worst iniquities of global capitalist culture, by forcing media producers other than the global giants out of business, engineering a 'race to the bottom' in terms of regulations and standards, and further embedding the global cultural hegemony of dominant Western political and economic interests.

The balance of Chapter 3 draws upon other perspectives, particularly those from institutionalism and economic geography, to develop an empirical critique of these arguments. In doing so, the purpose is not to reject activism around global media issues and inequalities as being somehow illegitimate, but rather to consider whether the arguments that drive such campaigns rest upon sound empirical foundations. Three points are made in this analysis. First, there is a general danger in these arguments of presenting large figures as being *prima facie* evidence of greater media concentration, partly because reversals of fortune happen (as in the cases of the AOL-Time Warner merger of 2000, or Vivendi's ill-fated attempts to become a global media conglomerate), but also because they may arise from specific and contingent factors, such as the boom in telecommunications mergers in the late 1990s 'dot.com boom' era.

Second, findings from the UNCTAD transnationality index indicate very clearly that there is not a large-scale trend towards the largest corporations becoming more global in their operations, but rather a gradual expansion of the scale and scope of operations outside of the corporate 'home base'. Moreover, the most 'transnational' corporations tend to be those that come from smaller domestic 'home bases', such as Switzerland, Belgium, Canada, and The Netherlands, rather than the United States, Japan, Britain, France or Germany. The UNCTAD data also indicates that media industries are laggards rather than leaders in globalization: by far the most 'global' corporations are those in mining and extractive industries, followed by manufacturing. Where media have a significant presence, it is in telecommunications rather than media and entertainment industries *per se*; the only significantly global media corporation is arguably News Corporation, and this arose at least in part from its having a home base in Australia until 2004, whereas the bulk of its operations are in the United States, Europe and, increasingly, Asia.

Finally, recent literature from economic geography indicates the dangers of automatically assuming that foreign direct investment by MNCs fosters by its very nature dependency relations between these MNCs and host nations.

Dunning's (2001) work on evaluating the *internalization* advantages of foreign direct investment, or the capacity to engage in knowledge capture and knowledge transfer across markets, rather than simply expanding in order to increase sales or reduce production costs, greatly complicates those models of global media that understand the international ambitions of the largest global media MNCs as simply being about expanding reach or cutting costs. This concept of globalization that aims to work with, rather than in opposition to, local producers and markets dovetails with Storper's (1997) critique of globalization as simply involving the cost-driven, 'winner-take-all' expansion of Western-based MNCs and their products and production lines to the rest of the world. Storper argues that, insofar as the globalization of economic production is occurring, it has developed around a two-track logic, where the cost-driven model, which assumes that anything an be produced anywhere because the labour is generic and the technology can be easily accessed, needs to be complemented by an awareness of those models of producing for global markets which rely upon high, specific labour and knowledge capacities. These are located in particular geographical sites, often clustered around particular institutional configurations, and generate the production of 'de-standardized' commodities, which draw upon difference and novelty or variety as being the sources of sustainable competitive advantage in global economic markets.

The Knowledge Economy and the Creative Industries: Different Ways of Thinking about Global Media

The 1990s and 2000s have seen a challenging of dominant models of thought in both the cultural and the economic spheres. In the cultural sphere, the question has been one of whether cultural policy can move away from traditional models based upon public subsidy of the arts, protection from imported media product, and social improvement based upon exposure to artistic excellence. The 'creative industries' paradigm has emerged as a policy discourse that emphasizes culture as a resource brought into other policy domains, the media and cultural sectors as exemplars of technological and organizational innovation, and the fluidity of global media markets as they intersect with increasingly diverse forms of cultural identity in a globalizing cultural economy.

This intersects with debates within economic theory, such as 'new growth' economics that presents innovation, ideas and intangibles rather than greater efficiency of use of existing resources as the primary drivers of economic development. This corresponds with the rise of a *knowledge economy*, where the rising stars of the global corporate world travel light on direct ownership of physical assets and control over skilled and creative labour, instead relying upon interaction with *knowledge and learning networks* outside of their own institutional structure, particularly when they are geographically co-located within particular cities or regions. This has been particularly important to corporate organizations that are internationalizing their operations, and are reliant upon an awareness of alternate forms of business culture and governance. This in turn arises from the continuing *social embeddedness* of market relations, which points to the limits of both conventional neo-classical economic models that separate economics from other social and cultural domains, and also of critical theories of globalization, such as the new international division of cultural labour (Miller *et al.*, 2001), that view globalization largely in terms of cost advantages derived from lower wages and state subsidies in order to attract 'footloose' and geographically mobile investment capital.

Chapter 4 draws attention to four concepts from media, cultural and communications studies that point to different ways of thinking about the relationship between the global and the local. First, Straubhaar's (1991, 1997) concept of *asymmetrical interdependence* indicates that the entry of global media into national markets is never simply a one-way street, or a transfer of the locus of control from the national to the global spatial domain. What instead occurs in many instances is a selective incorporation of the 'best practice' elements of dominant media formats by local players in order to advance the appeal of their own media product in a more competitive environment. Second, Canclini's concept of *cultural reconversion* indicates that the sense of loss of a national cultural project by governments is not synonymous with a decline in local cultural and creative energy. Rather, there are forms of adaptation which occur among both the large-scale commercial cultural producers and distributors and the more localized and community-based media and cultural producers: the latter have been particularly facilitated by the opening up of distribution channels enabled by networked media such as the Internet (Rennie, 2006).

Third, the implicit 'Global Effects Model' found in some of the key theories of 'cultural imperialism' is challenged not only by an awareness of the complexities of cross-cultural media reception, but by the increasingly multicultural and diasporic nature of much of the world's population. Moreover, there remain advantages of incumbency in national media markets, partly in terms of receptiveness to local cultural traditions and preferences, but also in terms of privileged access to key national policy agents and government decision-makers. Chan (2004) has observed that global media corporations remain, for the most part, 'first of all national players in their home countries', who seek 'cultural crossovers' as their basis for international expansion, rather than crossing the interscalar divide to become truly transnational corporate entities (Chan, 2004, p. 26). Finally, just as the rise of global production networks points to significant instances of knowledge capture and knowledge transfer by the host nations for foreign direct investment (Ernst and Kim, 2002), there has also been work on the relationship between global media and the rise of local production centres. Work on media capitals, particularly in Asia, suggests that there is scope to move from the 'world factory' or 'outsourcing' model towards cultural technology transfer, the creation of 'global niches' and the emergence of new creative clusters, as seen in cities such as Hong Kong, Vancouver and Seoul, and sought after in cities such as Shanghai, Sydney and Auckland (Curtin, 2003; Keane, 2006).

The significance of the concept of creative industries to these debates has been approached, not simply in terms of a retooling of arts, media and cultural policy, but rather as arising from new ways of thinking about culture and its relationship to other domains. In particular, it was argued in Chapter 5 that culture needs to be thought about not only in terms of the traditional dimensions of lived and shared experience and mediated symbolic communication, but also in terms of Yúdice's (2003) concept of *culture as resource*, and the notion of culture as an object of policy and instrument of government developed by Bennett (1992a, 1998) and others. In particular, the rise of creative industries as a policy discourse can be seen as arising from the intersection of: shifts in media policy from national protection of audiovisual industries to the promotion of the digital content industries; recognition in the post-'dot.com' environment of the need to move from ICT-centred information policies to wider debates about how to promote creativity, innovation and entrepreneurship; and the movement of policy towards the cultural and creative sectors from the relative margins of arts policy to the mainstream of national innovation policies in a 'knowledge economy' context. As UNCTAD (2004) has observed, there are explicit links between globalization and the rise of the creative industries at an economic level, as market liberalization, rising average global consumer incomes, networked ICTs, the global rise of service industries and expanding international trade in services are all conduits for the growth of creative industries sectors. From a different angle, Tomlinson (2003) has argued that, rather than suppressing unique cultural identities in order to homogenize global culture into what Barber (2000) termed a 'McWorld', globalization has in fact been a highly significant force in creating, galvanizing and proliferating cultural identities, as difference and identity become more central to a definition of self and participation in the social world.

The Politics of Globalization and Media Policy: Beyond Sanguinity and Critique

Understanding Global Media has sought to develop a perspective on the globalization of media industries, technologies, and products and services that gives equal weight to economic and cultural dimensions of globalization. This book has empirically tested a range of key propositions that arise from debates in the field of global media and communications, and has identified some important emerging points of intersection between recent developments in media, communications and cultural studies with those in institutionalism, economic and cultural geography, cultural policy studies, and theories of the creative industries. It could be argued that, in the course of questioning some of the key theoretical and empirical underpinnings of critical theory as applied to global communications media, the book is providing an endorsement – unwitting or otherwise – of the *status quo* in media relations and, by implication, endorsing the perspectives of the most powerful global media interests.

The counter-argument that is developed in this book is that we need to rethink two issues. The first is the easy equation that is often made between the presence of global media corporations in a variety of national markets, and the assumption that their presence therefore makes them dominant in these environments. The empirical evidence indicates that, from the benchmarks of corporate globalization developed by economic geographers such as Dunning (2001), Dicken (2003a) and others, it is only News Corporation that could be considered a 'global' corporation by such measures, and that its own global status is both a historical by-product of being established in Australia and highly contingent upon its ability to draw upon networks and institutional relations in the range of countries in which it operates.

Second, there is a need to think about the historical contingency of relationships between communications media, the nation-state, and cultural policy, and to recognize that the trajectories and configurations that held sway for much of the 20th century will not be as applicable to the media industries of the 21st century. The argument that a regulatory and protectionist state could draw upon the connection between nationally based media and the role of the nation-state in managing media and cultural policy in order to 'produce' national citizens has been under challenge for some time. The rise of global media is only part of the equation here, as increasingly culturally diverse populations, the proliferation of means by which to access digital content, contestation of 'top-down' nationalist cultural policy agendas, and the decline of popular belief in the nation-building project of cultural nationalism (as indicated in media consumption patterns) are elements that are as significant as the development of the emergence of media technologies with cross-border and potentially global reach.

It is argued in *Understanding Global Media* that we are moving from the 20th-century model of the regulatory and protective state, in a context where nation-states had variable degrees of control over media flows within their territories, to a 21st-century model of the *enabling state*, whereby the role of governmental authorities is increasingly promotional and performative, working with complex networks of non-governmental authority and agency. This policy shift has been associated with scalar shifts in the crucial *loci* of cultural policy energies and dynamics from the national level to that of the sub-national and the supra-national.

At the *sub-national* level, media and cultural policies have been strongly aligned with moves towards developing creative cities and creative clusters, in many cases strongly influenced by influential US academics such as the business strategy theorist Michael Porter, and the economic geographer Richard Florida. Creative-city strategies have been driven by a heterogeneous set of policy priorities, ranging from attracting geographically mobile capital and skilled labour to developing a more demand-driven approach to arts and cultural policy, renovating disused inner-urban industrial districts, and promoting cultural diversity and an innovation culture. Contrary to the assumption that globalization would generate greater homogeneity among the world's cities, the desire of 'place competitiveness' on a national, regional or global scale has in fact acted as a stimulus to innovative thinking in the field of urban planning, and greater attention to the cultural dimensions of place. At the same time, by bringing culture to the forefront of local development strategies, it has tended to efface the specific dimensions of cultural policy, working more explicitly with the 'culture as resource' approach identified by Yúdice (2003), and discussed in Chapter 5.

The *supra-national* sites of media and cultural policy have also become more central over the last two decades. While the concept of globalization was of minor significance as late as the early 1990s, it has moved to the front and centre of attention of those in the corporate world, governmental agents, academics and activists. This book has documented the rise of media globalization as an element of more general processes of economic and cultural globalization, but it is also important to understand two further dimensions of globalization. One is the rise of agreements reached at an international level that are legally binding upon the nations that are signatories to them. Some of the most significant of these have been the General Agreement on Trade in Services (GATS) and the Trade-Related Intellectual Property Services (TRIPS) agreement, and the transnational intergovernmental organizations (IGOs) established to both oversee national compliance with these agreements and to promote further economic liberalization, such as the World Trade Organization (WTO) and the World Intellectual Property Organization (WIPO). The second major dimension is the proliferation of international non-governmental organizations (INGOs), whose formal numbers range from 6,000 to over 50,000, depending upon how INGOs are classified. The importance of IGOs, INGOs and legally binding international agreements introduces a degree of multiscalarity into media and cultural policy processes, along the lines identified by Held *et al.* when they described how one consequence of globalization is that 'effective power is shared and bartered by diverse forces and agencies at national, regional and international levels' (Held *et al.*, 1999, p. 80). The World Summits on the Information society (WSIS) in Geneva (2003) and Tunis (2005) provide fascinating case studies of how international organizations such as those associated with the United Nations are seeking to extend transnational policy dialogue beyond nation-states, to include not only corporate actors, but agents of global civil society as represented by the INGO sector.

An issue raised at various points in this book, particularly through its references to creative industries policy discourse, is whether innovation in the media sphere is linked to broader development and innovation agendas. This issue has been canvassed around the question of whether new forms of digitally networked media, and broadening of access to the means of producing and distributing digital content (the rise of the so-called 'prod-user'), mark out the possibility of democratizing media access and distributing its means of production and distribution beyond its traditional institutional gatekeepers (Hartley, 2005; Cunningham, 2006; Deuze, 2006; Jenkins, 2006; cf. Bruns, 2005 for a discussion in relation to news media and journalism). This book has left open the question as to whether such developments in the digital domain will displace the traditional 'hourglass' structure of the media industries, where large numbers of creative producers exist alongside extensive and diverse consumer demands for culture, but access is regulated, and cultural and economic power accrued, through the distributional 'bottlenecks' that arise from concentration of the means of cultural distribution.

Rather, the core question raised in *Understanding Global Media* has been, even if such bottlenecks still exist and remain an important aspect of the media sector, have the last 25 years of media globalization simply represented a shift in the scalar dynamics of monopoly capitalism, so that bottlenecks in the media industries that arose from national oligopolies have now become global bottlenecks dominated by a much smaller number of global media monopolies? The argument of this book has been that it does not. Rather, a complex industrial and cultural geography of global media is emerging, whereby there certainly remain hegemonic media capitals, and dominant media capitalists, but where media globalization does not simply mean the reproduction of long-established core–periphery relations between 'Global Hollywood' and the rest of the world. Attempts to extend market dominance beyond national home bases by global media corporations will continue to have to engage in an ongoing manner with key national players, as well as with the diversity and heterogeneity of local and national cultures, and the available evidence thus far suggests that they are at some disadvantage in doing so, in contrast to our usual assumptions about the ubiquitous power of multinational corporations. More generally, what the rise of global media instead points to is a complex and shifting scalar dynamic between the local, the national and the global, whereby new centres of global media production may emerge from a variety of locales as immanent clusters of cultural creativity.

Notes

Chapter 1

1. See Zelizer (2004) for a discussion of how the role of journalists has been approached in various strands of media and social theory.
2. The term *agent* is used rather than *person*, as it recognizes that communication activities are engaged in by a range of social organizations, or by people acting on behalf of these institutions, and not just among people as autonomous individuals.
3. McQuail (2005) distinguishes between what he terms *media-centric* and *society-centric* models of social change, with the former identifying the media as a primary driver of social change, and the latter viewing the media as largely an extension of larger political, economic and social forces.
4. The wider tendency of such behavioural models of media influence was to generate scepticism about the nature and significance of media power, since virtually any direct empirical study of the impact of a media message upon individual behaviour would draw attention to the importance of *intervening variables*, or those factors external to the media itself – such as social status, prior psychological disposition, or personal background – that would impact upon an individual's receptiveness to any single media message. At the height of the influence of such models, Joseph Klapper could confidently observe that 'mass communication does not ordinarily serve as a necessary or sufficient cause of audience effects, but rather functions through a nexus of mediating factors' (cited in Newbold, 1995a, p. 119).
5. One of the central elements, which will not be discussed at length in this book, was a critique of theories of media effects, and the attention given to empirical studies of how certain types of media message (for example, the portrayal of violence) have behavioural effects upon the consuming audience. For an overview of the history of media effects research, see McQuail (2005), pp. 456–78. For a rejection of media effects research from a critical media-cultural studies perspective, see Gauntlett (1998).
6. The concept of 'relative autonomy' was developed by the French Marxist philosopher Louis Althusser, who argued that the political and ideological dimensions of a society should not be seen as being simply determined by the structure of economic relations, but that they developed in a complex process of interaction with the economic and political levels that was determining as well as determined, or what he also termed 'overdetermination' in any given society. While the detail of this can certainly get confusing – particularly given that Althusser, as a Marxist, maintained that economic relations were determinant 'in the last instance' – it nonetheless enabled the study of ideology, and with it the question of cultural power, to be developed in ways that did not simply refer back to relations of power and domination in the economic domain. For an overview of Althusser's analysis

of ideology, see Elliott (1987), Barrett (1991).

7. The proliferation of reviews of media products, and the tendency to use various consumer guide indicators such as stars to rate the vast range of media products, can be seen as being a response to this ongoing consumer uncertainty.

8. Perhaps the most famous attempt to own creative people through institutionalized contracts was the Hollywood 'studio system' that operated in the US film industry from the 1920s to the 1940s. The studio system finally broke down, partly because the 'Big Five' Hollywood majors were found to be in breach of US anti-trust laws, but also because the success of the movies gave the film stars celebrity status, and associated economic clout, such that they were able to successfully negotiate their way out of such binding contracts. On the Hollywood studio system, see Sklar (1994).

9. The question of the status of corporate law as distinctive when compared with common law, and whether it has generated pathological behaviour on the part of those working at the higher levels of corporations, is addressed in an interesting way in the documentary *The Corporation* (Achbar, Abbott and Bakan, 2004).

Chapter 2

1. One of the key early summaries of cultural studies was that of Graeme Turner, whose book is explicitly concerned with *British* cultural studies. See Turner (1990).

2. A major influence on cultural policy studies in Britain were the initiatives of Labour-led local governments in the 1980s to develop cultural industries as a response to the loss of traditional manufacturing jobs. Such strategies would evolve into creative industries policies in the 1990s.

3. Dicken (2003b) uses the example of Wal-Mart to illustrate this point. Wal-Mart was the world's largest private employer, with 1.14 million employees in 1999. Its sales outside of the US, however, account for only 14 per cent of total sales, and 85 per cent of its workforce is employed in the US. While Wal-Mart is significant in other aspects of globalization, most notably in how it globally sources the items that it stocks but perhaps also in how it encourages thinking about 'mega-marts' as a way of organizing retail activities, it is not a transnational corporation in terms of the bulk of its sales activities, the significance of its overseas investments, or where the majority of its workforce are located.

4. The 'Washington Consensus' was a term used to describe a commonly held set of views among economists at the IMF, the Word Bank and the US Treasury about the measures necessary to address structural imbalances in developing countries that required international assistance. They pointed in the direction of cutting government spending, privatizing state enterprises, reducing domestic tariff protection and opening up the economy to foreign investment, and moving toward exchange rates set by international financial markets and the removal of capital controls. The term is taken from an economist with the Washington-based Institute for International Economics, John Williamson, and his analysis in 1990 of the impli-

cations of economic policy reforms in Latin America in the 1980s. For an analysis of this literature, see Santino (2004).

5. MMOGs are Massive Multiplayer Online Games, where real-time interaction between globally dispersed players is a condition of game-playing. Examples of such MMOGs include *EverQuest*, *Counter-Strike* and *The Sims Online*.

Chapter 3

1. Strictly speaking, what is referred to can be described as a global media oligopoly rather than a monopoly, meaning dominance by a small number of corporations rather than control over the market by a single provider. I have used the term 'monopoly' rather than 'oligopoly' for two reasons. First, such arguments are clear in their implications that concentration of ownership necessarily entails a diminution of competition, even if it does not lead to control by a single producer. Second, the tendency towards monopoly points in this thesis to a shift in the dynamics of capitalist economies on a global scale that is akin to that described in the neo-Marxist theory of monopoly capitalism.

2. Alfred Hitchcock apparently used to reprimand British critics of his move to Hollywood, by saying that 'There are no Americans here. Hollywood is full of foreigners' (quoted in Miller *et al.*, 2001, p. 55).

3. In light of the rise of China, and also of South Korea and Taiwan, it is perhaps better to think of this as a North East Asian regional trading bloc.

4. The problems facing AOL-Time Warner were, however, minor when compared to those of another global media conglomerate, the France-based Vivendi Universal, established under CEO Jean-Marie Messier. Vivendi Universal's shares had been reduced to junk bond status by 2002, as Messier was turned on not only by the Hollywood hard-heads who had always doubted the capacity of a French 'outsider' to manage a US-based entertainment business, but also by the French political and economic establishment, who feared for the future of 'national champions' such as the Canal Plus cable TV provider. Compaine (2000) and Caves (2000) drew attention to some of the limitations of conglomeration strategies in the media sector, as they generate new problems of control across the diffuse organizational elements of the multidivisional media corporation, and to how it may stifle the original sources of creativity in the pre-merged entity.

5. With the merger of Vivendi Universal's North American media and entertainment assets with General Electric through the NBC corporation in 2003, Vivendi could no longer be considered to be a global media conglomerate, since its sole significant media asset is the French cable network Canal Plus, which has limited market penetration outside of France (The Economist, 2002a, 2003).

6. The UNCTAD list of the top 100 non-financial MNCs ranked by foreign assets in 2003 also included Vodafone (2), France Telecom (10), Deutsche Telekom AG (14), Telecom Italia Spa (24), Telefónica SA (36), Singtel (66), Nokia (69), Verizon (82) and Motorola (97) from the telecommunications sector (UNCTAD, 2005, pp.

269–71). All of these companies have a presence in media and entertainment industries, and one that is likely to grow over time. Whether they can be considered media corporations remains an important and open definitional question, as it is for companies such as General Electric and Microsoft. I would argue that they cannot as yet be considered to be media corporations in ways that support the hypothesis that they are increasingly dominating global media markets and, with it, the provision of media content.

7. Such exercises invariably draw attention to the blurriness of distinctions between the 'developed' and 'developing' world, particularly those arising from economic development in East Asia. Companies such as Hutchinson, Samsung, Hyundai, LG Electronics, Acer and Singtel are significant global players in their respective markets, and their 'home base' countries – Singapore, Hong Kong SAR, Republic of Korea and Taiwan – have been quickly moving out of 'developing country' status. The UNCTAD *World Development Report 2006* discusses at length the implications of the rise of TNCs from developing economies (UNCTAD, 2006).

Chapter 4

1. A common counter-example to this claim is that industrial production has not declined in significance, but has instead been relocated to the developing world. The rise of China as the world's pre-eminent location for manufacturing, or the 'world's factory', in the early 21st century has been seen as an exemplar of such a trend (see e.g. Deloitte Research, 2003). I don't consider China's rise as an industrial economy to invalidate claims that there is a transition towards a knowledge economy for two reasons. First, the global shift of investment in manufacturing goods production to China only intensifies the need for higher-wage economies to identify new sources of employment and economic growth which are not as sensitive to price-based international competition. Second, the Chinese are themselves intensely interested in how to develop more knowledge-intensive industries (Grewal *et al.*, 2002; Keane, 2004c).

2. A very important related development in economic theory has been the rise of *new growth economics*, associated with Paul David and others from the so-called 'Stanford School'. Paul Romer (1994) has pointed out that conventional economic thinking has tended to treat technology as exogenous 'manna from heaven', which influences economic systems from the outside. He instead proposes that there is a dynamic interrelationship between technological change and economic growth, and that socio-economic systems that develop institutional conditions that are conducive to new ideas and innovation experience cumulative technological change. David (1999) has also contributed to this literature, particularly with his observation about the time-lag between the emergence of new techno-economic regimes and socio-institutional adjustment which enables the opportunities of new technologies to be maximized, which may exist for up to 50 years.

3. The synonymy of Los Angeles with 'Hollywood' marks an interesting conflation of a city-region with a particular sub-region within it. Due to the historical correspondence of the rise of US cinema worldwide with the location of film studios in this sub-region, we continue to refer to 'Hollywood' cinema, even though most film and television production in Los Angeles County now occurs outside of the Hollywood area, and it is perhaps now best known as a centre for the adult film industry than for the film and television industry proper.

4. Nixon (2004) presents a fascinating case study of this in identifying the importance of inner-urban London regions such as Soho and Covent Garden to the advertising industry.

5. David Harvey, *The Limits to Capital* (Harvey, 1982) provides the definitive interpretation of Marx's political economy from a geographical perspective. In his later work *The Condition of Postmodernity*, Harvey argued that 'the history of capitalism has been characterized by speed-up in the pace of life, while so overcoming spatial barriers that the world sometimes seems to collapse inward upon us' (Harvey, 1989, p. 240).

6. While a detailed study of global telecommunications is outside of the scope of this book, these issues have been quite apparent in that sector. The telecommunications universe of the early 1980s, where state-run national monopolies provided a POTS (plain old telephone system) on a universal basis in 1994 is today almost inconceivable, and there have certainly emerged major international players, most notably AT&T and Vodafone. At the same time, the incumbent national telecommunications providers, while having lost their monopoly status and having been privatized in many instances, have only slowly lost market share and have often maintained privileged access to national governments and policy-makers. The largest providers, such as Telefónica (Spain), Deutsche Telekom (Germany) and France Telecom (France) have also internationalized and diversified their activities to operate in multiple markets, particularly in new media areas.

Chapter 5

1. Schlesinger quotes figures showing that 94 percent of total television viewing in Europe in 1994 was language-specific (Schlesinger, 1997, p. 384). This is consistent with observations that less than 10 per cent of programming made in one EU member nation is viewed in another member nation, in spite of a range of initiatives to promote pan-European audiovisual media content (Collins, 1998).

2. Examples of such policies included the US government's *National Information Infrastructure Task Force* report (1993); the European Union's *Europe and the Information Superhighway* (Bangemann Report) (1994); Singapore's *IT2000 – A Vision of an Intelligent Island* report (1992); the Canadian government's *The Canadian Information Highway: Building Canada' Information and Communications Infrastructure* report (1994); Japan's *Program for Advanced Information Infrastructure* report (1994); the Australian government's *Creative*

Nation (1994) and *Networking Australia's Future* (1995) reports; the Malaysian government's *Multimedia Super Corridor* strategy report (1995); Korea's *Infomatization Strategies for Promoting National Competitiveness* report (1996); and the OECD's *Global Information Infrastructure – Global Information Society* report (1997). See Northfield (1999) for an extended commentary on these.

3. One relatively benign example of such a trend has been seen in the reassertion of an English cultural identity. Tomlinson (2004) has observed that as devolution began to give Scotland and Wales more political power to match their distinctive cultural identity claims, there was the re-emergence of the Cross of St George as a flag of English identity, displacing the Union Jack at major sporting events such as the 2002 World Cup soccer tournament , the 2003 Rugby World Cup and the 2006 Ashes cricket tour of Australia. This can be seen as paralleling the earlier assertions of an English identity in popular music seen in mid-1990s 'Brit-pop', where bands such as Oasis explicitly connected themselves to an English musical patrimony derived from The Beatles, The Rolling Stones and The Who. Less benign examples of a reassertion of 'majority' cultural identities can be seen in the rise of a 'neo-nativist' movement in the United States that combines hostility to the federalist state with a discourse on the threatened nature of 'White' cultural identity, the electoral success of Jean-Marie Le Pen's National Front party in France, and the rise of the 'One Nation' Party in Australia, which opposed multiculturalism, globalization and the extension of rights to indigenous peoples on the basis of a traditional 'Anglo-Celtic' culture that had been betrayed by 'politically correct' governing elites (Hage, 1998).

4. It was rumoured, for instance, that copies of Huntington's book *The Clash of Civilizations* were unobtainable in Cairo in the immediate aftermath of 9/11.

5. See Buchanan (2004) for an admirably concise introduction to key concepts in Deleuzian thought.

Chapter 6

1. Whereas people in the West tend to refer to this as the First Gulf War, with the second being the invasion of Iraq by US-led forces in 2003, in the Arab world the Iran–Iraq war, which went from 1981 to 1989 and saw over 1 million people lose their lives, is known as the First Gulf War, and the liberation of Kuwait from Iraqi occupation in 1991 as the Second Gulf War.

2. The example of Australian indigenous art is interesting in this regard. Since the mid-1980s, there has been a growing international demand for artistic works produced by indigenous (Aboriginal) Australians, to the point where auctions of such works are held by the leading British auction house Christie's, and where the Musée du Quai Branly in Paris has had Australian indigenous artists painting its ceiling. While this generation of new international income from the sale of art works is welcome in Australian Aboriginal communities, which are among the most socio-economically disadvantaged groups in Australia by some margin, it

nonetheless generates three problematic issues. First, the art world's preference for payment to the original creator as author sits uncomfortably with the expectations of indigenous communities in remote areas, whose work is by far the most sought-after in international markets, of collective forms of ownership and responsibility. Second, it has set in train a conflict between the expectations of wealthy international art patrons that 'traditional' works will continue to be produced, and the fact that indigenous artists are increasingly working within a global circuit of artistic and cultural trade. Third, among an indigenous population that was routinely dispossessed of its land and identity in over 200 years of European settlement, there is the danger of reinforcing stereotypes of 'real' Aborigines living in remote settlements, and of those living in cities and regional centres as somehow not being 'authentic' in either their indigenous identity or the products of their artistic and creative work.

3. Article II, Most-Favoured-Nation Treatment, stipulates that each Member is required to 'accord immediately and unconditionally to services and service suppliers of any other Member treatment no less favourable than that it accords to like services and service suppliers of any other country'; Article XVI, Market Access, requires that 'each Member shall accord services and service suppliers of any other Member treatment no less favourable than that provided for under the terms, limitations and conditions agreed and specified in its Schedule'. This Article also requires that, if the cross-border movement of capital is an essential part of the service, the Member is required to permit such capital movements; Article XVII, National Treatment, requires that 'each Member shall accord to services and service suppliers of any other Member, in respect of all measures affecting the supply of services, treatment no less favourable than it accords to its own like services and service suppliers'.

4. To take one example, the payment for broadcast rights to the 2002 World Cup soccer tournament was considerably higher for Telemundo, broadcasting in Spanish, than for ESPN, which had the English-language rights. This is because the intensity of interest in international soccer is much greater among the US Hispanic community than among other communities within the US, which tend to see soccer as a sport of minor interest.

5. Sarikakis indicates that over 30 million people living in the EU have no citizenship (Sarikakis, 2005, p. 167). Many of these people are from Africa, the Middle East and Eastern Europe, and are among the most culturally disenfranchised within their national societies.

Bibliography

Abramovitz, Moses and David, Paul (2001) *Two Centuries of American Macroeconomic Growth: From Exploitation of Resource Abundance to Knowledge-Driven Development*. Stanford: Stanford Institute for Economic Policy Research, Discussion Paper 01–05, August.

Abramson, Bram Dov (2001) Media Policy after Regulation?. *International Journal of Cultural Studies* 4 (3), September, pp. 301–26.

Acland, Charles, and Buxton, William (eds) (1999) *Harold Innis in the New Century*. Montréal: McGill-Queen's University Press.

Ádám, Gyorgy (1975) Multinational Corporations and Worldwide Sourcing. In H. Radice (ed.) *International Firms and Modern Imperialism*. Harmondsworth: Penguin, pp. 89–103.

Aglietta, Michel (1987) *A Theory of Capitalist Regulation*. London: Verso.

— (1998) Capitalism at the Turn of the Century: Regulation Theory and the Challenge of Social Change. *New Left Review* 232, pp. 41–90.

Altvater, Elmar, and Mahnkopf, Birgit (1997) The World Market Unbound. In A. Scott (ed.) *The Limits of Globalization: Cases and Arguments*. London: Routledge, pp. 306–26.

Amin, Ash (2001) Globalization: Geographical Aspects. In N. J. Smelser and P. B. Baltes (eds) *International Encyclopedia of the Social and Behavioural Sciences*. Amsterdam: Elsevier Science, pp. 6271–7.

— (2002) Spatialities of Globalization. *Environment and Planning A* 34, pp. 385–99.

— and Thrift, Nigel (eds) (2004) *The Cultural Economy Reader*. Oxford: Blackwell.

Amin, Samir (2004) Unity and Changes in the Ideology of Political Economy. In P. Leistnya (ed.) *Cultural Studies: From Theory to Action*. Oxford and Malden: Blackwell, pp. 19–28.

Anderson, Benedict (1991) *Imagined Communities: Reflections on the Origins and Spread of Nationalism*. London: Verso.

Ang, Ien (1991) *Desperately Seeking the Audience*. London: Routledge.

— (1996a) Global Media/Local Meaning. In *Living Room Wars: Rethinking Media Audiences for a Postmodern World*. New York: Routledge, pp. 50–61.

— (1996b) In the Realm of Uncertainty: The Global Village and Capitalist Postmodernity. In *Living Room Wars: Rethinking Media Audiences for a Postmodern World*. New York: Routledge, pp. 162–80.

Angus, Ian, and Shoesmith, Brian (1993) Orality in the Twilight of Humanism: A Critique of the Communications Theory of Harold Innis. *Continuum: Journal of Media and Cultural Studies* 7 (1), pp. 1–28.

Appadurai, Arjun (1990) Disjuncture and Difference in the Global Cultural Economy. In M. Featherstone (ed.) *Global Culture: Nationalism, Globalization and Modernity*. London: Sage, pp. 295–310.

— (1996) *Modernity at Large: Cultural Dimensions of Globalization*. Minneapolis: University of Minnesota Press.

— (2003) Grassroots Globalization and the Research Imagination. In A. Appadurai (ed.) *Globalization*. Durham, NC: Duke University Press, pp. 1–21.

Arthur, Brian (1999) Competing Technologies, Increasing Returns and Lock-In by Historical Events. *Economic Journal* 99, pp. 116–31.

Auerbach, Paul (1988) *Competition: The Economics of Industrial Change*. Oxford: Basil Blackwell.

AusFILM (2000) *A Bigger Slice of the Pie: Policy Options for a More Competitive International Film and Television Production Industry in Australia*. Report prepared by Malcolm Long Associates, November.

Australian Broadcasting Tribunal (1991) *Oz Content: An Inquiry into Australian Content on Commercial Television*. Five volumes. Canberra: Australian Government Printing Service.

Australian Film Commission (AFC) (2002) *Foreign Film and Television Drama Production in Australia*. Sydney: AFC.

Bagdikian, Ben (2000) *The Media Monopoly*, 6th edition. Boston: Beacon.

Balibrea, Mari Paz (2001) Urbanism, Culture and the Post-Industrial City: Challenging the 'Barcelona Model'. *Journal of Spanish Cultural Studies* 2 (2), pp. 187–210.

Baran, Paul (1973) *The Political Economy of Growth*. Harmondsworth: Penguin.

— and Sweezy, Paul (1968) *Monopoly Capital*. Harmondsworth: Penguin.

Barber, Benjamin (2000) Jihad vs. McWorld. In F. J. Lechner and J. Boli (eds) *The Globalization Reader*. Oxford and Malden: Blackwell, pp. 21–6.

Barnes, Trevor (2003) Introduction: 'Never Mind the Economy: Here's Culture'. in K. Anderson, M. Domosh, S. Pile and N. Thrift (eds) *Handbook of Cultural Goegraphy*. London: Sage, pp. 89–97.

Barnet, Richard and Müller, Robert (1974) *Global Reach: The Power of the Multinational Corporations*. New York: Simon & Schuster.

Barney, Darin (2004) *The Network Society*. Cambridge: Polity.

Barrett, Michèle (1991) *The Politics of Truth: From Marx to Foucault*. Cambridge: Polity.

Barwise, Patrick, and Ehrenberg, Andrew (1988) *Television and its Audience*. London: Sage.

Bellamy, Robert and Traudt, Paul (2000) Television Branding as Promotion. In S. T. Eastman (ed.) *Research in Media Promotion*. Mahwah: Lawrence Erlbaum, pp. 127–59.

Beniger, James (1986) *The Control Revolution: Technological and Economic Origins of the Information Society*. Cambridge, MA: Harvard University Press.

Benkler, Yochai (2002) Coase's Penguin, or, Linux and the Nature of the Firm. *Yale Law Journal* 112 (3), pp. 369–446.

Bennett, Tony (1989) Culture: Theory and Policy. *Culture and Policy* 1 (1), pp. 9–11.

— (1992a) Putting Policy into Cultural Studies. In L. Grossberg, C. Nelson and P. Treichler (eds) *Cultural Studies*. New York: Routledge, pp. 23–37.

— (1992b) Useful Culture. *Cultural Studies* 6 (3), pp. 395–408.

— (1995) *The Birth of the Museum: History, Theory, Politics*. London: Routledge.

— (1998) *Culture: A Reformer's Science*. Sydney: Allen & Unwin.

— (2003) Culture and Governmentality. In J. Z. Bratich, J. Packer and C. McCarthy (eds) *Foucault, Cultural Studies, and Governmentaity*. Albany: State University of New York Press, pp. 47–63.

Best, Michael (1990) *The New Competition: Institutions of Industrial Restructuring.* Cambridge: Polity.

Bhabha, Homi (1994) *The Location of Culture.* London: Routledge.

Bicket, Douglas (2005) Reconsidering Geocultural Contraflow: Intercultural Information Flows through Trends in Global Audiovisual Trade. *Global Media Journal* 4 (6), pp. 1–26.

Blackburn, Robin (ed.) (1972) *Ideology in Social Science: Readings in Critical Social Theory.* London: Fontana.

Bocock, Robert (1992) The Cultural Formations of Modern Society. In S. Hall and B. Gieben (eds) *Formations of Modernity.* Cambridge: Polity with the Open University, pp. 229–74.

Bolter, Jay David and Grusin, Richard (2000) *Remediation: Understanding New Media.* Cambridge, MA: MIT Press.

Bordwell, David (2000) *Planet Hong Kong: Popular Cinema and the Art of Entertainment.* Cambridge, MA: Harvard University Press.

Botsman, Peter and Latham, Mark (2001) *The Enabling State: People Before Bureaucracy.* Sydney: Pluto.

Bourdieu, Pierre (1984) *Distinction: A Social Critique of the Judgement of Taste.* Trans. R. Nice. London: Routledge.

Boyd, Douglas (1999) *Broadcasting in the Arab World*, 3rd edition. Ames: Iowa State University Press.

Boyd-Barrett, Oliver (1998) Media Imperialism Reformulated. In D. K. Thussu (ed.) *Electronic Empires: Global Media and Local Resistance.* London: Edward Arnold, pp. 157–76.

Boyer, Robert (1987) Regulation. In J. Eatwell, M. Milgate and P. Newman (eds) *The New Palgrave: A Dictionary of Economics, Volume 4.* London: Macmillan (now Palgrave Macmillan), pp. 126–8.

— (1988) Technical Change and the Theory of Regulation. In G. Dosi, C. Freeman, R. R. Nelson, G. Silverberg and L. Soete (eds) *Technical Change and Economic Theory.* London: Pinter, pp. 67–94.

— (1990) *The Regulation School: A Critical Introduction.* New York: Columbia University Press.

— and Drache, Daniel (eds) (1996) *States Against Markets: The Limits of Globalization.* New York: Routledge.

Braithwaite, John (2000) The New Regulatory State and the Transformation of Criminology. *British Journal of Criminology* 40 (2), pp. 222–38.

— and Drahos, Peter (2000) *Global Business Regulation.* Cambridge: Cambridge University Press.

Brewer, Anthony (1980) *Marxist Theories of Imperialism: A Critical Survey.* London: Routledge & Kegan Paul.

Brown, Andy, O'Connor, Justin and Cohen, Sara (2000) Local Music Policies within a Global Music Industry: Cultural Quarters in Liverpool, Manchester and Sheffield. *Geoforum* 31 (4), pp. 431–51.

Bruns, Axel (2005) *Gatewatching: Collaborative Online News Production.* New York: Peter Lang.

Buchanan, Ian (2004) Introduction: Deleuze and Music. In I. Buchanan and M. Swiboda (eds) *Deleuze and Music.* Edinburgh: Edinburgh University Press, pp. 1–19.

Budd, Alan, Entman, Robert and Steinman, Clay (1990) The Affirmative Character of U.S. Cultural Studies. *Critical Studies in Mass Communication* 7 (2), pp. 169–84.

Burch, Sally (2004) Global Media Governance: Reflections from the WSIS Experience. *Media Development* 1, pp. 1–6.

Calabrese, Andrew (1999) The Information Age According to Manuel Castells. *Journal of Communication* 49 (3), pp. 172–86.

Campbell, John and Lindberg, Leon (1990) Property Rights and the Organization of Economic Activity by the State. *American Sociological Review* 55 (4), pp. 634–47.

Canclini, Néstor García (1992) Cultural Reconversion. In G. Yúdice, J. Franco and J. Flores (eds) *On Edge: The Crisis of Contemporary Latin American Culture*. Minneapolis: University of Minnesota Press, pp. 29–43.

— (1995) *Hybrid Cultures: Strategies for Entering and Leaving Modernity*. Minneapolis: University of Minnesota Press.

— (2000) Cultural Policy Options in the Context of Globalization. In G. Bradford, M. Gary and G. Wallach (eds) *The Politics of Culture: Policy Perspectives for Individuals, Institutions, and Communities*. New York: New Press, pp. 302–26.

— (2001) *Consumers and Citizens: Globalization and Multicultural Conflicts*. Intro. and trans. George Yúdice. Minneapolis: University of Minnesota Press.

Castells, Manuel (1978) *City, Class, and Power*. London: Verso.

__ (1996) *The Rise of the Network Society*. Volume 1 of *The Information Age: Economy, Society, and Culture*. Oxford: Blackwell.

— (1998) *The Power of Identity*. Volume 2 of *The Information Age: Economy, Society, and Culture*. Oxford: Blackwell.

— (2000a) *End of Millennium*. Volume 3 of *The Information Age: Economy, Society, and Culture*. Oxford: Blackwell.

— (2000b) Materials for an Exploratory Theory of the Network Society. *British Journal of Sociology* 51 (1), pp. 5–24.

— (2001) E-Business and the New Economy. In Manuel Castells, *The Internet Galaxy: Reflections on the Internet, Business, and Society*. Oxford: Oxford University Press, pp. 64–115.

— (2004) Afterword: Why Networks Matter. In H. McCarthy, P. Miller and P. Skidmore (eds) *Network Logic: Who Governs in an Interconnected World?* London: DEMOS, pp. 221–4.

Castles, Stephen (1997) Multicultural Citizenship: A Response to the Dilemma of Globalization And National Identity?. *Journal of Intercultural Studies* 18 (1), pp. 5–22.

— and Davidson, Alastair (2000) *Citizenship and Migration: Globalization and the Politics of Belonging*. Basingstoke: Macmillan (now Palgrave Macmillan).

Caughie, John (1990) Playing at Being American: Games and Tactics. In P. Mellencamp (ed.) *Logics of Television: Essays in Cultural Criticism*. Bloomington: Indiana University Press, pp. 44–58.

Caves, Richard (2000) *Creative Industries: Contracts Between Art and Commerce*. Cambridge, MA: Harvard University Press.

Centre for Cultural Policy Research (CCPR) (2003) *Baseline Study of Hong Kong's Creative Industries*. University of Hong Kong, September. Available from www.ccpr.hku.hk/BaselineStudyonHKCreativeIndustries-eng.pdf. Accessed 13 September 2006.

Chan, Joseph Man (2004) Global Media and the Dialectics of the Global. *Global Media and Communication* 1 (1), pp. 24–8.

Chandler, Alfred (1977) *The Visible Hand: The Managerial Revolution in American Business.* Cambridge, MA: Harvard University Press.

Chenoweth, Neil (2002) *Virtual Murdoch: Reality Wars on the Information Highway.* London: Vintage.

Chomsky, Noam (2001) *9-11.* New York: Seven Stories.

— and Herman, Edward S. (1988) *Manufacturing Consent: The Political Economy of the Mass Media.* New York: Pantheon.

Christensen, Clayton (1997) *The Innovator's Dilemma.* New York: HarperCollins.

Christopherson, Susan (2002) Why do National Labor Market Practices Continue to Diverge in the Global Economy? The 'Missing Link' of Investment Rules. *Economic Geographer* 78 (1), pp. 1–20.

Chua, Beng Huat (2004) Conceptualizing an East Asian Popular Culture. *Inter-Asia Cultural Studies* 5 (2), pp. 200–21.

Civil Society WSIS (2003) *Shaping Information Societies for Human Needs: Civil Society Declaration to the World Summit on the Information Society*, WSIS Civil Society Plenary, Geneva, 8 December.

Clegg, Stewart, Boreham, Paul and Dow, Geoff (1986) *Class, Politics and the Economy.* London: Routledge & Kegan Paul.

—, Kornberger, Martin and Pitsis, Tyrone (2005) *Management and Organizations.* London: Sage.

Cohen, Hart (2000) Revisiting McLuhan. *Media International Australia* 94, pp. 5–12.

Collins, Richard (1990) *Culture, Communication and National Identity: The Case of Canadian Television.* Toronto: University of Toronto Press.

— (1998) *From Satellite to Single Market: The Europeanization of Television 1982–1992.* London: Routledge.

—, Garnham, Nicholas and Locksley, Gareth (1988) *The Economics of Television: The UK Case.* London: Sage.

— and Murroni, Christina (1996) *New Media, New Policies.* Cambridge: Polity.

Compaine, Benjamin (2000) Distinguishing between Concentration and Competition. In B. M. Compaine and D. Gomery, *Who Owns the Media? Competition and Concentration in the Mass Media Industry*, 3rd edition. Mahwah: Lawrence Erlbaum, pp. 537–81.

— (2001) The Myths of Encroaching Global Media Ownership. *Open Democracy.* Available from www.opendemocracy.net/debates/debate-8-24.jsp. Posted 8 November. Accessed 14 November 2004.

Condit, Celeste (1989) The Rhetorical Limits of Polysemy. *Critical Studies in Mass Communication* 6 (1), pp. 103–22.

Connell, John and Gibson, Chris (2003) *Soundtracks: Popular Music, Identity and Place.* London: Routledge.

Considine, Mark (1994) *Public Policy: A Critical Approach.* Melbourne: Macmillan (now Palgrave Macmillan).

Control Room (2004). Director: Jehane Noujaim.

Cooke, Philip (2002) New Media and New Economy Cluster Dynamics. In L. Lievrouw and S. Livingstone (eds) *The Handbook of New Media*, 1st edition. London: Sage, pp. 287–303.

Cooper, David (1992) *A Companion to Aesthetics*. Oxford: Oxford University Press.

Corbridge, Stuart (1986) *Capitalist World Development: A Critique of Radical Development Geography*. Totowa: Rowman & Littlefield.

Coriat, Benjamin and Dosi, Giovanni (2002) The Institutional Embeddedness of Economic Change: An Appraisal of the 'Evolutionary' and 'Regulationist' Research Programmes. In G. Hodgson (ed.) *A Modern Reader in Evolutionary and Institutional Economics*. Cheltenham: Edward Elgar, pp. 95–123.

Couldry, Nick and Curran, James (2003) The Paradox of Media Power. In N. Couldry and J. Curran (eds) *Contesting Media Power: Alternative Media in a Networked World*. Lanham: Rowman & Littlefield, pp. 3–16.

Cowen, Tyler (2002) *Creative Destruction: How Globalization Is Changing the World's Cultures*. Princeton: Princeton University Press.

Cowling, Keith (1982) *Monopoly Capitalism*. New York: John Wiley.

Cox, Kevin (1997) Globalization and the Politics of Distribution. In K. Cox (ed.) *Spaces of Globalization: Reasserting the Power of the Local*. New York: Guilford, pp. 115–36.

Craik, Jennifer, Davis, Glyn and Sutherland, Naomi (2002) Cultural Policy and National Identity. In G. Davis and M. Keating (eds) *The Future of Governance: Policy Choices*. Sydney: Allen & Unwin, pp. 177–209.

Crotty, James, Epstein, Gerald and Kelly, Patricia (1998) Multinational Corporations in the Neo-Liberal Regime. In D. Baker, G. Epstein and R. Pollin (eds) *Globalization and Progressive Economic Policy*. Cambridge: Cambridge University Press, pp. 117–43.

Cunningham, Stuart (1992) *Framing Culture: Criticism and Policy in Australia*. Sydney: Allen & Unwin.

— (2002) From Cultural to Creative Industries: Theory, Industry and Policy Implications. *Media International Australia* 102, pp. 54–65.

— (2005a) Culture, Services, Knowledge: Television between Policy Regimes. In J. Wasko (ed.) *A Companion to Television*. Oxford and Malden: Blackwell, pp. 199–214.

— (2005b) Creative Enterprises. In J. Hartley (ed.) *Creative Industries*. Oxford: Blackwell, pp. 282–98.

— (2006) *What Price a Creative Economy?* Platform Papers No. 9. Sydney: Currency.

— and Jacka, Elizabeth (1996) Australian Television in World Markets. In J. Sinclair, E. Jacka and S. Cunningham (eds) *New Patterns in Global Television: Peripheral Vision*. Oxford: Oxford University Press, pp. 192–228.

— and Flew, Terry (2000) De-westernizing Australia? Media Systems and Cultural Co-ordinates. In J. Curran and M.-J. Park (eds) *De-Westernizing Media Studies*. London: Routledge, pp. 237–48.

—, Cutler, Terry, Hearn, Greg, Ryan, Mark and Keane, Michael (2004) An Innovation Agenda for the Creative Industries: Where is the R&D?. *Media International Australia* 112, pp. 174–85.

Curran, James (1977) Capitalism and Control of the Press, 1800–1975. In J. Curran, M. Gurevitch and J. Woollacott (eds) *Mass Communication and Society*. London: Edward Arnold, pp. 195–230.

— (1990) The New Revisionism in Mass Communication Research: A Reappraisal. *European Journal of Communication* 5 (2–3), pp. 135–64.

— (2002) Global Media Concentration: Shifting the Argument. *Open Democracy*.

Available from www.opendemocracy.net/debates/article-8-24-37.jsp. Posted 23 May. Accessed 12 August 2004.

— and Park, Myung-Jin (2000) Beyond Globalization Theory. In J. Curran and M.-J. Park (eds) *De-Westernizing Media Studies*. London: Routledge, pp. 3–18.

Curtin, Michael (2003) Media Capital: Towards the Study of Spatial Flows. *International Journal of Cultural Studies* 6 (2), pp. 202–28.

— (2005) Murdoch's Dilemma, or 'What's the Price of TV in China?'. *Media, Culture and Society* 27 (2), pp. 155–75.

— and Streeter, Thomas (2001) Media. In R. Maxwell (ed.) *Culture Works: The Political Economy of Culture*. Minneapolis: University of Minnesota Press, pp. 225–49.

Dahlgren, Peter (1995) *Television and the Public Sphere*. London: Sage.

Dajani, Nabil (2005) Television in the Arab East. In J. Wasko (ed.) *A Companion to Television*. Oxford and Malden: Blackwell, pp. 580–601.

David, Paul (1999) Digital Technology and the Productivity Paradox: After Ten Years, What Has Been Learned?. Paper prepared for *Understanding the Digital Economy: Data, Tools and Research*. Washington, DC: US Department of Commerce, 25–26 May.

— and Foray, Dominique (2002) An Introduction to the Economy of the Knowledge Society. *International Social Science Journal* 171, February–March, pp. 9–23.

Davis, Howard and Scase, Richard (2000) *Managing Creativity: The Dynamics of Work and Organization*. Buckingham and Philadelphia: Open University Press.

de Certeau, Michel (1984), *The Practice of Everyday Life*. Trans. S. Rendell. Berkeley: University of California Press.

de Kerckhove, Derrick (2001) *The Architecture of Intelligence*. Basel: Birkhäuser.

Dean, Mitchell (1999) *Governmentality: Power and Rule in Modern Society*. London: Sage.

Deleuze, Gilles and Guattari, Félix (1987) *A Thousand Plateaus*. Trans. B. Massumi. Minneapolis: University of Minnesota Press.

Deloitte Research (2003) *The World's Factory: China Enters the 21st Century*. Available from www.dc.com/research. Accessed 11 June 2005.

Demers, David (2002) *Global Media: Menace or Messiah?* Cresskill: Hampton.

Department of Communications and the Arts (DoCA) (1994) *Creative Nation: Commonwealth Cultural Policy*. Canberra: Commonwealth of Australia.

Department of Communications, Information Technology and the Arts (DCITA) (2004) *Digital Content Industry Action Agenda*. Available from www.cultureandrecreation.gov.au/actionagenda/. Accessed 30 July 2006.

Department of Culture, Media and Sport (1998) *Mapping the Creative Industries*. Available from www.culture.gov.uk/creative/creativeindustries.html. Accessed 5 May 2001.

Deuze, Mark (2006) Collaboration, Participation and the Media. *New Media and Society* 8 (4), pp. 691–8.

Dicken, Peter (2003a) *Global Shift: Reshaping the Global Economic Map in the 21st Century*. London: Sage.

— (2003b) 'Placing' Firms: Grounding the Debate on the 'Global'. In J. Peck and H. W. Yeung (eds) *Remaking the Global Economy*. London: Sage, pp. 27–44.

Di Maggio, Paul (1983) Cultural Policy Studies: What They Are and Why We Need Them. *Journal of Arts Management and Law* 13 (1), pp. 241–8.

—, Hargittai, Eszter, Neuman, W. Russell and Robinson, John (2001) Social Implications of the Internet. *Annual Review of Sociology* (27), pp. 307–26.

Dirlik, Arif (1994) The Postcolonial Aura: Third World Criticism in the Age of Global Capitalism. *Critical Inquiry* 20 (2), pp. 328–56.

Dodge, Martin and Kitchin, Rob (2001) *Mapping Cyberspace*. London: Routledge.

Dodgson, Mark, Gann, David and Salter, Ammon (2002) The Intensification of Innovation. *International Journal of Innovation Management* 6 (1), pp. 53–83.

Donald, James (1998) Perpetual Noise: Thinking about Media Regulation. *Continuum: Journal of Media and Cultural Studies* 12 (2), pp. 217–32.

Doremus, Paul, Keller, William, Pauly, Lewis and Reich, Simon (1998) *The Myth of the Global Corporation*. Princeton: Princeton University Press.

Dos Santos, Theodor (1973) The Structure of Dependence. In C. K. Wilber (ed.) *The Political Economy of Development and Underdevelopment*. New York: Random House, pp. 109–17.

Douglas, Mary (1987) *How Institutions Think*. London: Routledge & Kegan Paul.

Doyle, Gillian (2002a) *Media Ownership*. London: Sage.

— (2002b) *Understanding Media Economics*. London: Sage.

du Gay, Paul and Pryke, Michael (2002) Cultural Economy: An Introduction. In P. du Gay and M. Pryke (eds) *Cultural Economy: Cultural Analysis and Commercial Life*. London: Sage, pp. 1–19.

Dugger, William and Sherman, Howard (1994) Comparison of Marxism and Institutionalism. *Journal of Economic Issues* 28 (1), pp. 101–27.

Dunleavy, Patrick and O'Leary, Brendan (1987) *Theories of the State: The Politics of Liberal Democracy*. London: Macmillan (now Palgrave Macmillan).

Dunning, John (2000), Regions, Globalization and the Knowledge-Based Economy: The Issues Stated. In J. Dunning (ed.) *Regions, Globalization and the Knowledge-Based Economy*. Oxford: Oxford University Press, pp. 8–41.

— (2001) *Global Capitalism at Bay?* London: Routledge.

During, Simon (1997) Popular Culture on a Global Scale: A Challenge for Cultural Studies?. *Critical Inquiry* 23, pp. 808–33.

Eco, Umberto (1976) *A Theory of Semiotics*. Bloomington: Indiana University Press.

Economist, The (2002a) *Tangled Webs of Media*. Available from www.economist.com/printedition/displayStory.cfm?StoryID=S%27%29H%28%28P%217%24%20%40%224%0A. Posted 23 May. Accessed 5 August 2004.

Economist, The (2003) *A Media Giant is Born*. Available fromwww.economist.com/agenda/displaystory.cfm?storyid=2034123. Posted 4 September. Accessed 11 June 2006.

Elliott, Gregory (1987) *Althusser: The Detour of Theory*. London: Verso.

El-Nawawy, Mohammed and Iskandar, Adel (2002) *Al Jazeera: How the Free Arab News Network Scooped the World and Changed the Middle East*. Cambridge, MA: Westview.

El Oifi, Mohammed (2005) Influence without Power: Al Jazeera and the Arab Public Sphere. In M. Zayani (ed.) *The Al Jazeera Phenomenon: Critical Perspectives on New Arab Media*. London: Pluto, pp. 66–79.

Ernst, Dieter and Kim, Lin Su (2002) Global Production Networks, Knowledge Diffusion, and Local Capability Formation. *Research Policy* 31, pp. 1417–29.

European Cinema Journal (2003) The Korean Film Industry, Dramatic Movement over the Next Generation, pp. 4–5.

Fallows, James (2003) The Age of Murdoch. *The Atlantic Online*. Available from www.theatlantic.com/issues/2003/09/fallows.htm. Accessed 31 August 2003.

Ferguson, Marjory and Golding, Peter (eds) (1997) *Cultural Studies in Question*. London: Sage.

Fewsmith, Joseph (2001) The Political and Social Implications of China's Accession to the WTO. *China Quarterly* 167, pp. 573–91.

Financial Times (2006) *FT Global 500*. Available from www.ft.com/cms/adb61f66-f7bf-11da-9481-0000779e2340.html. Posted 9 June. Accessed 21 November 2006.

Fiske, John (1987) *Television Culture*. New York: Routledge.

— (1992) British Cultural Studies and Television. In R. C. Allen (ed.) *Channels of Discourse, Reassembled*. London: Routledge, pp. 284–326.

Fitzgerald, Brian and Montgomery, Lucy (2005) Copyright and the Creative Industries in China. *Proceedings of the 2005 Shanghai International IPR Forum: Intellectual Property Protection and Creative Industries Development*, Shanghai, China. Available from www.eprints.qut.edu.au/archive/00002961/01/2961.pdf. Accessed 26 June 2006.

Flew, Terry (2001) The 'New Empirics' in Internet Studies and Comparative Internet Policy. In H. Brown, G. Lovink, H. Merrick, N. Rossiter, D. Teh and M. Willson (eds) *Politics of a Digital Present*. Melbourne: Fibreculture, pp. 105–14.

— (2002) Broadcasting and the Social Contract. In M. Raboy (ed.) *Global Media Policy in the New Millennium*. Luton: University of Luton Press, pp. 113–29.

— (2003a) Creative Industries and the New Economy. In G. Argyrous and F. Stilwell (eds) *Economics as a Social Science: Readings in Political Economy*. Sydney: Pluto, pp. 309–14.

— (2003b) Television, Regulation and Citizenship in Australia. In P. Kitley (ed.) *Television, Regulation and Civil Society in Asia*. London: RoutledgeCurzon, pp. 148–66.

— (2003c) Creative Industries: From the 'Chicken Cheer' to the Culture of Services. *Continuum: Journal of Media and Cultural Studies* 17 (1), pp. 89–94.

— (2004) Creativity, the 'New Humanism' and Cultural Studies. *Continuum: Journal of Media and Cultural Studies* 18 (2), pp. 161–78.

— (2005a) *New Media: An Introduction*. Melbourne: Oxford University Press.

— (2005b) Creative Economy. In J. Hartley (ed.) *Creative Industries*. Oxford: Blackwell, pp. 344–60.

— (2005c) Sovereignty and Software: Rethinking Cultural Policy in a Global Creative Economy. *International Journal of Cultural Policy* 11 (3), pp. 243–59.

— (2006a) The Social Contract and Beyond in Broadcast Media Policy. *Television and New Media* 7 (3), pp. 282–305.

— (2006b) Media and Citizenship. In A.-V. Anttiroiko and M. Malika (eds) *Encyclopedia of Digital Government*. Hershey: Idea, pp. 905–10.

— and Cunningham, Stuart (1997) Media Policy. In A. Parkin, J. Summers and D. Woodward (eds) *Government, Politics, Power and Policy in Australia*, 5th edition. Melbourne: Longman, pp. 468–85.

—, Ching, Gillian, Stafford, Andrew and Tacchi, Jo (2001) *Music Industry Development and Brisbane's Future as a Creative City*. Brisbane: Creative Industries Research and Applications Centre and Brisbane City Council.

— and McElhinney, Stephen (2005) Globalization and New Media Industries. In L. Lievrouw and S. Livingstone (eds) *The Handbook of New Media*, paperback edition. London: Sage, pp. 287–306.

Florida, Richard (2002) *The Rise of the Creative Class*. New York: Basic Books.

Footer, Mary and Graber, Christoph Beat (2000) Trade Liberalization and Cultural Policy. *Journal of International Economic Law* 3 (1), pp. 1–32.

Forgacs, David (1993) National-Popular: Genealogy of a Concept. In S. During (ed.) *The Cultural Studies Reader*. London: Routledge, pp. 177–90.

Foster, John Bellamy (1987) Paul Malor Sweezy. In J. Eatwell, M. Milgate and P. Newman (eds) *The New Palgrave: A Dictionary of Economics, Volume 4*. London: Macmillan (now Palgrave Macmillan), pp. 350–5.

— (2000) Monopoly Capital at the Turn of the Millennium. *Monthly Review* 51 (11), pp. 1–17.

Foucault, Michel (1982) The Subject and Power. In H. L. Dreyfus and P. Rabinow (eds) *Michel Foucalt: Between Structuralism and Hermeneutics*. Chicago: University of Chicago Press, pp. 208–26.

— (1984) Space, Knowledge and Power. In P. Rabinow (ed.) *The Foucault Reader*. London: Penguin, pp. 239–56.

— (1986) Of Other Spaces. Trans. J. Miskowiec. *Diacritics* (16), pp. 22–7.

— (1988) On Power. In L. Kritzman (ed.) *Michel Foucault: Politics, Philosophy, Culture: Interviews and Other Writing 1977–1984*. Trans. A. Sheridan. New York: Routledge, pp. 96–109.

— (1991) Governmentality. In G. Burchell, C. Gordon and P. Miller (eds) *The Foucault Effect: Studies in Governmentality*. Brighton: Harvester Wheatsheaf, pp. 87–104.

Freedman, Des (2003) Who Wants to be a Millionaire? The Politics of Television Exports. *Information, Communication and Society* 6 (1), pp. 24–41.

Friedland, Roger and Robertson, A. F. (1990) Beyond the Marketplace. In R. Friedland and A. F. Robertson (eds) *Beyond the Marketplace: Rethinking Economy and Society*. New York: de Gruyter, pp. 3–49.

Fröbel, Folker, Heinrichs, Jürgen and Kreye, Otto (1980) *The New International Division of Labour*. Cambridge: Cambridge University Press.

Frow, John and Morris, Meaghan (1996) Australian Cultural Studies. In J. Storey (ed.) *What Is Cultural Studies? A Reader*. London: Edward Arnold, pp. 344–67.

Galbraith, John Kenneth (1973) *Economics and the Public Purpose*. Harmondsworth: Penguin.

Galperin, Hernan (1999) Cultural Industries Policy in Regional Trade Agreements: The Case of NAFTA, the European Union and MERCOSUR. *Media, Culture and Society* 21 (5), pp. 627–48.

Gandy, Oscar H., Jr (2002) The Real Digital Divide: Citizens versus Consumers. In L. Lievrouw and S. Livingstone (eds) *Handbook of New Media*, 1st edition. Thousand Oaks: Sage, pp. 448–60.

García, Beatriz (2004) Urban Regeneration, Arts Programming and Major Events: Glasgow, 1990, Sydney, 2000, Barcelona, 2004. *International Journal of Cultural Policy* 10 (1), pp. 103–18.

Garnham, Nicholas (1987) Public Policy and the Cultural Industries. *Cultural Studies* 1 (1), pp. 23–37.

— (1990) *Capitalism and Communications*. London: Sage.

— (1995) Political Economy and Cultural Studies: Reconciliation or Divorce? *Critical Studies in Mass Communication* 12 (1), pp. 62–71.

— (2004) Information Society Theory as Ideology. In F. Webster (ed.) *The Information Society Reader*. London: Routledge, pp. 165–83.

— (2005) From Cultural to Creative Industries: An Analysis of the Implications of the 'Creative Industries' Approach To Arts And Media Policy Making in the United Kingdom. *International Journal of Cultural Policy* 11 (1), pp. 15–29.

Gasher, Mike (2002) *Hollywood North: The Feature Film Industry in British Columbia*. Vancouver: UBC Press.

Gauntlett, David (1998) Ten Things Wrong with the 'Effects' Model. In R. Dickinson, R. Harindranath and O. Linné (eds) *Approaches to Audiences: A Reader*. London: Edward Arnold, pp. 120–30.

— (ed.) (2004) *Web.Studies*. London: Arnold.

Gellner, Ernest (1983) *Nations and Nationalism*. Oxford: Basil Blackwell.

Gertler, Meric (2003a) A Cultural Economic Geography of Production. In K. Anderson, M. Domosh, S. Pile and N. Thrift (eds) *Handbook of Cultural Geography*. London: Sage, pp. 131–46.

— (2003b) The Spatial Life of Things: The Real World of Practice within the Global Firm. In J. Peck and H. W. Yeung (eds) *Remaking the Global Economy*. London: Sage, pp. 101–13.

Gibson, Chris (2003) Cultures at Work: Why 'Culture' Matters in Research on the 'Cultural' Industries. *Social and Cultural Geography* 4 (2), pp. 201–15.

Giddens, Anthony (1990) *The Consequences of Modernity*. Oxford: Polity.

— (2000) *The Third Way and its Critics*. Oxford: Polity.

— (2002) Media and Globalization. Keynote presentation to the 22nd Conference of the International Association for Media and Communications Research, Barcelona, Spain, 17–22 July. Broadcast on *The Media Report*, 19 September. Available from www.abc.net.au/rn/talks/8.30/mediarpt/stories/s678261.htm. Accessed 9 October 2003.

Gilder, George (1994) *Life After Television*. New York: W. W. Norton.

Girard, Augustin (1982) Cultural Industries: A Handicap or a New Opportunity for Cultural Development?. In *Cultural Industries: A Challenge for the Future of Culture*. Paris: UNESCO, pp. 24–39.

Glyn, Andrew and Sutcliffe, Bob (1999) Still Underwhelmed: Indicators of Globalization and their Misinterpretation. *Review of Radical Political Economics* 31 (1), pp. 111–31.

Golding, Peter and Murdock, Graham (1973) For a Political Economy of Mass Communication. In R. Miliband and J. Saville (eds) *The Socialist Register 1973*. London: Merlin, pp. 205–34.

— (1989) Information Poverty and Political Inequality: Citizenship in the Age of Privatized Communication. *Journal of Communication* 39 (3), pp. 180–95.

— (2000) Culture, Communications, and Political Economy. In J. Curran and M. Gurevitch (eds) *Mass Media and Society*, 3rd edition. London: Edward Arnold, pp. 70–92.

Goldsmith, Ben (2002) Cultural Diversity, Cultural Networks and Trade. *Media International Australia* 102, pp. 35–53.

— and O'Regan, Tom (2003) *Cinema Cities, Media Cities: The Contemporary International Studio Complex*. Sydney: Australian Film Commission.

Gordon, David (1988) The Global Economy: New Edifice or Crumbling Foundations?. *New Left Review* 168, pp. 24–65.

Gordon, Ian and McCann, Philip (2001) Industrial Clusters: Complexes, Agglomeration, and/or Social Networks?. *Urban Studies* 37 (3), pp. 513–32.

Grant, Peter and Wood, Chris (2004) *Blockbusters and Trade Wars: Popular Culture in a Globalized World*. Vancouver: Douglas & McIntyre.

Granovetter, Mark (1985) Economic Action and Social Structure. *American Journal of Sociology* 91 (3), pp. 481–510.

Grewal, Bhajan, Xue, Lan, Sheehan, Peter and Sun, Fiona (eds) (2002) *China's Future in the Knowledge Economy: Engaging the New World*. Melbourne: Centre for Strategic Economic Studies/Tsinghua University Press.

Grossberg, Lawrence (1995) Cultural Studies vs. Political Economy: Is Anyone Else Bored with this Debate?. *Critical Studies in Mass Communication* 12 (1), pp. 72–81.

Habermas, Jürgen (1977) The Public Sphere. In A. Mattelart and S. Siegelaub (eds) *Communications and Class Struggle, Volume 1*. New York: International, pp. 199–202.

Hage, Ghassan (1998) *White Nation: Fantasies of White Supremacy in a Multicultural Society*. Sydney: Pluto.

Hagström, Peter and Hedlund, Gunnar (1999) A Three-Dimensional Model of Changing Internal Structure in the Firm. In A. D. Chandler, Jr, P. Hagström and Ö. Sölvell (eds) *The Dynamic Firm: The Role of Technology, Strategy, Organization, and Regions*. Oxford: Oxford University Press, pp. 166–91.

Hall, Peter (1998) *Cities in Civilization: Culture, Innovation and Urban Order*. London: Phoenix Grant.

— (2000) Creative Cities and Economic Development. *Urban Studies* 37 (4), pp. 639–49.

— and Taylor, Rosemary (1996) Political Science and the Three New Institutionalisms. *Political Science* 44, pp. 936–57.

Hall, Stuart (1977) Culture, the Media, and the 'Ideological Effect'. In J. Curran, M. Gurevitch and J. Woollacott (eds) *Mass Communication and Society*. London: Edward Arnold, pp. 315–48.

— (1982) The Rediscovery of 'Ideology': Return of the Repressed in Media Studies. In M. Gurevitch, T. Bennett, J. Curran and J. Woollacott (eds) *Culture, Society and the Media*. London: Methuen, pp. 56–90.

— (1986) Cultural Studies: Two Paradigms. In R. Collins, J. Curran, N. Garnham, P. Scannell, P. Schlesinger and C. Sparks (eds) *Media, Culture and Society: A Reader*. London: Sage, pp. 33–48.

— (1993a) Culture, Community, Nation. *Cultural Studies* 7 (1), pp. 349–63.

— (1993b) Encoding, Decoding. In S. During (ed.) *The Cultural Studies Reader*. London: Routledge, pp. 90–103.

— (1996) On Postmodernism and Articulation: An Interview with Stuart Hall (with Lawrence Grossberg). In D. Morley and K.-H. Chen (eds) *Stuart Hall: Critical Dialogues in Cultural Studies*. London: Routledge, pp. 131–50.

— and Jefferson, Tony (eds) (1976) *Resistance Through Rituals: Youth Sub-Cultures in Post-War Britain*. London: Hutchinson.

Ham, Christopher, and Hill, Michael (1993) *The Policy Process in the Modern Capitalist State*. Brighton: Harvester Wheatsheaf.

Hamelink, Cees (1997) MacBride with Hindsight. In P. Golding and P. Harris (eds) *Beyond Cultural Imperialism: Globalization, Communication and the New International Order*. London: Sage, pp. 69–93.

Hardt, Michael and Negri, Antonio (2000) *Empire*. Cambridge, MA: Harvard University Press.

— and — (2005) *Multitude*. London: Penguin.

Harries, Dan (ed.) (2002) *The New Media Book*. London: British Film Institute.

Hartley, John (1996) *Popular Reality: Journalism, Modernity, Popular Culture*. London: Edward Arnold.

— (1999) *Uses of Television*. London: Routledge.

— (2002) *Communication, Cultural and Media Studies: The Key Concepts*. London: Routledge.

— (2003) *A Short History of Cultural Studies*. London: Sage.

— (ed.) (2005) *Creative Industries*. Oxford: Blackwell.

Harvey, David (1982) *The Limits to Capital*. Oxford: Blackwell.

— (1985) The Geopolitics of Capitalism. In D. Gregory and J. Urry (eds) *Social Relations and Spatial Structures*. London: Macmillan (now Palgrave Macmillan), pp. 128–63.

— (1989) *The Condition of Postmodernity*. Cambridge, MA: Blackwell.

Hassan, Robert (2004) *Media, Politics and the Network Society*. Maidenhead: Open University Press.

Hawkins, Gay (1993) *From Nimbin to Mardi Gras: Constructing Community Arts*. Sydney: Allen & Unwin.

Headrick, Daniel (1981) *The Tools of Empire: Technology and European Imperialism in the Nineteenth Century* New York: Oxford University Press.

Held, David (2004) *Global Covenant: The Social Democratic Alternative to the Washington Consensus*. Cambridge: Polity.

—, McGrew, Anthony, Goldblatt, David and Perraton, Jonathon (1999) *Global Transformations: Politics, Economics and Culture*. Stanford: Stanford University Press.

— and McGrew, Anthony (2002) *Globalization/Anti-Globalization*. Cambridge: Polity.

Henderson, Jeffrey, Dicken, Peter, Hess, Martin, Coe, Neil and Yeung, Henry Wai-Chung (2002) Global Production Networks and the Analysis of Economic Development. *Review of International Political Economy* 9 (3), pp. 436–64.

Herman, Edward S. (1981) *Corporate Control, Corporate Power*. New York: Twentieth Century Fund.

— (1997) The Externalities Effects of Commercial and Public Broadcasting. In P. Golding and G. Murdock (eds) *The Political Economy of the Media, Volume 1*. Cheltenham: Edward Elgar, pp. 374–404.

— and Chomsky, Noam (1988) *Manufacturing Consent: The Political Economy of the Media*. New York: Pantheon.

— and McChesney, Robert W. (1997) *The Global Media: The New Missionaries of Global Capitalism*. London: Cassell.

Herz, J. C. (2002) The Broadband Capital of the World. *WIRED* 10.08, August.

Hesmondhalgh, David (2001) Ownership Is Only Part of the Media Picture. *Open Democracy*. Available from www.opendemocracy.net/debates/debate-8-24.jsp. Posted 29 November. Accessed 12 August 2004.

— (2002) *The Cultural Industries*. London: Sage.

— and Pratt, Andy (2005) Cultural Industries and Cultural Policy. *International Journal of Cultural Policy* 11 (1), pp. 1–13.

Hilferding, Rudolf (1985 [1910]), *Finance Capital*. London: Routledge & Kegan Paul.

Hill, Michael (1997) *The Policy Process in the Modern State*. New York: Prentice-Hall.

Hindess, Barry (1989) *Political Choice and Social Structure: An Analysis of Actors, Interests and Rationality*. Aldershot: Edward Elgar.

— (1991) Imaginary Presuppositions of Democracy. *Economy and Society* 20 (2), pp. 173–95.

— (1993) Multiculturalism and Citizenship. In C. Kukathas (ed.) *Multicultural Citizens: The Philosophy and Politics of Identity*. Sydney: Centre for Independent Studies, pp. 33–45.

Hirst, Paul and Thompson, Grahame (1996) *Globalization in Question*. Cambridge: Polity.

Ho, K. C., Kluver, Randolph and Yang, Kenneth (2003) *Asia.com: Asia Encounters the Internet*. London: RoutledgeCurzon.

Hobsbawm, Eric (1990) *Nations and Nationalism Since 1780: Programme, Myth, Reality*. Cambridge, Cambridge University Press.

Hodgson, Geoffrey (1988) *Economics and Institutions*. Cambridge: Polity.

— (2000) Socio-economic Consequences of the Advance of Complexity and Knowledge. In Organization for Economic Co-operation and Development, *The Creative Society of the 21st Century*. Paris: OECD, pp. 89–112.

— (2002) Varieties of Capitalism and Varieties of Economic Theory. In G. Hodgson (ed.) *A Modern Reader in Institutional and Evolutionary Economics*. Cheltenham: Edward Elgar, pp. 201–29.

Hofstede, Geert (1980) *Culture's Consequences: International Differences in Work-Related Values*. London: Sage.

Hoogvelt, Ankie (2001) *Globalization and the Postcolonial World: The New Political Economy of Development*. Baltimore: Johns Hopkins University Press.

Horwitz, Robert (1989) *The Irony of Regulatory Reform: The Deregulation of American Telecommunications*. New York: Oxford University Press.

Hoskins, Colin, McFadyen, Stuart and Finn, Adam (1997) *Global Television and Film: An Introduction to the Economics of the Business*. Oxford: Clarendon.

Howells, Jeremy (2000) Knowledge, Innovation and Location. In J. R. Bryson, P. Daniels, N. Henry and J. Pollard (eds) *Knowledge, Space, Economy*. London: Routledge, pp. 50–62.

Howkins, John (2001) *The Creative Economy: How People Make Money from Ideas*. London: Allen Lane/Penguin.

— (2005) The Mayor's Commission on the Creative Industries, London. In J. Hartley (ed.) *Creative Industries*. Oxford: Blackwell, pp. 117–25.

Hunter, Ian (1988) Setting Limits to Culture. *New Formations* 4, pp. 103–22.

— (1994) *Rethinking the School*. Sydney: Allen & Unwin.

Huntington, Samuel (2000) The Clash of Civilizations?. In F. Lechner and J. Boli (eds) *The Globalization Reader*. Oxford and Malden: Blackwell, pp. 27–33.

Hutchison, David (2004) Protecting the Citizen, Protecting Society. In R. C. Allen and A. Hill (eds) *The Television Studies Reader*. London: Routledge, pp. 64–78.

Hymer, Stephen (1975) The Multinational Corporation and the Law of Uneven Development. In H. Radice (ed.) *International Firms and Modern Imperialism*. Harmondsworth: Penguin, pp. 37–64.

Innis, Harold A. (1991 [1951]) *The Bias of Communication*. Intro. P. Heyer and D. Crowley. Toronto: University of Toronto Press.

International Journal of Cultural Studies (2006) Special Issue on 'Creative Industries and Innovation in China' 9 (3), September.

Iwabuchi, Koichi (2002) *Recentering Globalization: Popular Culture and Japanese Transnationalism*. Durham, NC: Duke University Press.

— (2004) Feeling Glocal: Japan in the Global Television Format Business. In A. Moran and M. Keane (eds) *Television Across Asia: Television Industries, Programme Formats and Globalization*. London: RoutledgeCurzon, pp. 21–35.

Jenkins, Henry (2006) *Convergence Culture: Where Old and New Media Collide*. New York: New York University Press.

Jessop, Bob (1990) *State Theory: Putting Capitalist States in their Place*. University Park: Pennsylvania State University Press.

— (2002) The Social Embeddedness of the Economy and its Implications for Economic Governance. In F. Adaman and P. Devine (eds) *Economy and Society: Money, Capitalism and Transition*. Montréal: Black Rose, pp. 192–222.

Johnson, Gerry, Scholes, Kevan and Whittington, Richard (2005) *Exploring Corporate Strategy: Text and* Cases, 7th edition. London: Prentice-Hall.

Johnston, Les (1986) *Marxism, Class Analysis and Socialist Pluralism*. London: Allen & Unwin.

Jordan, Tim (1999) *Cyberpower: The Culture and Politics of Cyberspace and the Internet*. London: Routledge.

Keane, Michael (2004a) Asia: New Growth Areas. In A. Moran and M. Keane (eds) *Television Across Asia: Television Industries, Programme Formats and Globalization*. London: RoutledgeCurzon, pp. 9–20.

— (2004b) A Revolution in Television and a Great Leap Forward for Innovation? China in the Global Television Format Business. In A. Moran and M. Keane (eds) *Television Across Asia: Television Industries, Programme Formats and Globalization*. London: RoutledgeCurzon, pp. 88–104.

— (2004c) Brave New World: Understanding China's Creative Vision. *International Journal of Cultural Policy* 10 (3), pp. 265–79.

— (2005) Television Drama in China: Remaking the Market. *Media International Australia* 105, May, pp. 82–93.

— (2006) Once Were Peripheral: Creating Media Capacity in East Asia. *Media, Culture and Society* 28 (6), pp. 833–55.

Keen, Steve (2001) *Debunking Economics: The Naked Emperor of the Social Sciences*. Sydney: Pluto.

Kellner, Douglas (1990) *Television and the Crisis of Democracy*. Boulder: Westview.

— (1995) Cultural Studies, Multiculturalism and Media Culture. In G. Dines and J. M. Humez (eds) *Gender, Race and Class in Media: A Text-Reader*. Thousand Oaks: Sage, pp. 5–17.

Klein, Hans (2003) *Understanding WSIS: An Institutional Analysis of the UN World Summit on the Information Society*. Atlanta: Internet and Public Policy Project, School of Public Policy, Georgia Institute of Technology.

Klein, Naomi (2000) *No Logo*. London: Flamingo.

Korean Film Observatory (2004) *A Review of the 2004 Korean Film Industry*. Seoul: Korean Film Council.

Korzeniewicz, Miguel (2000) Commodity Chains and Marketing Strategies: Nike and the Global Athletic Footwear Industry. In F. J. Lechner and J. Boli (eds) *The Globalization Reader*. Malden and Oxford: Blackwell, pp. 155–66.

Landry, Charles (2000) *The Creative City: A Toolkit for Urban Innovators*. London: Earthscan.

— (2005) London as a Creative City. In J. Hartley (ed.) *Creative Industries*. Oxford: Blackwell, pp. 233–43.

—, Greene, Lesley, Matarasso, François and Bianchini, Franco (1996) *The Art of Urban Regeneration: Urban Renewal through Cultural Activity*. London: Comedia.

— and Wood, Phil (2003) *Harnessing and Exploiting the Power of Culture for Competitive Advantage*. A report by Comedia for Liverpool City Council and the Core Cities Group. London: Comedia, March.

Larrain, Jorge (1983) *Marxism and Ideology*. London: Macmillan (now Palgrave Macmillan).

Lash, Scott and Urry, John (1987) *The End of Organized Capitalism*. Cambridge: Polity.

— and — (1994) *Economies of Signs and Space*. London: Sage.

Lavery, David (ed.) (2002) *This Thing of Ours: Investigating the Sopranos*. New York: Columbia University Press.

Lenin, V. I. (1983 [1917]) *Imperialism: The Highest Stage of Capitalism*. Moscow: Progress.

Leo, Petrina and Lee, Terence (2004) The 'New' Singapore: Mediating Culture and Creativity. *Continuum: Journal of Media and Cultural Studies* 18 (2), pp. 205–18.

Leong, Anthony C. Y. (2002) *Korean Cinema: The New Hong Kong*. Victoria, BC: Trafford.

Lerner, Daniel (1958) *The Passing of Traditional Society: Modernizing the Middle East*. New York: Free Press.

Levinson, Paul (2001) *Digital McLuhan: A Guide to the Information Millennium*. London: Routledge.

Lewis, Glen (2003) The Thai Movie Revival and Thai National Identity. *Continuum: Journal of Media and Cultural Studies* 17 (1), pp. 69–78.

Lewis, Justin and Miller, Toby (2003) Introduction. In J. Lewis and T. Miller (eds) *Critical Cultural Policy Studies: A Reader*. Oxford and Malden: Blackwell, pp. 1–9.

Lievrouw, Leah and Livingstone, Sonia (2005) Introduction to the Updated Student Edition. In L. Lievrouw and S. Livingstone (eds) *Handbook of New Media*, Updated Student Edition. London: Sage, pp. 1–14.

Lim, Tania (2004) Let the Contests Begin! 'Singapore Slings' into Action. In A. Moran and M. Keane (eds) *Television Across Asia: Television Industries, Programme Formats and Globalization*. London: RoutledgeCurzon, pp. 105–21.

Lipietz, Alain (1987) *Mirages and Miracles: The Crises of Global Fordism*. London: Verso.

Litman, Barry (1990) Network Oligopoly Power: An Economic Analysis. In T. Balio (ed.) *Hollywood in the Age of Television*. Boston: Unwin Hyman, pp. 115–44.

Livingstone, Sonia (1999) New Media, New Audiences. *New Media and Society* 1 (1), pp. 59–68.

Looseley, David (1995) *The Politics of Fun: Cultural Policy and Debate in Contemporary France*. Oxford: Berg.

Lull, James (1991) *China Turned On: Television, Reform, and Resistance*. New York: Routledge.

Lury, Celia (1994) Planning a Culture for the People?. In R. Keat, N. Whiteley and N. Abercrombie (eds) *The Authority of the Consumer*. London: Routledge, pp. 138–53.

Ma, Eric Kit-Wai (1999) *Culture, Politics and Television in Hong Kong*. London: Routledge.

MacBride, Sean and Roach, Colleen (2000) The New International Information Order. In F. J. Lechner and J. Boli (eds) *The Globalization Reader*. Oxford and Malden: Blackwell, pp. 286–92.

MacBride Report (1980) *Many Voices, One World: Communications and Society Today and Tomorrow*. International Commission for the Study of Communication Problems. Paris: UNESCO.

Magder, Ted (2004a) The End of TV 101: Reality Programs, Formats, and the New Business of Television. In S. Murray and L. Ouellette (eds) *Reality TV: Remaking Television Culture*. New York: New York University Press, pp. 137–56.

— (2004b) Transnational Media, International Trade and the Idea of Cultural Diversity. *Continuum: Journal of Media and Cultural Studies* 18 (3), pp. 380–97.

Makeham, Paul (2005) Performing the City. *Theatre Research International* 30 (2), pp. 1–12.

Malmberg, Anders and Maskell, Peter (2002) The Elusive Concept of Localization Economies: Towards a Knowledge-Based Theory of Spatial Clustering. *Environment and Planning A* 34, pp. 429–49.

Mani, Lata (1992) Cultural Theory, Colonial Texts: Reading Eyewitness Accounts of Widow Burning. In L. Grossberg, C. Nelson and P. Treichler (eds) *Cultural Studies*. New York: Routledge, pp. 392–408.

March, James G. and Olsen, Johan P. (1989) *Rediscovering Institutions: The Organizational Basis of Politics*. New York: Free Press.

Markusen, Ann (1996) Sticky Places in Slippery Space: A Typology of Industrial Districts. *Economic Geography* 72 (3), pp. 293–313.

Marshall, Alfred (1961 [1890]) *Principles of Economics*. New York: Macmillan (now Palgrave Macmillan).

Marshall, David (2000) The Mediation Is the Message: The Legacy of McLuhan for the Digital Era?. *Media International Australia* 94, pp. 29–38.

— (2004) *New Media Cultures*. London: Arnold.

Marshall, T. H. (1949) Citizenship and Social Class. In T. H. Marshall, *Class, Citizenship and Social Development*. Chicago: University of Chicago Press, pp. 81–121.

Martin, Hans-Peter and Schumann, Harald (1997) *The Global Trap: Globalization and the Assault on Democracy and Prosperity*. Trans P. Camiller. London: Zed.

Martin, Ron and Sunley, Peter (2003) Deconstructing Clusters: Chaotic Concept or Policy Panacea?. *Journal of Economic Geography* 3, pp. 3–35.

Martín-Barbero, Jesús (1993) *Communication, Culture and Hegemony: From the Media to Mediations*. Intro. Philip Schlesinger. Trans. Elizabeth Fox and Robert A. White. London: Sage.

Marx, Karl (1976 [1867]) *Capital: A Critique of Political Economy, Volume 1*. Intro. Ernest Mandel. Trans. Ben Fowkes. London: Penguin.

Mason, Sir Anthony (1996) The Internationalization of Domestic Law. 'Reshaping Australian Institutions', Australian National University Public Lecture, 2 August.

Massey, Doreen (1984) *Spatial Divisions of Labour: Social Structures and the Geography of Production*. London: Macmillan (now Palgrave Macmillan).

— (1985) New Directions in Space. In D. Gregory and J. Urry (eds) *Social Relations and Spatial Structures*. London: Macmillan (now Palgrave Macmillan), pp. 9–19.

Mastrini, Guillermo and de Charras, Diego (2005) Twenty Years Mean Nothing: From NWICO to WSIS. *Global Media and Communication* 1 (3), pp. 273–88.

Mathijs, Ernest and Jones, Janet (eds) (2004) *Big Brother International: Formats, Critics and Publics*. London: Wallflower.

Mattelart, Armand (1994) *Mapping World Communication: War, Progress, Culture*. Trans. S. Emanuel and J. A. Cohen. Minneapolis: University of Minnesota Press.

— (2003) *The Information Society: An Introduction*. Trans. S. G. Taponier and J. A. Cohen. London: Sage.

McChesney, Robert (1999) *Rich Media, Poor Democracy: Communication Politics in Dubious Times*. Urbana: University of Illinois Press.

— (2001a) Global Media, Neoliberalism, and Imperialism. *Monthly Review* 52 (10), pp. 1– 19.

— (2001b) Policing the Unthinkable. *Open Democracy*. Available from www.open-democracy.net/debates/article-8-24-56.jsp. Posted 25 October. Accessed 14 November 2004.

— (2003) Corporate Media, Global Capitalism. In S. Cottle (ed.) *Media Organization and Production*. London: Sage, pp. 27–40.

— and Foster, John Bellamy (2003) The Commercial Tidal Wave. *Monthly Review* 54 (10), pp. 1–16.

— and Schiller, Dan (2003) The Political Economy of International Communication: Foundations for the Emerging Global Debate about Media Ownership and Regulation. United Nations Research Institute for Social Development. Technology, Business and Society, Programme Paper No. 11, October.

—, Wood, Ellen Meiskins and Foster, John Bellamy (1998) *Capitalism and the Information Age: Political Economy of the Global Communications Revolution*. New York: Monthly Review Press.

McGuigan, Jim (1996) *Culture and the Public Sphere*. London: Routledge.

McKee, Alan (2002) I Don't Want to be a Citizen (If It Means I Have to Watch the ABC). *Media International Australia* 103, pp. 14–23.

— (2005) *The Public Sphere: An Introduction*. Melbourne: Cambridge University Press.

McLuhan, Marshall and Powers, B. R. (1969) *The Global Village*. Oxford: Oxford University Press.

McQuail, Denis (2005) *Mass Communication Theory*, 5th edition. London: Sage.

McRobbie, Angela (1996) All the World's a Stage, Screen or Magazine: When Culture Is the Logic of Late Capitalism. *Media, Culture and Society* 18 (3), pp. 335–42.

— (2005a) Clubs to Companies. In J. Hartley (ed.) *Creative Industries*. Oxford: Blackwell, pp. 375–90.

— (2005b) *The Uses of Cultural Studies*. London: Sage.

Meier, Werner and Trappel, Josef (1998) Media Concentration and the Public Interest. In D. McQuail and K. Siune (eds) *Media Policy: Convergence, Concentration and Commerce*. London: Sage, pp. 38–59.

Mercer, Colin (1994) Cultural Policy: Research and the Governmental Imperative. *Media Information Australia* 73, August, pp. 16–22.

Meredyth, Denise (1997) Invoking Citizenship: Education, Competence and Social Rights. *Economy and Society* 26 (2), pp. 273–95.

Meyrowitz, Joshua (1994) Medium Theory. In D. Crowley and D. Mitchell (eds) *Communication Theory Today*. Cambridge: Polity, pp. 50–77.

Michael, James (1990) Regulating Communications Media: From the Discretion of Sound Chaps to the Arguments of Lawyers. In M. Ferguson (ed.) *Public Communications: The New Imperatives*. London: Sage, pp. 40–60.

Miège, Bernard (1989) *The Capitalization of Cultural Production*. Paris: International General.

Miliband, Ralph (1973) *The State in Capitalist Society*. London: Quartet.

Miller, Daniel and Slater, Don (2000) *The Internet: An Ethnographic Approach*. Oxford: Berg.

Miller, Peter and Rose, Nikolas (1992) Political Power Beyond the State: Problematics of Government. *British Journal of Sociology* 43 (2), pp. 173–205.

Miller, Toby (1994) Culture with Power: The Present Moment in Cultural Policy Studies. *Southeast Asian Journal of Social Science* 22, pp. 264–82.

—, Govil, Nitin, McMurria, John and Maxwell, Richard (2001) *Global Hollywood*. London: British Film Institute.

— and Yúdice, George (2002) *Cultural Policy*. London: Sage.

Milner, Andrew (1991) *Contemporary Cultural Theory*, 2nd edition. Sydney: Allen & Unwin.

Ministry of Trade and Information (MTI) (2003) *Economic Contribution of Singapore's Creative Industries*. Singapore: Ministry of Trade and Information.

Mitchell, Don (2000) *Cultural Geography: A Critical Introduction*. Oxford: Blackwell.

Mitchell, William, Inouye, Alan and Blumenthal, Marjory (2003) *Beyond Productivity: Information Technology, Innovation and Creativity*. Committee on Information Technology and Creativity, National Research Council of the National Academies. Washington, DC: National Academies Press.

Mittell, Jason (2004) A Cultural Approach to Television Genre Theory. In R. C. Allen and A. Hill (eds) *The Television Studies Reader*. New York: Routledge, pp. 171–81.

MKW Wirtschaftsforschung GmbH (2001) *Exploitation and Development of the Job Potential in the Cultural Sector in the Age of Digitization*. Final Report – Summary. Commissioned by European Commission DG Employment and Social Affairs, June.

Modelski, George (2000) Globalization. In D. Held and A. McGrew (eds) *The Global Transformations Reader*. Cambridge: Polity, pp. 55–9.

Mommaas, Hans (2004) Creative Clusters and the Post-Industrial City: Towards the Remapping of Urban Cultural Policy. *Urban Studies* 41 (3), pp. 507–32.

Moran, Albert (1998) *Copycat Television: Globalization, Program Formats and Cultural Identity*. Luton: University of Luton Press.

— (2004) Television Formats in the World/The World of Television Formats. In A. Moran and M. Keane (eds) *Television Across Asia: Television Industries, Programme Formats and Globalization*. London: RoutledgeCurzon, pp. 1–8.

— and Keane, Michael (eds) (2004) *Television Across Asia: Television Industries, Programme Formats and Globalization*. London: RoutledgeCurzon.

Morley, David (1980) *The 'Nationwide' Audience*. London: British Film Institute.

— (1992) *Television, Audiences, and Cultural Studies*. London: Routledge.

— and Robins, Kevin (1997) *Spaces of Identity: Global Media, Electronic Landscapes and Cultural Boundaries*. London: Routledge.

Morris, Meaghan (1992) The Man in the Mirror: David Harvey's 'Condition' of Postmodernity. In E. Jacka (ed.) *Continental Shift: Globalization and Culture*. Sydney: Local Consumption, pp. 25–51.

Mosco, Vincent (1996) *The Political Economy of Communication: Rethinking and Renewal*. London: Sage.

Mulgan, Geoff (1989) *Communications and Control*. Cambridge: Polity.

— and Wilkinson, Helen (1992) The Enabling State. In P. Ekins and M. Max-Neef (eds) *Real-Life Economics: Understanding Wealth Creation*. London: Routledge, pp. 340–57.

Murdock, Graham (1992) Citizens, Consumers and Public Culture. In M. Skovmand and K. C. Schrøder (eds) *Media Cultures: Rethinking Transnational Media*. London: Routledge, pp. 17–41.

— (1993) Communications and the Constitution of Modernity. *Media, Culture and Society* 15 (3), pp. 521–39.

— (2000) Reconstituting the Ruined Tower: Contemporary Communications and Questions of Class. In J. Curran and M. Gurevitch (eds) *Mass Media and Society*, 3rd edition, pp. 7–26.

— (2004) Past the Posts: Rethinking Change, Retrieving Critique. *European Journal of Communication* 19 (1), pp. 19–38.

— and Golding, Peter (1973) For a Political Economy of Mass Communications. In R. Miliband and J. Saville (eds) *The Socialist Register 1973*. London: Merlin, pp. 205–34.

— and Golding, Peter (1977) Capitalism, Communication and Class Relations. In J. Curran, M. Gurevitch and J. Woollacott (eds) *Mass Communication and Society*. London: Edward Arnold, pp. 12–43.

Murray, Susan and Ouellette, Laurie (eds) (2004) *Reality TV: Remaking Television Culture*. New York: New York University Press.

Nelson, Cary, Treichler, Paula and Grossberg, Lawrence (1992) Cultural Studies: An Introduction. In L. Grossberg, C. Nelson and P. Treichler (eds) *Cultural Studies*. New York: Routledge, pp. 1–22.

Neuman, W. Russell (1991) *The Future of the Mass Audience*. Cambridge: Cambridge University Press.

Newbold, Chris (1995a) The Media Effects Tradition. In O. Boyd-Barrett and C. Newbold (eds) *Approaches to Media: A Reader*. London: Edward Arnold, pp. 118–23.

— (1995b) Approaches to Cultural Hegemony within Cultural Studies. In O. Boyd-Barrett and C. Newbold (eds) *Approaches to Media: A Reader*. London: Edward Arnold, pp. 328–31.

Nielsén, Tobias (2004) *Understanding the Experience Industry: A Swedish Perspective on Creativity*. Stockholm: QNB Analys & Kommunikation AB.

Nixon, Sean (2004) *Advertising Cultures*. London: Sage.

Noam, Eli (1991) *Television in Europe*. New York: Oxford University Press.

Nolan, Peter (2004) *Transforming China: Globalization, Transition and Development*. London: Anthem.

Nordenstreng, Kaarle and Schiller, Herbert (eds) (1993), *Beyond National Sovereignty: International Communications in the 1990s*. Norwood, NJ: Ablex.

Northfield, Diane (1999) *The Information Policy Maze: Global Challenges – National Responses*. Melbourne: Centre for International Research into Communications and Information Technologies.

Nye, Joseph (2004) *Soft Power: The Means to Success in World Politics*. New York: Public Affairs.

Oakley, Kate (2004) Not so Cool Britannia: The Role of the Creative Industries in Economic Development. *International Journal of Cultural Studies* 7 (1), pp. 67–77.

Obar, Jonathon (2004) Designing Globality: An Examination of the Relationship between Globalization and Popular Film Content. Paper presented to

'Communication and Globalization' meeting, Centre for Global Media Studies, Seattle, 16–17 July.

O'Connor, Justin (1999) *The Definition of 'Cultural Industries'*. Manchester Institute for Popular Culture. Available from www.mipc.mmu.ac.uk/iciss/reports/defin.pdf. Accessed 2 August 2004.

— (2004) 'A Special Kind of City Knowledge': Innovative Clusters, Tacit Knowledge and the Creative City. *Media International Australia* 112, August, pp. 131–49.

— (2005) Cities, Culture and 'Transitional Economies': Developing Cultural Industries in St Petersburg. In J. Hartley (ed.) *Creative Industries*. Oxford: Blackwell, pp. 244–58.

Ohmae, Kenichi (1995) *The End of the Nation-State*. New York: Free Press.

Ong, Aihwa (1999) *Flexible Citizenship: The Cultural logic of Transnationalism*. Durham, NC: Duke University Press.

O'Regan, Tom (1993) *Australian Television Culture*. Sydney: Allen & Unwin.

— (2002) Too Much Culture, Too Little Culture: Trends and Issues for Cultural Policy-Making. *Media International Australia* 102, February, pp. 9–24.

— (2004) The Utility of a Global Forum: UNESCO's Significance for Communication, Culture and ICTs. *Media International Australia* 111, May, pp. 63–80.

Organization for Economic Co-operation and Development (OECD) (1998) *Content as a New Growth Industry*. Paris: OECD.

— (1999) *Policy and Regulatory Issues for Network-based Content Services*. Paris: OECD.

— (2001) *The New Economy: Beyond the Hype*. Paris: OECD.

Ó Siochrú, Seán (2004) Civil Society Participation in the WSIS Process: Promises and Reality. *Continuum: Journal of Media and Cultural Studies* 18 (3), pp. 330–44.

— and Girard, Bruce, with Mahan, Amy (2003) *Global Media Governance: A Beginner's Guide*. Lanham: Rowman & Littlefield.

Owen, Bruce, Beebe, Jack and Manning, Willard (1974) *Television Economics*. Lexington: D. C. Heath.

Padovani, Claudia (2005) Debating Communication Imbalances from the MacBride Report to the World Summit on the Information Society: An Analysis of a Changing Discourse. *Global Media and Communication* 1 (3), pp. 316–38.

— and Tuzzi, Arjuna (2004) The WSIS as a World of Words: Building a Common Vision of the Information Society?. *Continuum: Journal of Media and Cultural Studies* 18 (3), pp. 360–79.

Pakulski, Jan (1997) Cultural Citizenship. *Citizenship Studies* 1 (1), pp. 73– 86.

Paquet, Darcy (2005) A Short History of Korean Film. Available from www.korean-film.org/history.html. Accessed 22 July 2005.

Paré, Daniel (2003) *Internet Governance in Transition: Who Is the Master of the Domain?* Lanham: Rowman & Littlefield.

Park, Myung-Jin, Kim, Chang-Nam and Sohn, Byung-Woo (2000) Modernization, Globalization and the Powerful State: The Korean Media. In J. Curran and M.-J. Park (eds) *De-Westernizing Media Studies*. London: Routledge, pp. 111–23.

Park, Sangyoub and Shin, Eui Hang (2004) Patterns of Market Polarization and Market Matching in the Korean Film Industry. *Journal of East Asian Studies* 4, pp. 285–300.

Pasquali, Antonio (2005) The South and the Imbalance in Communication. *Global Media and Communication* 1 (3), pp. 289–300.

Pearce, Matthew (2000) Perspectives on Australian Broadcasting Policy. *Continuum: Journal of Media and Cultural Studies* 14 (3), pp. 367–82.

Peck, Jamie (2002) Political Economies of Scale: Fast Policy, Interscalar Relations, and Neoliberal Workfare. *Economic Geography* 78 (3), pp. 331–60.

— (2005) Struggling with the Creative Class. *International Journal of Urban and Regional Research* 29 (4), pp. 740–70.

Peters, R. Guy (1999) *Institutional Theory in Political Science: The New Institutionalism.* London: Continuum.

Picard, Robert (1989) *Media Economics: Concepts and Issues.* Newbury Park: Sage.

Piertse, Jan Nederveen (2004) *Globalization and Culture: Global Mélange.* Lanham: Rowman & Littlefield.

Pine, B. Joseph and Gilmore, James H. (1999) *The Experience Economy: Work Is Theatre and Every Business a Stage.* Boston: Harvard Business School Press.

Pink, Daniel (2004) The MFA Is the New MBA. *Harvard Business Review* February, pp. 21–2.

Polanyi, Karl (1944) *The Great Transformation: The Political and Economic Origins of Our Time.* New York: Rinehart.

— (1957) The Economy as an Instituted Process. In K. Polanyi, C. M. Arensberg and H. W. Pearson (eds) *Trade and Market in the Early Empires: Economies in History and Theory.* New York: Free Press, pp. 29–52.

Polodny, Joel and Page, Karen (1998) Network Forms of Organization. *Annual Review of Sociology* 24, pp. 57–76.

Pontusson, Jonas (1995) From Comparative Public Policy to Political Economy: Putting Political Institutions in Their Place and Taking Interests Seriously. *Comparative Political Studies* 28 (1), pp. 117–47.

Porter, Michael (1998a) Clusters and the New Economics of Competition. *Harvard Business Review* 76 (6), pp. 77–91.

— (1998b) *Competitive Advantage: Creating and Sustaining Superior Performance.* New York: Free Press.

— (1998c) *On Competition.* Cambridge, MA: Harvard Business School Press.

— (2001) Location, Competition and Economic Development. *Economic Development Quarterly* 14 (1), pp. 15–34.

— and Sölvell, Örjan (1999) The Role of Geography in the Process of Innovation and the Sustainable Competitive Advantage of Firms. In A. D. Chandler, Jr, P. Hagström and Ö. Sölvell (eds) *The Dynamic Firm: The Role of Technology, Strategy, Organization, and Regions.* Oxford: Oxford University Press, pp. 440–57.

Poster, Mark (ed.) (1988), *Jean Baudrillard: Selected Writings.* Cambridge: Polity.

— (2005) Culture and New Media. In L. Lievrouw and S. Livingstone (eds) *Handbook of New Media*, 2nd edition. Thousand Oaks: Sage, pp. 134–40.

Poulantzas, Nicos (1972) The Problem of the Capitalist State. In R. Blackburn (ed.) *Ideology in Social Science: Readings in Critical Social Theory.* London: Fontana, pp. 238–53.

Pratt, Andy (2000) New Media, the New Economy and New Spaces. *Geoforum* 31 (4), pp. 425–36.

— (2002) Hot Jobs in Cool Places: The Material Cultures of New Media Product Spaces: The Case of South of the Market, San Francisco. *Information, Communication and Society* 5 (1), pp. 27–50.

Price, Monroe E. (1995) *Television, the Public Sphere, and National Identity*. Oxford: Clarendon.

Raboy, Marc (2002) Media Policy in the New Communications Environment. In M. Raboy (ed.) *Global Media Policy in the New Millennium*. Luton: University of Luton Press, pp. 3–16.

— (2004) The WSIS as a Political Space in Global Media Governance. *Continuum: Journal of Media and Cultural Studies* 18 (3), pp. 345–59.

Redhead, Steve (2004a) Creative Modernity: The New Cultural State. *Media International Australia* 112, August, pp. 9–27.

— (2004b) *Paul Virilio: Theorist for an Accelerated Culture*. Edinburgh: Edinburgh University Press.

Reich, Robert (1992) *The Work of Nations*. New York: Vintage.

Rennie, Elinor (2005). Creative World. In J. Hartley (ed.) *Creative Industries*. Oxford: Blackwell, pp. 42–54.

— (2006) *Community Media: A Global Introduction*. Lanham: Rowman & Littlefield.

Rentschler, Ruth (2002) *The Entrepreneurial Arts Leader: Cultural Policy, Change and Reinvention*. Brisbane: University of Queensland Press.

Ritzer, George (1993) *The McDonaldization of Society*. London: Sage.

Roach, Colleen (1997) The Western World and the NWICO? United They Stand?. In P. Golding and P. Harris (eds) *Beyond Cultural Imperialism: Globalisation, Communication and the New International Order*. London: Sage, pp. 94–116.

Robbins, Bruce (1998) Actually Existing Cosmopolitanism. In P. Cheah and B. Robbins (eds) *Cosmopolitics: Thinking and Feeling Beyond the Nation*. Minneapolis: University of Minnesota Press, pp. 1–19.

Roberts, J. Timmons and Hite, Amy (eds) (2000) *From Modernization to Globalization: Perspectives on Development and Social Change*. Oxford: Blackwell.

Robertson, Roland (1991) Mapping the Global Condition: Globalization as the Central Concept. In M. Featherstone (ed.) *Global Culture: Nationalism, Globalization and Modernity*. London: Sage, pp. 15–30.

Rogers, Mark, Epstein, Michael and Reeves, Jimmie (2002) *The Sopranos* as HBO Brand Equity: The Art of Commerce in the Age of Digital Reproduction. In D. Lavery (ed.) *This Thing of Ours: Investigating The Sopranos*. New York: Columbia University Press, pp. 42–57.

Rohm, Wendy Goldman (2002) *The Murdoch Mission: The Digital Transformation of a Media Empire*. New York: John Wiley.

Romer, Paul (1994) The Origins of Endogenous Growth. *Journal of Economic Perspectives* 8 (1), pp. 3–22.

Rosaldo, Renato (1994) Cultural Citizenship and Educational Democracy. *Cultural Anthropology* 9 (3), pp. 402–11.

Roscoe, Jane (2004) *Big Brother* Australia: Performing the 'Real' Twenty-Four Seven. In R. C. Allen and A. Hill (eds) *The Television Studies Reader*. New York: Routledge, pp. 311–21.

Rose, Nikolas (1999) *Powers of Freedom: Reframing Political Thought*. Cambridge: Cambridge University Press.

Rugman, Alan (2000) *The End of Globalization*. London: Random House.

Rutherford, Malcolm (1996) *Institutions in Economics: The Old and the New Institutionalism*. Cambridge: Cambridge University Press.

Ryan, Bill (1992) *Making Capital from Culture: The Corporate Form of Capitalist Cultural Production*. Berlin: de Gruyter.

Sakr, Naomi (2001) *Satellite Realms: Transnational Television, Globalization and the Middle East*. London: I.B. Tauris.

— (2005) Maverick or Model? Al Jazeera's Impact on Arab Satellite Television. In J. Chalaby (ed.) *Transnational Television Worldwide*. London: I.B. Tauris, pp. 66–95.

Sánchez-Tabernero, Alfonso, Trabanco, Alfonso, Denton, Alison, Lochon, Pierre-Yves, Mounier, Philippe and Woldt, Runar (1993), *Media Concentration in Europe: Commercial Enterprise and the Public Interest*. Dusseldorf: European Institute for the Media.

Santino, Carlos (2004) The Contentious Washington Consensus: Reforming the Reforms in Developing Markets. *Review of International Political Economy* 11 (4), pp. 828–44.

Sarikakis, Katharine (2005) Defending Communicative Spaces: The Remits and Limits of the European Parliament. *Gazette: The International Journal for Communication Studies* 67 (2), pp. 155–72.

Sassen, Saskia (2000) *Cities in a World Economy*. Oxford: Blackwell.

— (2001) *The Global City: New York, London, Tokyo*, 2nd edition. Princeton: Princeton University Press.

— (2002) Locating Cities on Global Circuits. In S. Sassen (ed.) *Global Networks, Linked Cities*. New York: Routledge, pp. 1–36.

Sayer, Andrew (1995) *Radical Political Economy: A Critique*. Oxford: Blackwell.

Schiller, Dan (1999) *Digital Capitalism: Networking the Global System*. Cambridge, MA: MIT Press.

Schiller, Herbert I. (1969) *Mass Communications and American Empire*. Boston: Beacon.

— (1976) *Communication and Cultural Domination*. New York: International Arts and Sciences Press.

— (1996) *Information Inequality: The Deepening Social Crisis in America*. London: Routledge.

— (1997) Not Yet the Post-Imperialist Era. In T. O'Sullivan and Y. Jewkes (eds) *The Media Studies Reader*. London: Edward Arnold, pp. 361–71.

Schlesinger, Philip (1991a) *Media, State and Nation: Political Violence and Collective Identities*. London: Sage.

— (1991b) Media, the Political Order and National Identity. *Media, Culture and Society* 13 (3), pp. 297–308.

— (1997) From Cultural Defence to Political Culture: Media, Politics and Collective Identity in the European Union. *Media, Culture and Society* 19 (3), pp. 369–91.

Schramm, Wilbur (1964) *Mass Media and National Development: The Role of Information in the Developing Countries*. Stanford: Stanford University Press.

Schudson, Michael (1994) Culture and the Integration of Modern Societies. *International Social Science Journal* 46 (1), pp. 63–80.

Schultz, Julianne (ed.) (1994) *Not Just Another Business: Journalists, Citizens and the Media*. Sydney: Pluto.

Schuster, J. Mark (2002) Sub-national Cultural Policy – Where the Action Is? Mapping State Cultural Policy in the United States. *International Journal of Cultural Policy* 8 (2), pp. 181–96.

Scott, Allen (1999) Regional Motors of the World Economy. In W. E. Halal and K. B. Taylor (eds) *Twenty-First Century Economics: Perspectives of Socio-Economics for a Changing World*. New York: St. Martin's, pp. 77–105.

— (2000) *The Cultural Economy of Cities: Essays on the Geography of Image-Producing Industries*. London: Sage.

— (2004a) The Other Hollywood: The Organizational and Geographical Bases of Television-Program Production. *Media, Culture and Society* 26 (2), pp. 183–205.

— (2004b) Cultural-Products Industries and Urban Economic Development: Prospects for Growth and Market Contestation in Global Context. *Urban Affairs Review* 39 (4), pp. 461–90.

Scott, John (1985) *Corporations, Classes and Capitalism*, 2nd edition. London: Hutchinson.

Scott, W. Richard (1995) *Institutions and Organizations*. Thousand Oaks: Sage.

Shaw, Martin (1997) The Theoretical Challenge of Global Society. In A. Sreberny-Mohammadi, D. Winseck, J. McKenna and O. Boyd-Barrett (eds) *Media in Global Context: A Reader*. London: Edward Arnold, pp. 27–36.

Shawcross, William (1992) *Rupert Murdoch: Ringmaster of the Information Circus*. London: Chatto & Windus.

Shrikhande, Seema (2001) Competitive Strategies in the Internationalization of Television: CNN and BBC World in Asia. *Journal of Media Economics* 14 (3), pp. 147–68.

Sinclair, John (1997) The Business of International Broadcasting: Cultural Bridges and Barriers. *Asian Journal of Communication* 7 (1), pp. 137–55.

— (1999) *Latin American Television: A Global View*. New York: Oxford University Press.

— and Harrison, Mark (2004) Globalization, Nation and Television in Asia. *Television and New Media* 5 (1), pp. 41–54.

—, Jacka, Elizabeth and Cunningham, Stuart (1996) Peripheral Vision. In J. Sinclair, E. Jacka and S. Cunningham (eds) *New Patterns in Global Television: Peripheral Vision*. Oxford: Oxford University Press, pp. 1–32.

Sklar, Robert (1994) *Movie-Made America: A Cultural History of American Movies*. New York: Vintage.

Skocpol, Theda (1985) Bringing the State Back In: Current Research. In P. B. Evans, D. Rueschmeyer and T. Skocpol (eds) *Bringing the State Back In*. Cambridge: Cambridge University Press, pp. 3–37.

Smeers, Joost (2004) A Convention on Cultural Diversity: From WTO to UNESCO. *Media International Australia* 111, May, pp. 81–96.

Smith, Anthony (1991) Towards a Global Culture?. In M. Featherstone (ed.) *Global Culture: Nationalism, Globalization and Modernity*. London: Sage, pp. 171–92.

Smith, Lenny (2001) The New Golden Age of Korean Cinema. *MovieMaker* 44. Available from www.moviemaker.com/issues/44/index.html. Accessed 22 July 2005.

Smith, Neil (1990) *Uneven Development*. Oxford: Blackwell.

— (2000) Whatever Happened to Class?. *Environment and Planning A* (32), pp. 1011–32.

Söderstrom, Ola (2005) Representation. In D. Atkinson, P. Jackson, D. Sibley and N. Washbourne (eds) *Cultural Geography: A Critical Dictionary of Key Concepts*. London: I.B. Tauris, pp. 11–15.

Soja, Edward (1989) *Postmodern Geographies: The Reassertion of Space in Critical Social Theory.* Oxford: Blackwell.

Sparks, Colin (2004) The Impact of the Internet on Existing Media. In A. Calabrese and C. Sparks (eds) *Towards a Political Economy of Culture: Capitalism and Communication in the Twenty-First Century.* Lanham: Rowman & Littlefield, pp. 307–26.

— (2005) What's Wrong with Globalization?. Paper presented to International Communications Association Conference, New York, May.

Spivak, Gaytari Chakravorty (1990) *The Post-Colonial Critic: Interviews, Strategies, Dialogues.* Ed. S. Harasym. New York: Routledge.

Star, Susan Leigh and Bowker, Geoffrey C. (2005) How to Infrastructure. In L. Lievrouw and S. Livingstone (eds) *Handbook of New Media*, 2nd edition. London: Sage, pp. 230–45.

Steger, Manfred (2003) *Globalization: A Very Short Introduction.* Oxford: Oxford University Press.

Stevenson, Deborah (2004) 'Civic Gold' Rush: Cultural Planning and the Politics of the 'Third Way'. *International Journal of Cultural Policy* 10 (1), pp. 119–31.

Stevenson, Nick (1995) *Understanding Media Culture: Social Theory and Mass Communications.* London: Sage.

Stiglitz, Joseph (2002) The Roaring Nineties. *Atlantic Monthly* 290 (3), pp. 75–89.

Stilwell, Frank J. B. (2002) *Political Economy: The Contest of Economic Ideas.* Melbourne: Oxford University Press.

Storper, Michael (1997a) *The Regional World.* New York: Guilford.

— (1997b) Territories, Flows and Hierarchies in the Global Economy. In K. Cox (ed.) *Spaces of Globalization: Reasserting the Power of the Local.* New York: Guilford, pp. 19–44.

— (2000) Geography and Knowledge Flows: An Industrial Geographer's Perspective. In J. Dunning (ed.) *Regions, Globalization and the Knowledge-Based Economy.* Oxford: Oxford University Press, pp. 42–62.

— (2001) The Poverty of Radical Theory Today: From the False Promises of Marxism to the Mirage of the Cultural Turn. *International Journal of Urban and Regional Research* 25 (1), pp. 155–79.

— and Walker, Richard (1989) *The Capitalist Imperative: Territory, Technology and Industrial Growth.* Oxford: Blackwell.

Strange, Susan (1988) *States and Markets: An Introduction to International Political Economy.* London: Pinter.

Stratton, Jon and Ang, Ien (1996) On the Impossibility of a Global Cultural Studies: 'British' Cultural Studies in an 'International' Frame. In D. Morley and K.-H. Chen (eds) *Stuart Hall: Critical Dialogues in Cultural Studies.* London: Routledge, pp. 361–91.

Straubhaar, Joseph (1991) Beyond Media Imperialism: Assymetrical Interdependence and Cultural Proximity. *Critical Studies in Mass Communication* 8 (1), pp. 39–59.

— (1997) Distinguishing the Global, Regional and National Levels of World Television. In A. Sreberny-Mohammadi, D. Winseck, J. McKenna and O. Boyd-Barrett (eds) *Media in Global Context: A Reader.* London: Edward Arnold, pp. 284–98.

Streeter, Thomas (1995) *Selling the Air: A Critique of the Policy of Commercial Broadcasting in the United States.* Chicago: University of Chicago Press.

Sweezy, Paul (1987) Monopoly Capitalism. In J. Eatwell, M. Milgate and P. Newman (eds) *The New Palgrave: Marxian Economics*. London: Macmillan (now Palgrave Macmillan), pp. 297–303.

Syvertsen, Trine (2003) Challenges to Public Television in the Era of Convergence and Commercialization. *Television and New Media* 4 (2), pp. 155–75.

Tambini, Damian (2002) The New Public Interest. Paper presented to the Australian Broadcasting Authority Conference, Canberra, 26–28 May.

Tay, Jinna (2005) Creative Cities. In J. Hartley (ed.) *Creative Industries*. Oxford: Blackwell, pp. 220–32.

Taylor, Peter (1996) Embedded Statism and the Social Sciences: Opening Up to New Spaces. *Environment and Planning A* 28 (11), pp. 1917–28.

—, Walker, D. R. F. and Beaverstock, J. V. (2002) Firms and Their Global Service Networks. In S. Sassen (ed.) *Global Networks, Linked Cities*. New York: Routledge, pp. 93–115.

The Corporation (2004). Documentary by M. Achbar, J. Abbott and J. Bakan. Produced by M. Achbar and B. Simpson.

Thomas, Amos Owen (2005) *Imagi-Nations and Borderless Television: Media, Culture and Politics Across Asia*. New Delhi: Sage.

Thompson, Grahame (2003) *Between Hierarchies and Networks: The Logic and Limits of Network Forms of Organization*. Oxford: Oxford University Press.

Thompson, John B. (1991) *Ideology and Modern Culture*. Cambridge: Polity.

— (1995) *The Media and Modernity: A Social Theory of the Media*. Cambridge: Polity.

Thorburn, David (2004) *The Sopranos*. In H. Newcomb (ed.) *Encyclopedia of Television*, 2nd edition. New York: Taylor & Francis, pp. 2134–7.

Thrift, Nigel (2000) Pandora's Box: Cultural Geographies of Economies. In G. Clark, M. Feldman and M. Gertler (eds) *The Oxford Handbook of Economic Geography*. Oxford: Oxford University Press, pp. 689–704.

— (2005) *Knowing Capitalism*. London: Sage.

Thussu, Daya Kishan (2006) *International Communication: Continuity and Change*, 2nd edition. London: Edward Arnold.

Tomlinson, John (1991) *Cultural Imperialism*. London: Pinter.

— (1999) *Globalization and Culture*. Chicago: University of Chicago Press.

— (2003) The Agenda of Globalization. *New Formations* 50, pp. 10–21.

— (2004) Globalization and National Identity. In J. Sinclair and G. Turner (eds) *Contemporary World Television*. London: British Film Institute, pp. 24–8.

Tracey, Michael (1988) Popular Culture and the Economics of Global Television. *Intermedia* 16 (3), pp. 53–69.

Turner, Bryan (1997) Citizenship Studies: A General Theory. *Citizenship Studies* 1 (1), pp. 5–18.

Turner, Graeme (1990) *British Cultural Studies: An Introduction*. London: Unwin Hyman.

United Nations Conference on Trade and Development (UNCTAD) (2000) *World Investment Report: Cross Border Mergers and Acquisitions and Development*. New York and Geneva: United Nations.

— (2003) *World Investment Report: FDI Policies for Development: National and International Perspectives*. New York and Geneva: United Nations.

— (2004) *High Level Panel on Creative Industries*. Eleventh session, São Paulo. Summary prepared by the UNCTAD Secretariat, 13 June. Available from www.unctad.org/en/docs/tdl379en.pdf. Accessed 27 February 2005.

— (2005) *World Investment Report 2005: Transnational Corporations and the Internationalization of R&D*. New York and Geneva: United Nations.

— (2006) *World Investment Report 2006: FDI from Developing and Transitional Economies – Implications for Development*. New York and Geneva: United Nations.

United Nations Educational, Scientific and Cultural Organization (UNESCO) (1982) *World Conference on Cultural Policies: Final Report*. Paris: UNESCO.

— (2001) *Universal Declaration on Cultural Diversity*. Adopted by the 31st session of the General Conference of UNESCO, Paris, 2 November. Paris: UNESCO.

— (2003) *Culture, Trade and Globalization: Questions and Answers*. Available from www.unesco.org/culture/industries/trade/htmleng. Accessed 4 June 2003.

— (2004) *UNESCO and the Question of Cultural Diversity: Review and Strategy, 1946–2004*. Division of Cultural Policies and Intercultural Dialogue. Paris: UNESCO.

— (2005a) *International Flows of Selected Cultural Goods and Services, 1994–2003: Defining and Capturing the Flows of Global Cultural Trade*. Paris: UNESCO.

— (2005b) *Convention on the Protection and Promotion of the Diversity of Forms of Cultural Expression*. Paris: UNESCO, 20 October.

Urry, John (1989) The End of Organized Capitalism. In S. Hall and M. Jacques (eds) *New Times: The Changing Face of Politics in the 1990s*. London: Lawrence & Wishart, pp. 94–102.

van Zoonen, Liesbet and Aslama, Minna (2006) Understanding Big Brother: An Analysis of Current Research. *Javnost – The Public* 13 (2), pp. 85–96.

Venturelli, Shalini (2005) Culture and the Creative Economy in the Information Age. In J. Hartley (ed.) *Creative Industries*. Oxford: Blackwell, pp. 391–8.

Verhulst, Stefan (2005) The Regulation of Digital Content. In L. Lievrouw and S. Livingstone (eds) *The Handbook of New Media*, Updated Student Edition. London: Sage, pp. 329–49.

Waisbord, Silvio (2000) Media in South America: Between the Rock of the State and the Hard Place of the Market. In J. Curran and M.-J. Park (eds) *De-Westernizing Media Studies*. London: Routledge, pp. 50–62.

— (2002) *Grandes Gigantes*: Media Concentration in Latin America. *Open Democracy*. Available from www.opendemocracy.org/debates/article-8-24-64.jsp. Posted 27 February. Accessed 12 August 2004.

Wallerstein, Immanuel (1991) The National and the Universal: Can There Be Such a Thing as World Culture?. In A. D. King (ed.) *Culture, Globalization and the World-System*. Albany: State University of New York Press, pp. 91–106.

Wang, Jing (2004) The Global Reach of a New Discourse: How Far Can 'Creative Industries' Travel?. *International Journal of Cultural Studies* 7 (1), pp. 9–19.

Wark, McKenzie (1994) *Virtual Geographies*. Bloomington: Indiana University Press.

— (1998) *The Virtual Republic*. Sydney: Allen & Unwin.

— (2003) *How Hollywood Works*. London: Sage.

Wasko, Janet (2003) *How Hollywood Works*. London: Sage.

Waters, Malcolm (1995) *Globalization*. London: Routledge.

Wayne, Michael (2003) Post-Fordism, Monopoly Capitalism, and Hollywood's Media Industrial Complex. *International Journal of Cultural Studies* 6 (1), pp. 82–103.

Weber, Steven (2004) *The Success of Open Source*. Cambridge, MA: Harvard University Press.

Webster, Frank (2002) *Theories of the Information Society*, 2nd edition. London: Routledge.

Weiss, Linda (1997) Globalization and the Myth of the Powerless State. *New Left Review* 225, pp. 3–27.

— (2003) Introduction: Bringing Domestic Institutions Back In. In L. Weiss (ed.) *States in the Global Economy: Bringing Domestic Institutions Back In*. Cambridge: Cambridge University Press, pp. 1–33.

Wellman, Barry (2004) The Three Ages of Internet Studies: Ten, Five and Zero Years Ago. *New Media and Society* 6 (1), pp. 123–9.

Williams, Raymond (1965) *The Long Revolution*. Harmondsworth: Penguin.

— (1976) *Keywords: A Vocabulary of Culture and Society*. London: Fontana.

— (1977) *Marxism and Literature*. Oxford: Oxford University Press.

— (1980) *Problems in Materialism and Culture*. London: Verso.

— (1981) *Culture*. London: Fontana.

— (1989) Politics and Policies: The Case of the Arts Council. In R. Williams, *The Politics of Modernism: Against the New Conformists*. London: Verso, pp. 141–50.

Williamson, Oliver E. (1975) *Markets and Hierarchies*. New York: Free Press.

— (1985) *The Economic Institutions of Capitalism*. New York: Free Press.

Winseck, Dwayne (2002a) Wired Cities and Transnational Communications: New Forms of Governance for Telecommunications and the New Media. In L. Lievrouw and S. Livingstone (eds) *The Handbook of New Media*, 1st edition. London: Sage, pp. 393–409.

— (2002b) The WTO, Emerging Policy Regimes and the Political Economy of Transnational Communication. In M. Raboy (ed.) *Global Media Policy in the New Millennium*. Luton: University of Luton Press, pp. 19–38.

World Summit on the Information Society (WSIS) (2003) *Declaration of Principles. Building the Information Society: A Global Challenge in the New Millennium*. United Nations and International Telecommunications Union. Available from www.itu.int/dmspub/itu-s/md/03/wsis/doc/S03-WSIS-DOC-0004!!PDF-E.pdf. Accessed 15 February 2004.

— (2005) *Tunis Agenda for the Information Society*. United Nations and International Telecommunications Union. Available from www.itu.int/wsis/docs2/tunis/off/6rev1.pdf. Accessed 13 September 2006.

Yeatman, Anna (1998) Activism and the Policy Process. In A. Yeatman (ed.) *Activism and the Policy Process*. Sydney: Allen & Unwin, pp. 16–35.

Yeung, Henry Wai-chung (2002) The Limits to Globalization Theory: A Geographical Perspective on Global Economic Change. *Economic Geography* 78 (3), pp. 285–305.

Young, Robert (1990) *White Mythologies: Writing History and the West*. London: Routledge.

Yúdice, George (1992) Postmodernity and Transnational Capitalism in Latin America. In G. Yúdice, J. Franco and J. Flores (eds) *On Edge: The Crisis of Contemporary Latin American Culture*. Minneapolis: University of Minesota Press, pp. 1–28.

— (2003) *The Expediency of Culture: Uses of Culture in the Global Era*. Durham, NC: Duke University Press.

Yusuf, Shahid (2003) *Innovative East Asia: The Future of Growth*. Washington, DC: World Bank.

Zamagni, Stefano (1987) *Microeconomic Theory: An Introduction*. Oxford: Basil Blackwell.

Zayani, Mohamed (2005) Introduction – Al Jazeera and the Vicissitudes of the New Arab Mediascape. In M. Zayani (ed.) *The Al Jazeera Phenomenon: Critical Perspectives on New Arab Media*. London: Pluto, pp. 1–46.

Zelizer, Barbie (2004) *Taking Journalism Seriously: News and the Academy*. London: Sage.

Zha, Jainying (1995) *China Pop: How Soap Operas, Tabloids, and Bestsellers are Transforming a Culture*. New York: New Press.

Zhu, Tianbiao (2003) Building Institutional Capacity for China's New Economic Opening. In L. Weiss (ed.) *States in the Global Economy: Bringing Domestic Institutions Back In*. Cambridge: Cambridge University Press, pp. 142– 60.

Index